Biopolitics after Truth

To Marina and Pauliina

BIOPOLITICS AFTER TRUTH

Knowledge, Power and Democratic Life

SERGEI PROZOROV

EDINBURGH
University Press

Edinburgh University Press is one of the leading university presses in the UK. We publish academic books and journals in our selected subject areas across the humanities and social sciences, combining cutting-edge scholarship with high editorial and production values to produce academic works of lasting importance. For more information visit our website: edinburghuniversitypress.com

Edinburgh University Press Ltd
The Tun – Holyrood Road
12(2f) Jackson's Entry
Edinburgh EH8 8PJ

First published in hardback by Edinburgh University Press 2022

Typeset in 11/13 Adobe Sabon by
IDSUK (DataConnection) Ltd

A CIP record for this book is available from the British Library

ISBN 978 1 4744 8578 4 (hardback)
ISBN 978 1 474485791 (paperback)
ISBN 978 1 4744 8580 7 (webready PDF)
ISBN 978 1 4744 8581 4 (epub)

Contents

INTRODUCTION

The word of the year

Handel's opera *Agrippina* premiered in Venice in 1709. It is a satirical comedy describing Agrippina's efforts to install her son Nero as Roman emperor in a series of deceitful intrigues. Having heard that Emperor Claudius has perished in a storm, Agrippina ensures the support of court nobles Pallas and Narcissus for her plan, deceiving them with declarations of her love.

When it turns out that Claudius is in fact alive and returning to Rome, Agrippina does not abandon her plan. As Claudius promises the throne to Otho, the commander of his army, for saving his life during the storm, she seeks to damage Otho's reputation in order to make Claudius rescind his promise. The key figure in her intrigue is Poppaea, the object of affection of all three men involved in the struggle for the throne: Claudius, Nero and Otho. Agrippina falsely informs Poppaea that Otto had struck a deal with Claudius, whereby he would get the throne but leave Poppaea to Claudius. She then advises Poppaea to complain to Claudius that Otho ordered her to refuse his attentions. The cunning plan works: Poppaea is furious about Otho's alleged betrayal, while Claudius is equally enraged by the latter's ingratitude. Otho is denounced as a traitor and abandoned by friends and allies, while Claudius agrees to give up the throne for Nero, his mind set on the pursuit of Poppaea.

However, Poppaea remains unconvinced about Otho's betrayal and takes pity on him. She pretends to recount Agrippina's accusations in her sleep and, as Otho finds out what he is being accused

1

of, he understands Agrippina's deception and protests his innocence. Poppaea believes him and seeks to avenge him by, as it were, deceiving the deceiver and ruining Agrippina's designs for Nero's coronation. She invites both Claudius and Nero to her house, telling the former that it was actually Nero rather than Otho that she meant to accuse in the first place. It was Nero who had pursued her all this time and forbidden her to meet with Claudius. She then arranges it so that Claudius discovers Nero hiding in the house and angrily walks out.

In the meantime, the freedmen, Pallas and Narcissus, also understand that Agrippina has been lying to them all along and confess their participation in her intrigues to Claudius. Enraged, Claudius confronts Agrippina, but she presents her actions not as deception and treason but rather as a defence of Claudius's throne against stronger challengers. Faced with the rumours of his death, she placed her son on the throne only as a means to safeguard it, in case Claudius might be alive and return to Rome. At first, Claudius decides that Nero and Poppaea should be married, while Otho would receive the throne, yet after both Poppaea and Otho affirm their love for each other, he reverses his decision, giving the throne to Nero and letting the two lovers be united.

It would be nice to conclude that everyone lived happily ever after, but as we know from history this was not to be the case. In fact, all the major characters would go on to die violent or at least suspicious deaths. Pallas and Narcissus would be executed soon after Nero's ascent to power. Claudius would eventually be poisoned by Agrippina, who in turn would be murdered by Nero. Poppaea's marriage to Otho would not last and she would eventually marry Nero and die while pregnant with their second child, after being hit by Nero in the abdomen. Nero would go on to enjoy a period of extravagant and tyrannical rule until his defeat in the revolt of Vindex and Galba, assisted by none other than Otho, whom Nero had previously demoted and sent away to a far off province after forcing him to divorce Poppaea. In his defeat Nero would decide to take his own life and would die after being stabbed by his attendant at his request. In the chaotic period after Nero's fall, Otho would briefly be emperor but would eventually be overthrown as well and commit suicide.

This is why David McVicar's 2019 staging of the work at the Metropolitan Opera sets the action in a mausoleum, the characters recounting the story by rising from and ultimately returning to their sarcophagi. This is not the only innovation in the staging, as the action is set in the vaguely contemporary period, the characters drinking Heineken and using smart phones. Yet even without this modernisation, the theme of the opera has a highly contemporary ring to it, evoking both the intrigues and lies of the Trump presidency and more generally the contemporary condition that we have come to know as *post-truth*.

Agrippina is a story of deceit and power, of using deceit to come to power, of deceiving the powers that be, of lying to avenge those who have been deceived and of ending up deceiving oneself. There is not a single character in the opera who does not engage in deceit – Otho comes closest yet still participates in Poppaea's intrigue. None of them is a match for Agrippina herself, who manages to transform her apparent defeat into a triumph by casting what seems like an evident act of betrayal into the proof of utmost loyalty, making Claudius feel bad for ever doubting her. After this masterstroke of what we now call *gaslighting*, the hapless Claudius appears to have lost the will to fight for the throne and is ready to give it up to whomsoever, Otho or Nero. In her aria 'Se vuoi pace' ('If You Want Peace') Agrippina urges him to abandon the search for truth, let go of hatred and find peace, presumably no longer as the emperor. This is what he does at the end, utterly deflated and indifferent. The peace thus attained is of course entirely based on lies, so the eventually dismal fate of all the characters should not really surprise us.

What does the contemporary relevance of the opera mean? Does the resonance between Agrippina's lies and Trump's deceit entail that what we call the post-truth era is actually nothing new and has been there since Handel or even Nero himself? And how should we respond to this resonance – by taking it as a call to arms or by letting it lull us into passivity, since post-truth is, as it were, nothing new?

The word 'post-truth' was chosen as the 'word of the year' by Oxford Dictionaries in 2016, joining the privileged club whose members also include 'youthquake', 'toxic', 'climate emergency' and 'emoji'. Nonetheless, the term itself dates back at least two decades. Its first occurrence is usually traced back to a 1992 article in *The Nation*, written by Steve Tesich and entitled 'A Government of Lies' (Tesich 1992). The article dealt with the transformations in the relation of the American society to truth in politics after Watergate and offered a chilling diagnosis that has only become ever more relevant since then:

> All the dictators up to now have had to work hard at suppressing the truth. We, by our actions, are saying that this is *no longer necessary*, that we have acquired a spiritual mechanism that can *denude truth of any significance*. In a very fundamental way we, as a free people, have freely decided that we want to live in some post-truth world. (Ibid.: 12, emphasis added)

A similar argument, also focused on American politics, was offered in a 2004 book by Eric Alterman entitled *When Presidents Lie: A History of Official Deception and its Consequences* (Alterman 2004). The same year saw the publication of the book by Ralph Keyes called *The Post-Truth Era: Dishonesty and Deception in Contemporary Life* (Keyes 2004), whose diagnosis goes beyond the political sphere and addresses the spread of deception and dissimulation in the wider American society, including the fields of academia, religion, mass media, business and arts.

The same tendency continued in the subsequent decade: post-truth was used both to analyse specific political events – for example, the 2012 American elections (Parmar 2012) – and as a blanket term for the new 'regime' characterising culture and society more generally (Harsin 2015). After 2016, the year of the Brexit referendum and the election of Trump, 'post-truth' became a catchword, ceaselessly debated in various fields and disciplines. While before 2016 the term was largely used as a criticism of the tendencies in mainstream politics, intended as a warning about their negative aspects or effects, after 2016 the term began to denote a new era, marked by the breakdown of 'normal politics', the dissolution of the mainstream and the victorious challenge to it from formerly marginal forces (see Andersen 2017; Tallis 2016; D'Ancona 2017).

Yet, any announcement of a new era usually elicits a sceptical response. The problematic of post-truth is easy to dismiss as 'nothing new', a mere journalistic fad that will soon pass: who remembers what 'youthquake' even meant and why anyone cared about it enough to make it the word of 2017? The case of *Agrippina* clearly demonstrates that we will never lack in historical examples of politicians lying or mass media publicising falsehoods to legitimise their policies, and of entire societies becoming receptive to demagogues and charlatans of all sorts, political or otherwise. Moreover, even a casual acquaintance with debates in philosophy would appear to suggest that today's controversies over post-truth merely reprise, in a particularly heated way, a millennia-old debate between sophists and philosophers, those for whom there are only opinions and those who affirm the existence of truths without necessarily also affirming their knowledge of them.

There is something comforting in claiming, in a world-weary yet sombre tone, that there is nothing new under the sun. The speaker of these words thereby claims surplus wisdom over the others who also happen to live under the sun, yet so easily yield to superficial claims of novelty made by Oxford Dictionaries and other media outlets. Moreover, this surplus wisdom appears almost irrefutable, since it is always possible to reduce the new to the old in such a way that nothing new remains of it. Yet, rather than indicate surplus wisdom, such a reduction rather points to one's failure to recognise the new amidst the old, as well as the refusal to admit even the possibility of such failure. By steadfastly refusing to be duped by superficial novelties, one ends up fundamentally disoriented by nothing other than the familiar signposts that no longer provide any reassurance and seem only to exacerbate one's errancy.

A better approach, therefore, would be to try to isolate that in the present condition which is not so easily reducible to the familiar stories of intrigue and deceit, of broken promises and insidious lies. This approach would also be more faithful to Tesich's original insight about post-truth, which, after all, did not simply claim that governments lie, sometimes, frequently or always, but that these lies have become insignificant and inconsequential because it is 'no longer necessary' to suppress the truth as it is 'denuded of any significance'. What defines post-truth and accounts for its novelty is this insignificance of or indifference to truth, which alone permits us to speak of being *post*-truth, that is, definitively past it: if we were merely outraged at the lies told by politicians, wouldn't this be sufficient evidence that our era is still eminently that of truth?

From contestation to indifference: Defining post-truth

Before beginning to analyse the features of the post-truth condition we must therefore distinguish it from events and phenomena that at first glance appear related to it but in fact belong to a different historical condition or trajectory altogether. Firstly, post-truth does not refer to the sheer occurrence or even increased frequency of lies, fakes or falsehoods uttered in political discourse. Even when it is exceptionally frequent, this occurrence still presupposes the *difference* between truth and untruth, in the absence of which we could never even begin to lament the relative growth of lies and falsehoods in politics. In contrast, it is rather the *indistinction* between the two or *indifference* to the very possibility of their distinction that constitutes post-truth as an epistemico-political regime. In other words, to speak of a post-truth politics does not mean that previously our politics was based on truth, while now it is based on lies, but rather to argue that contemporary politics is becoming increasingly indifferent to the affirmation and contestation of truths that were previously essential to it. While a politics based on lies could still be rectified by the revelation of the truth, a politics indifferent to truth would not even register such a revelation. Of course, this indifference may well be an effect of the prevalence of lies in the prior historical periods, as Hannah Arendt has argued:

> [The] result of a consistent and total substitution of lies for factual truth is not that the lies will now be accepted as truth, and the truth be defamed as lies, but that the sense by which we take our bearings in the real words – and the category of truth vs falsehood is among the mental means to this end – is being destroyed. Consistent lying, metaphorically speaking, pulls the ground from under our feet and provides no other ground on which to stand. (Arendt 2006: 252–3)

It is this experience of groundlessness that in our view defines the post-truth disposition. For this reason, the study of post-truth politics must go beyond the focus on the familiar instances of lying politicians and misleading media towards outlining the more general regime, which serves to increasingly normalise these instances. In Chapter 1 we shall attempt precisely that by charting what we shall call the *regime of equivalence*, governing the formation and functioning of statements in contemporary political and other discourses.

Secondly, by post-truth we do *not* mean the presence or even intensification of millennia-old philosophical dispositions such as *relativism* and *scepticism* or any contemporary philosophical approaches problematising the truth claims of particular disciplines or discourses. As we shall argue at length in Chapter 2, the criticism of specific truths or even entire theories of truth in these philosophical approaches must presuppose the sheer *existence* of truth, even as it might challenge various approaches to finding it or even insist on its inherently elusive nature. Indifference to truth would make this criticism utterly redundant, as there is no reason to get worked up about something that does not exist. Thus, the most fiery contestation of truth claims or methods of reaching the truth must at the same time affirm that truths *do* exist, which is the only reason why it is worthwhile to question some or even most of them as possibly untrue. For this reason, the study of post-truth would gain little from looking for the precursors of this disposition among philosophers and social critics who have gained notoriety for opposing or debunking various truth claims throughout history: Nietzsche, Foucault, Derrida, and so on. It might, on the other hand, gain quite a lot from these and other authors if it approaches their works less as evidence of their complicity in post-truth than as inquiries into the meaning and function of truth, that would also help us understand the retreat from truth that we observe today.

Thirdly, by post-truth we do not mean the wider social conditions of disenchantment, scepticism and cynicism that accompany the decline or demise of hegemonic ideological orders. While the discourses on these conditions come close to post-truth in lamenting how the former order was 'built on a lie' and that there is no truth to be found in its ruins, the very fact of these lamentations suggests that truth remains *desirable* and its absence renders political orders ineffective or illegitimate. What constitutes the post-truth condition proper in our view is the conversion of this perception of the deficiency of order due to the lack or absence of truth into a *positive* condition, whereby truth is no longer something lacking yet still wanted but rather something impossible or meaningless, so that its absence is no longer viewed as a defect but rather as an advantage or a blessing. In Chapter 3 we shall trace this conversion by analysing the emergence of the post-truth disposition in postcommunist Russia and its consolidation under Putinism.

In short, we know that we are inhabiting a post-truth condition not when we are enraged that our politicians lie to us, or when our philosophers tell us that what we held to be true was a historical accident, but when we no longer understand how it could even be *otherwise*, what it would mean for political discourse to be adjudicated as to its truth or falsity or for scientific truths to be anything more than products of historical circumstances. While we might not dwell in this condition yet, since 2016 we at least have a good idea of what it would look like.

This understanding of post-truth permits us to counter a somewhat complacent understanding of this phenomenon in the current debates. It is all too easy to reject the very idea of post-truth politics by arguing that politics was never about truth to begin with but rather about deliberation, debate and struggles about numerous issues, including the question of truth. It is just as easy to point out that science, the 'proper' domain of the question of truth, also happens to have its own politics, in which what is true and what is false is ceaselessly debated and this debate is rarely settled. Yet, what these objections miss is precisely the novelty of the present condition that consists not in the intensification of debates about truth in politics, science or any other domain, but, on the contrary, in the increased *indifference* to the question of truth, which itself becomes indistinct from an *opinion*. If the period preceding the current predicament is to be called 'truth politics', it is certainly not in the sense that the question of truth was *settled* in it, but precisely in the sense that this question remained at the heart of debates, be they political or scientific, which presupposes that truth actually exists, however elusive it might be.

In contrast, when we speak of the post-truth condition today, it is to highlight the displacement of the very *question* of truth to the margins. Debates may still go on and even become more combative and toxic than ever, but what is at stake in them is no longer the pursuit of truth but rather something else: the expression of one's identity, standpoint, experience, preference or opinion, which may be interesting or dull, privileged or subaltern, trivial or quaint, but cannot be either true or false. It is this shift from what we might call an *argumentative* logic, still concerned with the question of truth, towards the *expressionist* logic entirely indifferent to it that in our view constitutes the essence of the post-truth predicament, which remains all but invisible to us, as long as we try to console ourselves by saying that things were not so simple with regard to truth before. Indeed, *they were not, but they are now*, as truth gives way to expressiveness, authenticity, degree of circulation or any other criterion.

Thus, our approach to post-truth in this book defines it not in terms of the disappearance of truths but in terms of the *decline of their efficacy*. This approach also guides the affirmative intention of this study. Our alternative to post-truth politics, which we elaborate in Chapter 4, does not seek to advance this or that truth or set it against the apparent falsehoods of today's politics but rather to affirm truth-telling *as such* as a disposition that ruptures the regime of equivalence, which reduces every statement to a mere opinion devoid of truth. Any advance beyond the post-truth condition must begin by restoring the *difference* of truth from opinion and thereby reviving its *performative efficacy*.

The key argument of this book is that this performative efficacy is not entirely contained in the semantic content of the statement but also inheres in the subjective disposition of truth-telling, which asserts that what it says is more than a mere opinion. The truth, as we shall insist throughout this book, *won't tell itself*. This is why the widespread appeals to 'follow the science' so rarely work in contemporary politics: not because the science in question is wrong, but because the act of truth-telling is not scientific but *ethico-political*, constituting the speaker as subject in the very act of enunciation. Since the post-truth condition is constituted by indifference to truth, it can only be resisted by letting truth *make a difference* through subjective investment in truth-telling. For this reason, in this book we shall be less concerned with epistemological approaches to truth, than with the effects of truth denials and truth-telling on our ethics and politics.

Thus, the intention of the book is not to offer a path 'back to normal', withdrawing from the post-truth condition into some kind of a pre-post-truth era. Post-truth has become the *new normal* – not in the sense of absolute domination but in the sense of defining a field of contestation that our politics will continue to be practised in and affected by for a long time to come. Particular practitioners of post-truth politics may be discredited and descend into oblivion, but it is difficult to imagine micro-targeting, disinformation through social media, foreign interference disappearing from election campaigns or everyday functioning of liberal democracies. Another reason why it is impossible to go 'back to normal' is that the 'normal' in question was also an exception. Every period has its own abnormalities and the one immediately preceding the rise of post-truth was characterised by the exceptional degree of *consensus* on the fundamentals of politics, economy and culture that lasted from the end of the Cold War until the 2008 economic crisis. If current politics appears to us as too conflictual, we should recall that during the 1990s and the early 2000s politics appeared as far too consensual and many political philosophers built successful careers on advocating the return to conflict, antagonism, dissensus or even enmity.

While we remain unconvinced that dissensus is necessarily preferable to consensus, we definitely do not wish to endorse a return to this particular consensus, whose foundation on neoliberal economics appears barely credible today. Yet, it certainly matters whether this consensus is resisted on the basis of the *fallibility* of the knowledge underlying it (which presupposes the existence of truths, in terms of which this knowledge is to be evaluated) or on the basis of the *equivalence* of all statements, as opinions expressing one's identity or interest, between which no adjudication in terms of truth and falsity is possible. While the former contestation is constitutive of any notion of democratic politics, the latter can only undermine democracy, paving the way for today's prevalent form of post-ideological authoritarianism that sneers at all claims to truth and contaminates public discourse by flooding it with toxic content. If this authoritarianism now appears as 'the new normal', it need not *remain* normal but may always be contested and possibly even defeated. This contestation will not, however, gain much from the nostalgia about the 'age of truth', when truth presumably reigned supreme, everyone trusted the scientists, and the media fulfilled their gatekeeping role. A discourse *about* truth will not suffice to bring the truth back into politics – it takes political acts of truth-*telling* to take us beyond post-truth.

OUTLINE OF THE ARGUMENT

Chapter 1 locates the problematic of post-truth in the context of the relation between democracy and biopolitics. We take our points of departure from Alain Badiou's critique of contemporary 'democratic materialism' that only recognises the existence of bodies and language rather than truths, and Michel Foucault's discussion of the doubly paradoxical relationship between democracy, governance and truth in Ancient Greece. From its very inception, democracy has had a problematic relationship to truth, enabling *both* the generation of true discourses underlying rationalities of governance *and* their continuous contestation on the basis of the equal right to speech. However, the post-truth condition introduces a new twist to this problematic relationship, insofar as it erases the distinction between *parrhesia* and *isegoria, true* speech and *free* speech. We then proceed to elaborate this condition in terms of a move from an argumentative to an expressionist logic (post-proof), which valorises free, unconstrained and undistorted expression of one's self, identity or interest (post-shame) that no longer seeks to persuade one's interlocutor (post-consensus). The result of this transformation is what we term the *regime of equivalence*, which renders all statements equivalent (but not equal!) as opinions that could not possibly be adjudicated in terms of truth and falsity.

In Chapter 2 we shall further elaborate the notion of regime of equivalence by addressing it in a more philosophical context. Firstly, we shall discuss the attempts to present postmodern or post-structuralist philosophers as somehow complicit in the rise of post-truth due to their sceptical or relativist approach to truth. We shall argue that the philosophical problematisation of particular truth claims or entire theories of truth must necessarily presuppose their existence, which differentiates these approaches clearly from the post-truth disposition that renders truths indistinct from opinions. Moreover, we shall demonstrate how the philosophical critique of truth, undertaken by such authors as Michel Foucault, Alain Badiou and Giorgio Agamben, actually helps us understand what is at stake in the post-truth condition. In their own different ways these authors are concerned less with the epistemological questioning of truths than with illuminating their ethico-political functioning in our subjectivation. If the meaning and function of truth consist primarily in the way it participates in the subjectivation of speaking beings, then the effects of the post-truth disposition are even more thoroughgoing than we have hitherto imagined, since they destabilise the very core of our subjectivity.

In Chapter 3 we shall reconstruct a particularly important episode in the genealogy of post-truth politics: the emergence of the regime of equivalence in the Russian postcommunist society and culture during the 1990s and its subsequent consolidation and weaponisation by the Putin regime. The frantic discussion of Russia's 'hybrid war' on the West after 2014 has largely ignored the fact that this strategy was only deployed in Russia's foreign policy after being successfully applied domestically for over a decade. The optimistic expectations of the Westernisation of Russia in the post-Soviet period have given way to the fears about the Russification of the West, which turned out to be just as receptive to post-truth strategies and technologies as the Russian postcommunist society was since the late 1990s. We will retrace the emergence of the post-truth disposition in the late-Soviet period, marked by ideological disenchantment and societal disengagement from the political space, the intensification of this disengagement during the reform period of the 1990s, marked by the rise of a cynical and conspiracist mindset, and the eventual adoption of this disposition by the Putin regime as its quasi-ideological foundation, permitting the consolidation of authoritarianism and the marginalisation of all opposition. We conclude this chapter by addressing what is perhaps the most famous instance of resistance to this regime, Pussy Riot's 2012 'punk prayer'. Drawing on Agamben's critical reinterpretation of J. L. Austin's theory of performative speech acts, we shall argue that the force of Pussy Riot's performance consists less in their scandalous blasphemy of the Orthodox prayer than in their rupture of the regime of equivalence and the forceful insistence on the truth of their discourse.

In Chapter 4 we shall offer an interpretation of this and other acts of truth-telling as a form of *affirmative biopolitics*, a politics of bringing truth into life or living life in truth. Drawing on Foucault's analysis of Cynic *parrhesia* in his final lecture course and the experience of East European dissident movements that he actively supported in the early 1980s, we shall reconstruct truth-telling as a practice of political subjectivation. We shall then venture to construct a model of truth-telling that would be adequate for the post-truth era, which differs from both Antiquity and socialist authoritarianism in no longer even pretending to practise what it preaches, since it no longer preaches anything at all. In this new condition, truth-telling cannot be content with living in accordance with the truth but must forcefully restore truth to existence, giving it surplus illocutionary force in one's speech acts that, as it were, speak *both* the truth and one's very act of speaking it. We shall analyse the statements of environmental activist Greta Thunberg as precisely such parrhesiastic acts that add to the semantic content of established scientific truths the force of their affirmation as truths rather than opinions. The chapter concludes by demonstrating the centrality of such affirmation to a genuinely *democratic biopolitics*, in which the principles of freedom, equality and community are not merely retained as transcendental conditions but enter our very experience of, and experiment in, living.

The title of this book thus plays on two meanings of being 'after' something. 'Biopolitics after truth' refers both to the *status* of biopolitics in the post-truth era, marked by the destabilisation of the foundations of governmental rationalities in scientific and other truths, and to the *quest* of affirmative biopolitics after truth, the attempt of political actors to transform their lives and the world they live in by putting themselves at stake in their speech acts. To be after truth does not entail becoming resigned to its absence but rather means being attuned to the possibilities of its pursuit.

CHAPTER ONE

The regime of equivalence

DIAGNOSIS: THERE ARE ONLY BODIES AND LANGUAGES

In his 2006 book *Logics of Worlds* Alain Badiou anticipated today's proclamations of the post-truth era by describing contemporary Western societies as governed by the ideology of 'democratic materialism', whose fundamental maxim is that 'there are only bodies and languages' with their particular desires and opinions (Badiou 2009a: 1–9). This ideology is a *materialism* because '[the] contemporary world recognizes the objective existence of bodies alone. Who does not *de facto* subscribe to the dogma of our finitude, of our carnal exposition to enjoyment, suffering and death?' (ibid.: 2). If there are only bodies, if existence is only conceivable in terms of biological life, humanity is reduced to an 'overstretched version of animality':

> 'Human rights' are the same as the rights of the living. The humanist protection of all living bodies: this is the norm of contemporary materialism. Today, this norm has a scientific name: 'bioethics', whose progressive reverse borrows its name from Foucault: 'biopolitics'. Our materialism is therefore a materialism of life. It is a bio-materialism. (Ibid.)

Why is this bio-materialism *democratic*? It is because it recognises all the *languages* that these bodies use as formally or juridically equal:

> [The] assimilation of humanity to animality culminates in the identification of the human animal with the diversity of its subspecies and the democratic rights that inhere in this diversity. Communities and cultures, colours and pigments, religions and clergies, uses and customs: everything and everyone deserves to be recognised and protected by the law. (Ibid.)

The only standpoint that does not merit this recognition and protection is the refusal to recognise this universal equality of bodies and languages that claims the superiority of some of them over others. In the democratic-materialist disposition this standpoint is branded as 'totalitarianism' and dismissed as an illegitimate desire of some bodies and languages to dominate and subjugate others.

What democratic materialism abhors is any form of universalism that affirms something that goes beyond the pluralistic particularism of bodies and languages. Just as individual bodies are characterised by particular desires irreducible to any universal principle, so individual languages affirm particular identities, values or interests, which cannot be adjudicated in terms of any universal standard. The universality that this disposition affirms pertains only to the space in which bodies and languages circulate freely.

Insofar as these plural bodies and languages are in themselves ethically indifferent, their sheer plurality constitutes a space of *general equivalence* in which they are all substitutable for one another:

> Capital demands a permanent creation of subjective and territorial identities in order for its principle of movement to homogenize its space of action; identities, moreover, that never demand anything but the right to be exposed in the same way as others to the uniform prerogatives of the market. The capitalist logic of the general equivalent and the identitarian and cultural logic of communities or minorities form an articulated whole. (Badiou 2001b: 10)

This is why Badiou is so scathing about identity politics that only serves to prop up the system it pretends to resist, maintaining a market-like free space in which all possible identities can interact without ever forming anything like a general will: 'black homosexuals, disabled Serbs, Catholic paedophiles, moderate Muslims, married priests, ecologist yuppies, the submissive unemployed, prematurely aged youth' (ibid.).

Badiou's diagnosis of the contemporary regime as *both* democratic and biopolitical is quite controversial, since the two terms are usually viewed in opposition: 'the onset of life into *dispositifs* of power marks the eclipse of democracy' (Esposito 2008b: 644; see more generally Prozorov 2019). What is even more interesting is that both terms are opposed by him to the idea of *truth:* '[The] contemporary conjuncture, believing itself to possess a stable, guaranteed foundation (democratic materialism) wages against the evidence of truths

15

an incessant propaganda war' (Badiou 2009a: 8). While it is easy to oppose democracy and truth from a quasi-Platonist perspective that Badiou espouses, it is more difficult to oppose biopolitics and truth, insofar as biopolitics, at least in the Foucauldian formulation, is constituted by grounding governmental practices in the ostensibly true knowledge of life sciences, economics and sociology. How can a materialism of life be opposed to truth?

The puzzle is resolved if we consider Badiou's highly specific understanding of truth. After briefly toying with the idea of naming his own approach 'aristocratic idealism' (ibid.: 3), Badiou settles on the term 'materialist dialectic', which introduces into the dualistic axiomatic of bodies and languages a third term in the manner of the *exception*: 'there are only bodies and language, except that there are truths': 'There is no doubt whatsoever concerning the existence of truths which are not bodies, languages or combinations of the two. These truths are incorporeal bodies, languages devoid of meaning, generic infinities, unconditional supplements' (ibid.: 4). Badiou does not disagree with the fact that what there is are, for the most part, bodies and languages, manifested to us in their difference that is of no political or philosophical consequence. Yet, that is not *all* there is in the world, and what is relevant and consequential is precisely that which transcends bodies, languages and the market in which they are rendered equivalent. Truths occur as an exception to what is – they are reducible to neither bodies nor languages, even though, as we shall see, their unfolding in the world is dependent on both.

Since it does not recognise the exceptional existence of truths, the biopolitics of democratic materialism remains hostile to the Idea as such, proclaiming 'the end of ideologies' as the good news, making it possible for speaking bodies to finally 'live without Idea'. While it is ostensibly a humanist ideology, democratic materialism only affirms that within the human which is reducible to the animal, and fears that 'inhuman' capacity for truths that, for Badiou, makes us human in the first place:

> If one fails to recognize the effects of those traces in which the inhuman commands humanity to exceed its being-there, it will be necessary, in order to maintain a purely animalistic, pragmatic notion of the human species, to annihilate both these traces and their infinite consequences. The democratic materialist is a fearsome and intolerant enemy of every human – which is to say inhuman – life worthy of the name. (Ibid.: 4)

16

What is this life worthy of the name? It is a life constituted by the participation in the body of truth that alone makes an individual or a community into a *subject*. In the final chapter of *Logics* entitled 'What is it to Live?' the difference between the life of democratic materialism and Badiou's 'true life' is accentuated most starkly: '"To live" obviously not in the sense of democratic materialism (persevering in the free virtualities of the body) but rather in the sense of Aristotle's enigmatic formula: "to live as an Immortal"' (ibid.: 507). Thus, whereas democratic materialism correlates 'life and individuals', Badiou's materialist dialectics correlates 'truth and subjects' (ibid.: 34). This statement clearly demonstrates Badiou's eagerness to take distance from biopolitics: while democratic materialism can only envision politics in terms of the regulation of the actualisation by bodies of their vital resources, for materialist dialectics politics presupposes the appearance of new bodies of truth, and of the subject (individual or collective) that is constituted by incorporation into these bodies. Thus, democratic materialism can only imagine a biopolitics without truth, while materialist dialectics promises a politics of truth that would abandon biopolitics.

In Chapter 2 we shall return to Badiou's diagnosis and venture to overcome this rigorous separation of the politics of truth from the biopolitics of living bodies. At this point it is important to emphasise that this diagnosis is definitely not anything novel. Badiou himself has on numerous occasions presented his own approach as the defence of philosophy, an enterprise concerned with *truths*, from *sophistry*, which denies the existence of truth and only affirms the game of opinions. The problematic status of truth in a democracy is not a contemporary problem but arguably a problem constitutive of the democratic regime as such, from its very inception in Ancient Greece.

Michel Foucault addressed this problematic relationship between truth, democracy and what he termed governmentality in Antiquity at length in his 1982–3 lecture course *The Government of Self and Others*. In these lectures he focused on the relationship between acts of truth-telling (*parrhesia*) and the equal right to speak (*isegoria*) afforded to all citizens in the Athenian democracy. According to the principle of *isegoria*, one's right to free speech was not affected by one's rank, origin or wealth. It was also not dependent on the truth content of one's enunciations (Foucault 2010: 149–51, 156–8). While these acts of free speech would often make claims to be true for rhetorical purposes in order to please or convince their audience, acts of *parrhesia* were distinguished by one's taking a risk of speaking frankly and directly, perhaps even at the cost of antagonising one's audience (ibid.: 182–3). We must emphasise that while *isegoria* is a *principle* that affirms the equal right to speak irrespective of the content of one's speech, *parrhesia* refers to a particular *mode* of speaking, whose value consists precisely in its claim to be true, even at the cost of negative consequences for the speaker. The principle of *isegoria* makes *parrhesia* legitimate but at the same time it also legitimises the proliferation of opinions that claim no truth value but enjoy the same freedom to be expressed. It is this opposition between truth-telling and free speech that will accompany us throughout this book, as it sets the stage for the familiar conflicts and controversies of the post-truth era: in a regime where one is entitled to say whatever one pleases, how can truth be identified and what is its status and function?

Foucault identified two paradoxes in the relation between truth and democracy, both of which are of relevance for contemporary liberal democracies. Firstly, even as true discourse is possible only on the basis of the democratic *isegoria*, it is not reducible to it and in fact introduces difference into democracy by endowing its practitioners with a certain ascendancy over others. One can only speak the truth if one is free to say anything one wants, but the truth, once it is told, is no longer just a product of free speech but a different kind of speech associated with certain powers and privileges. This is how governmentality in the most general sense begins to be possible in the democratic system:

> There can only be true discourse, the free play of true discourse, an access to true discourse for everybody where there is democracy. [However], true discourse is not and cannot be distributed equally in a democracy according to the form of *isegoria*. Not everyone can tell the truth just because everybody may speak. True discourse introduces a difference, or rather is linked, both in its conditions and its effects, to a difference: only a few can tell the truth. And once only a few can tell the truth, a difference is produced which is that of the ascendancy exercised by some over others. The emergence of true discourse underpins the process of governmentality. (Ibid.: 183–4)

On the one hand, it is only in democracies that discourses of truth can emerge as non-necessary, that is, *contingent*. While authoritarian regimes claim to found their power on the already established truths of tradition, religion or ideology, democracy alone is sustained by the affirmation of radical contingency that makes every truth non-necessary. This assumption of non-necessity ensures that no truth is ever given finally and definitively, which means that true discourses can *continue* to emerge. At the same time, the articulation of a true discourse inevitably contradicts this principle of contingency, insofar as this discourse subjectivises its practitioners in specific ways, often involving their ascendancy over others as 'experts' entitled to guide and direct others in various spheres. The governmentality that is enabled by the existence of true discourses inevitably comes into conflict with the basic presuppositions of democracy.

This paradox has only become more pronounced in the modern era, where government has taken the living processes of the population as its object, becoming biopolitical. Biopolitics is a mode of government that claims a foundation in the scientific knowledge of life, which enables it to discriminate between governmental practices that are properly knowledgeable and hence 'true' and those that do not accord with the scientific foundations and must be rejected as false. Yet, this discrimination contradicts the equality of speech acts under the democratic regime that presupposes that truth is *not* already given but keeps emerging as a matter of contingency out of the free play of opinions. On the one hand, biopolitics insists on a particular truthful way to govern the population as an *object*. On the other hand, the same population is the *subject* of democratic self-government, from which all truths, including the one underlying biopolitics, emanate.

This conflict leads to the perpetual reactualisation of the second paradox, which consists in the fact that while true discourse is needed for democracy to be maintained, democracy itself threatens the existence of this very discourse by exposing it to the challenge of confrontation with the opinions that the principle of *isegoria* permits to be expressed freely:

> [True] discourse must have its place for democracy actually to be able to take its course and to be maintained through misadventures, events, jousts and wars. But on the other hand, inasmuch as this true discourse in democracy only comes to light in the joust, in conflict, in confrontation or rivalry, it is always threatened by democracy. No true discourse without democracy, but true discourse introduces difference into democracy. No democracy without true discourse, but democracy threatens the very existence of true discourse. (Ibid.: 184)

Once again, the biopolitical turn of modernity only exacerbated this paradox: even as biopolitical governance is enabled by democratisation that placed the life of the population on the political agenda, it is also threatened at every point by the democratic challenge. The biopolitical claim to govern on the basis of truth contradicts the foundations of democratic government, which must remain open to contingency and chance and authorises the expression of opinions and even the election of officials who have nothing whatsoever to do with truth. While contemporary theorists of biopolitics have tended to focus on the ways in which biopolitical governance may *undermine* democracy (Agamben 1998: 121–2; Esposito 2008b: 643–4), they have paid a lot less attention to the reverse process whereby the democratic political process may disrupt every attempt to found governance on truth.

Foucault's account of the paradoxical relation between truth, democracy and governance suggests that today's post-truth condition arises from the fundamental constellation of power and knowledge that defines democracy as such, even in its most distant and archaic forms. Democracy both enables the continuous generation of discourses of truth that it relies on in its rationalities of governance and exposes these truths to confrontation and conflict with opinions without the status of truth, which nonetheless enjoy an equal right to be expressed. If that were all there was to post-truth politics, we could dismiss today's concerns by calling it democratic business as usual.

And yet, Foucault's account also attunes us to the specificity of the contemporary moment. As we shall demonstrate repeatedly in this book, the contemporary 'post-truth' constellation has less to do with its questioning and problematising discourses of truth, which defines democracy as such, than with the tendency to reduce all truth to opinion, which can be neither true nor false and whose contestation is therefore meaningless. If Badiou's diagnosis of the contemporary moment is at all correct, if there are indeed only 'bodies and languages' and every body has an equal right to express its desire in its own language, then there is simply no place for discourses of truth to emerge.

Thus, today's post-truth politics does more than replay the originary oscillation between founded governmental rationalities and their democratic contestation on the basis of the principle of *isegoria*. Instead, it renders truth and opinion indistinct, which makes the democratic contestation of authoritative truth claims no longer possible, simply because these claims are no longer authoritative and, in the infamous one-liner of Michael Gove, 'the people have had enough of experts' (Mance 2016: n.p.). They are nothing more than opinions, which deserve the same protection as other opinions – no less but definitely no more. Every statement is nothing other than a body's use of its language to express its desires and needs, which are no more true or false than those of other bodies.

This universal reign of opinions with no criteria to adjudicate between them appears to point to the ultimate triumph of democratic *isegoria* over *parrhesia*. Yet, as Foucault's analysis shows, democracy needs *both* free speech *and* true discourse, and the triumph of one over the other would end up undermining the democratic regime. Badiou's identification of the 'bio-materialist' regime of bodies and languages with democracy thus appears to be somewhat premature. As we shall demonstrate in detail in Chapter 3, it is hardly a coincidence that the idea of the indifference between truth and opinion is most aggressively promoted by regimes and movements advocating and implementing authoritarian and outright repressive policies: if politics is devoid of truth, then all that is left is power that can be exercised without any limitation. If every opinion is as good as any other, why not the opinion of those already in power? And if the discourse of power is itself an opinion, how can it be contested? The assumption of the non-existence of truths appears to leave us entirely disarmed before the worst excesses of power.

Besides being a challenge to democracy, this assumption is an even greater challenge to biopolitical governance, as contemporary controversies regarding Covid dissidence, vaccination scepticism and climate change denialism demonstrate. It is important to differentiate the claims involved in these controversies from the long-standing critical tradition that targets this or that particular truth claim (or set thereof) made in particular sciences, without debunking the category of truth as such. Gove's quip that the 'people in this country have had enough of experts' should not be confused with the time-honoured tradition of the critique of particular kinds of expertise on which governmental policies are based. This critical tradition never sought to dispense with the idea of truth and scientific method but rather problematised the truth claims of particular theories or entire disciplines, be they economics or psychiatry, precisely in the light of this method that exposed them as scientifically dubious and interwoven with rationalities of government (see Foucault 2006; see also Prozorov 2020). This is a far cry from the conspiracist insights of 'truthers' regarding the coronavirus, vaccinations and the shape of planet Earth, whose 'truth claims' are exhausted in the blanket debunking of all recognised truths as lies, based solely on the presumed authority of the speaker.

If the equal right to express one's opinion trumps the foundation of a policy on truth, then biopolitical governance ends up devoid of secure grounds and subjected to the vagaries of democratic decision-making. Yet if democracy is simultaneously undermined by the reduction of truths to opinions, then the problem is exacerbated even further. If the founded knowledge underlying biopolitical governance could previously be contested in democratic settings, now it can simply be ignored, dismissed and ridiculed as a particular opinion, whose status is equal to its blanket dismissal, mockery and ridicule. Unless, of course, it happens to be a very powerful opinion, in which case it can reign freely, no longer constrained by either democracy or truth.

Thus, the post-truth condition risks disrupting both democratic politics and biopolitical governance. While many pages have been devoted to elucidating the fundamental contradictions between democracy and biopolitics (see, for example, Foucault 1977: 222; Agamben 1998: 10; Esposito 2008b: 643–4), it appears that in the post-truth era they can be brought together by having a common enemy. Whereas in our previous book *Democratic Biopolitics* (Prozorov 2019) we have argued for the conceivability, realisability and sustainability of a positive synthesis between democracy and biopolitics, in this book we shall contextualise this synthesis in the contemporary condition of post-truth politics, analysing both the dangers this condition poses to a democratic biopolitics and the possibilities that a democratic reconfiguration of biopolitics offers for addressing the key challenges of post-truth. Before we begin to inquire into a possible cure, let us first dwell on the diagnosis and attempt to define the post-truth condition in a more rigorous manner.

DEFINITION: POST-PROOF, POST-SHAME, POST-CONSENSUS

We suggest that the post-truth condition may be defined in terms of three shifts. In *epistemic* terms, it consists in the move from an *argumentative* logic, in which statements are validated by evidence, proof or logical reasoning, to the *expressionist* logic, in which statements express the speaker's opinion that does not need to be supported by proofs or evidence. In *affective* terms, this condition consists in the tendency to privilege the authenticity of such expressive statements and the downgrading of any sense of shame that might accompany the expression of the self. Finally, in *normative* terms, this condition entails the move away from communication driven by the teleology of *consensus* towards communication driven by the desire to express oneself that no longer seeks consensus and no longer minds *dissent*. In other words, we have moved from a mode of discourse in which parties sought to arrive at consensus by offering proofs and evidence and were ready to yield to the force of the better argument to a mode of discourse in which parties seek to express their authentic selves in the manner that is not ashamed of exposing one's self and not concerned about the dissensual effects of such exposition. Let us briefly consider these three aspects in turn.

Post-proof

From the epistemic perspective, what we are dealing with in the post-truth condition is the increasing indistinction between *argument* and *opinion*, which leads to dispensing with the need for evidence and proof. Post-truth is less a post-fact (as it is sometimes also called) than a post-*proof* era. Facts remain in circulation; in fact, there are more of them than ever in the contemporary condition of information overload. 'There has simply been such a proliferation of facts and fact-producers that trivialization was a natural consequence; oversupply has led to depreciation in value' (Kalpokas 2019: 14).

Precisely because of this proliferation of facts, it becomes increasingly difficult to adjudicate between competing factual claims, trace the evidence for and against them, and thereby separate true factual claims from false ones. Instead, all facts become reducible to opinions or preferences, which need no evidence in their support and can never be either proven or disproven. 'What we call opinions are representations without truth, the anarchic debris of circulating knowledge' (Badiou 2001a: 50).

Badiou argues that opinions are the '[cement] of sociality, a primary element of all communication' (ibid.), sustaining the existence of human beings as 'social animals'. While these opinions, whose object may be anything at all, are certainly important for our being in the world, they remain 'beneath the true and the false' (ibid.: 51). One may communicate endlessly about 'the weather, the latest film, children's diseases, poor salaries, the government's villainy, the performances of the local football team, television, holidays, atrocities far away or closer to home' (ibid.: 50). Yet, this is precisely because this discourse is incapable of producing truths that could put an end to the exchange of opinions by establishing the truth of one and the falsity of the other. Since such an endpoint is barely thinkable, the exchange in question may go on interminably and the speaker could easily substitute one opinion for another in the very course of exchange.

This notion of opinion should be distinguished from that of *argument*, which would find its place in the middle of the spectrum from opinion to truth. An argument is something whose truth cannot be definitely demonstrated or incontestably proven but which nonetheless differs from an opinion insofar as it presupposes the possibility of being supported by evidence, including recognised factual truths, which would permit us to speak of a 'better argument' that should, in the ideal situation, win the contest. When Hannah Arendt uses the notion of opinion to describe the mode of discourse that defines politics, she arguably has in mind precisely arguments rather than mere opinions in Badiou's sense:

> [I] form an opinion by considering a given issue from different viewpoints, by making present to my mind the standpoints of those who are absent. The very process of opinion formation is determined by those in whose places somebody thinks and uses his own mind, and the only condition for this exertion of the imagination is disinterestedness, the liberation from one's own private interests. (Arendt 2006: 237)

It is easy to recognise in this description Kant's account of the aesthetic judgement, which Arendt relies on in her attempt to tease out Kant's political philosophy (Arendt 1992). Yet, Badiou's notion of opinion is entirely devoid of this presupposition of 'enlarged mentality', of taking into account the standpoints of others in a disinterested fashion. While Arendt is able to argue that 'no opinion is self-evident' (Arendt 2006: 238), insofar as it depends on discourse and deliberation by which alone it may ascend from particular standpoints to 'some impartial generality' (ibid.), Badiou's opinions are foreclosed from ever attaining any such generality and remain particular no matter the amount of discourse spent expounding them. While the generality that Arendt speaks could be conceived in terms of a provisional or tentative truth, in Badiou's account opinions could never transcend their particularity and attain any measure of disinterest: on the contrary, the exchange of opinions depends for its continuation on our interest in expressing our opinion and hearing the opinion of the other.

The post-proof syndrome that we are describing here may thus be grasped in terms of the lapse from the Arendtian argumentative notion of opinion to the Badiouan expressive one. For example, a statement 'asparagus is good for your health' is an argument, which could be supported or undermined by the available scientific evidence, however equivocal and tentative. It could also be advanced in a disinterested fashion, taking into account numerous alternative standpoints in order to establish at least a measure of the general consensus about the dietary value of asparagus that we could hold as true. In contrast, a statement 'asparagus is good' merely expresses one's subjective preference, dispensing with any need for evidence or proof that could lead to this consensus. Any consensus that might result from enunciating this statement is purely contingent, explained by nothing but the factual predominance of asparagus lovers in one's audience. Even if everyone in one's audience agreed with it, this statement would not become any more true and, conversely, even if all our interlocutors could not stand asparagus, the statement about its goodness could not be treated as false. Of course, this statement could be expressed by someone with intention to deceive or simply out of sheer politeness, but this 'falsity' would pertain not to the content of the statement but the intention of the speaker – a distinction we will return to when we address the performative dimension of truth in Chapter 4. Since opinions express preferences that cannot be true or false, the reduction of all statements to opinions renders the question of truth as such irrelevant.

Thus, it is not facts that are missing, but *proofs*, which makes all facts equally admissible, but only as opinions. As long as we are dealing with an opinion rather than an argument or a truth claim, it is unnecessary for the speaker to prove it, offer evidence in support of it, or ensure its correspondence with prior knowledge or even its non-contradictory character. The law of non-contradiction does not prevail in the realm of opinions, in which we may well prefer and even desire contrary things at the same time. The statement of opinion needs neither verification nor falsification but immediately counts as an *expression* of one's self, identity or interest. If this opinion is strange, baffling, ridiculous, then so be it – as soon as we are in the realm of opinions, the stranger the opinion, the better chance for circulation it has.

Dispensing with the need to prove one's statement is the key epistemic aspect of post-truth. What has so far gone almost unnoticed is the way this post-proof condition enables authoritarian power. At first glance, this should not necessarily be the case: after all, if all statements are reducible to opinions, one is entitled to pick and state any arbitrary opinion, including those against authoritarianism. Yet, once such opinions are no longer grounded in evidence (of violations of rights, crimes against humanity, etc.) or argumentation (for a better alternative, a more humane way of governing, etc.), they can only be advanced in an arbitrary fashion, as opinions *like any other*, including the opinions in favour of authoritarian government. The dissenting views can no longer rely on the privilege of being true (undistorted by governmental propaganda, official ideology, etc.), but must compete with propaganda and ideology, which in contrast become enabled and empowered by being freed from any burden of justification or proof, which legitimises the very arbitrariness that characterises authoritarian regimes to begin with. Thanks to twentieth-century critical theory's exposure of the complicity of science in politics, today we are more accustomed to see truth claims as operating in the service of powers that be. However, truth-telling has historically served to fortify the powerless who otherwise remain at the mercy of opinions expressed more loudly and fortified by the threat of the use of force against those disagreeing with them (see Foucault 2014: 13–17). In contrast, where there are only opinions, the opinion that prevails is usually the one with a better chance of circulation and better apparatuses of amplification, that is, the opinion of those already in power.

Post-shame

In the field of affects, post-truth is expressed in the *post-shame* disposition. The free expression of one's opinion is a constitutional right in contemporary liberal democracies, which thereby goes further than the ancient principle of *isegoria* in not merely permitting the equal right of speech but also protecting its exercise from censorship, sanction or retribution. With numerous exceptions concerning, for example, obscenity, fraud, libel or incitement to violence, one's right to express one's opinion is legally protected even when there is widespread consensus that the opinion in question is not worthy of being expressed.

This entails that there is no shame involved in expressing even the wildest and weirdest opinions, especially as one no longer is expected to back them up with evidence or proof. One might be ashamed of committing an *error* but since there are no erroneous opinions, all can be said without shame. One no longer argues one's point according to certain rules (a process in which one can succeed or fail) but *expresses* one's opinion or preference, in which one cannot really go wrong. In fact, a purportedly shameless expression of opinion might even enhance the force of one's expression, simply because it is more *expressive*, suggesting greater authenticity (Fieschi 2019: 35–9). This is why the politicians of the post-truth age, often misleadingly labelled populists despite their frequently manifest contempt for the people, including their supporters, so often contradict themselves and established facts, assuming incoherent or inconsistent standpoints. If they sought to *argue* their point, the argument would surely be damaged by its incoherence or contradictions, which would be a great shame. Yet, since they only seek to *express* themselves, all their contradictions and incoherence only serve to render this expression more authentic: however untrue the content of their discourse, its clumsy form ensures that it is 'for real':

> [Such] claims to authenticity go a long way towards justifying all manner of careless pronouncements since expressing your 'true, spontaneous self' cannot be held against you. Authenticity is also a trump card that can be played when caught in a lie – lying and covering up is what real humans do. Claims to authenticity can grant the most disingenuous behavior a measure of sincerity. And, short of producing a measure of sincerity, this kind of bombastic authenticity achieved through lying is often worn as a badge of 'chutzpah' – a willingness to game the system shamelessly and designed to highlight the arcane morality and stupidity of the person, or institution, being deceived. (Ibid.: 36)

The difference between the two logics is clear: in the argumentative logic, one's claim is never the final word in the discussion but is followed by an evaluation, criticism, debate, that result either in its (conditional) acceptance or a refutation. This is what Arendt refers to as 'giving an account' of one's opinion, which necessarily involves the judgement of others and the assumption of responsibility for what one says (Arendt 1992: 41). Yet, an opinion expressed is not necessarily followed by any another speech act, other than a perfunctory mark of recognition of its utterance. The speech act of expression is *complete* when the opinion is uttered. One cannot give account of one's opinion, since it has not been formed in a discursive and deliberative manner but rather simply *is*: as the saying goes, there is no accounting for taste. My opinions regarding the latest pop hit, the weather in Helsinki or Donald Trump's hairstyle cannot be accounted for: they are *thus*, but they could be *otherwise* at any moment in the exchange of opinions, for no reason whatsoever. I can neither account for nor assume responsibility for the opinions that are entirely contingent. Precisely for this reason, I can also express these opinions without any shame involved: an opinion that is neither true nor false, which can be both thus and otherwise, which is not developed in the process of critical judgement but simply happens to me, is not liable to being evaluated by others.

Insofar as such an opinion is to be evaluated at all, it is not with regard to its truth content but with regard to the *mode* of its expression, which must be authentic in the sense of expressing the self as it is, unadorned by the superficial masks or roles one tends to adopt in various social settings. While it is all but impossible for observers to adjudicate whether what is expressed is indeed the authentic self, the perception of authenticity is enhanced precisely by the brazenly unashamed manner of expression. If this expression also happens to be incoherent, contradictory or even openly fraudulent, this merely shows that the self that is being expressed is torn, fractured and conflicted, which no doubt testifies to its being authentic.

Post-consensus

Thirdly, on the level of social normativity, post-truth is manifested in the shift from the value of *consensus* to the valorisation of *dissent*. This shift becomes fully intelligible when we take into account the post-proof and post-shame syndromes discussed above. When politics and government are practised on the basis of the knowledge that can be questioned or contested as to its truth or falsity, the process of argumentation can be viewed as at least ideally leading towards a certain consensus, whereby the 'better argument' prevails, if only in a tentative and transient manner. Even when things do not work ideally and the 'better argument' is revealed to be contaminated by a hegemonic ideology, we are still in the realm of argumentative discourse, in which the aim of the speaker is to gain the adherence of the audience, so consensus remains the ultimate end, even if the paths towards it might be dubious.

When discourse moves from the logic of argumentation to the logic of expression, consensus or adherence ceases to be its ultimate horizon. It is both *more difficult* to attain, since the opinions or preferences one expresses might be idiosyncratic and incommensurable, and *less important* to attain, since it is not clear what value the adherence of the other to the content of my expressed self would be. To recall Badiou, the exchange of opinions sustains our very sociality, yet for this exchange to go on the opinions in question must be different, otherwise there will be little sense in exchanging them.

For this reason, the goal of self-expression is no longer the production of agreement or consensus but, on the contrary, bringing forth disagreement, for the sake of pluralism and diversity, or perhaps even for the purposes of polemic or confrontation, whereby speakers try to outdo each other in expressing themselves more shamelessly and hence authentically. The tendency towards consensus thus gives way to a perpetually reinforced polarisation: 'in the presence of competing voices, one tends to embellish their pitch to make it more appealing, but then everybody starts doing the same, so something even more exciting and appealing is necessary, producing a vicious circle of gratification' (Kalpokas 2019: 22). If the logic of argumentation privileged the formation of majorities, coalitions and alliances, in which a modicum of consensus was attained, the expressionist logic rewards the sheer expression of difference, which leads individuals and groups to adopt ever more extreme positions in order to accentuate how different they are.

Once again, a comparison with Arendt's account of judgement is instructive. In Arendt's reading of Kant, the development of one's judgement through comparison and confrontation with the standpoints of others serves the 'enlargement of the mind', which now incorporates and appropriates the many judgements and perspectives into one's standpoint. This enlargement does not necessarily produce consensus but it certainly enables it: firstly, by separating the formation of judgements from one's particular interests and, secondly, by weaving the judgements of others into one's own, so that the judgements are never mutually exclusive but, as it were, all contain elements of one another. A judgement that is disinterested and enlarged by the judgements of others makes consensus both possible and likely.

In contrast, the expressionist exchange of opinions requires neither subtraction from interest, since interested opinions might well be more interesting, nor their enlargement by the opinions of others, since such enlargement might make the exchange repetitive when all the expressed opinions express a little bit of one another. Instead, the shift from argumentation to expression produces not the enlargement but the contraction of the speaker's 'mind', as it privileges and rewards opinions that are ever more particular, original and even idiosyncratic. The post-shame valorisation of authenticity exacerbates this contraction, insofar as it invites framing these already particular opinions in a hyperbolically individualised manner, as the expression of one's innermost self that displays it in its entirety, with all the quirks and oddities. Rather than aim at producing a judgement by comparison with all possible judgements of all possible others, one seeks to produce an opinion that would be like no other and yet easily substitutable for any other in the process of communication. Our contemporary complaints about filter bubbles and echo chambers miss the target when they put the blame on the latest innovations in social media and information technologies, which only amplify and exacerbate much wider tendencies in public discourse.

As a result of these three intertwined processes, truth claims, which, while fallible and contestable, nonetheless served as building blocks towards the establishment of a modicum of consensus, become entirely superfluous in a discourse, whose statements rather derive their value from being expressed in a free, direct, unadorned fashion.

In his study of post-truth Ignas Kalpokas has defined this shift in somewhat similar terms as the move from information to experience (2019: 33–42). While the 'age of information' was characterised by the unprecedented expansion of the sources of information and an even more dramatic acceleration of access to it, the 'age of experience' responds to this information overload by discriminating between those numerous sites and sources of information by introducing the affective criterion, filtering the diverse information in such a way as to retain only that which increases one's satisfaction. Faced with the overwhelming supply of information, we behave like consumers, choosing that which we most enjoy. The providers of information adapt to this shift by tailoring the information to the audiences with the help of big data on our preferences. In this manner, in the absence of any imposition of hegemonic content or even the manipulation of consumer choices, there occurs a 'collusion' between the providers and the consumers of information (ibid.: 18):

> From the perspective of the audience, experience is the primary expectation: audiences have no desire of being merely passively exposed to information; instead, they expect affective connection, something that makes the story stick emotionally and allows people to be part of it. The capacity to create data-informed accumulations of individuals also reinforces the expectation, on behalf of the audiences, of tailor-made, individual-specific, and unchallenging content. (Ibid.: 34)

This explains why the attempts to confront the unpalatable excesses of the post-truth condition through fact-checking and debunking 'fake news' have been so ineffective: there is no guarantee whatsoever that the fact-checking information would actually be selected by the audience already accustomed and attuned to the 'experience' or 'enjoyment' filter. While false facts or narratives may be selected as enjoyable, their debunking, which does not provide the same enjoyment, would then be ignored, unless of course it is presented '[with] an even stronger emotional load than that of the original statement. But then, making facts attractive almost necessarily involves cropping and framing them, in turn defeating the very purpose of fact-checking' (ibid.: 39).

The effects of this shift go beyond the field of media and communication technology and pertain to the epistemic status of the information filtered through the imperatives of enjoyment. This filtering does not merely perform a quantitative reduction in the amount of information consumed, but transforms the information in a qualitative way. When the information is selected on the basis of the enjoyment it offers, it is no longer thinkable in terms of the categories of what we have termed the argumentative logic, simply because what is experienced as enjoyable need not be an argument, in whole or in part, on its own or in comparison with others, but might just as well be an opinion, a taste preference, a colourful turn of phrase, a funny accent or a seductive glance – *anything* as long as it contributes to one's enjoyable experience. While Kalpokas focuses primarily on the reception of this filtered information and

31

hence defines it in terms of *experience*, we would supplement this focus with the production of the information in question, which leads us to focus on *expression* as the correlate of experience. What we experience by filtering the information in accordance with the imperatives of our enjoyment is something that is no longer argued, verified or proven (or even arguable, verifiable or provable) but rather something *expressed* – an opinion, a preference, approval or disapproval, like or dislike.

This content is not evaluated in accordance with truth criteria (be they those of correspondence, consistency, coherence, consensus or any other theory of truth) but in accordance with whether and how it expresses the speaker's self, identity, beliefs or feelings, which are at once held to be *deserving* of free expression (the right to which may even be enshrined in law) and *not* subject to criticism, contestation or debunking (which may even be prohibited by law as offensive, insulting, hate speech, etc.). This explains the frequently discussed tendency in the post-truth era to ascribe value or even privilege to emotive and affective expressions over rational, discursive and deliberative arguments, the tendency well captured by Jayson Harsin's notion of 'emo-truth' (Harsin 2017: 514). This is not simply because we, as consumers of information, happen to like more emotively coloured information as opposed to dry facts but because in the absence of argumentative value, statements have nothing other to fall back on than expressive value, for example their presumed authenticity, sincerity or frankness.

In terms of J. L. Austin's theory of performativity that we shall return to in detail in subsequent chapters, we may say that the move from the argumentative to the expressionist logic entails a relative devaluation of the locutionary content of statements (their lexical meaning that *could* be true or false) in favour of their illocutionary force (what is being done *in* saying something) and perlocutionary effects (what is attained *by* saying something) (Austin 1975: 98–132). Neither of the latter can be evaluated in terms of truth and falsity: an act may be *unsuccessful* (or, in Austin's wording, 'unhappy') in terms of its illocutionary force or *ineffective* in terms of its perlocutionary effects, but it does not make it false in any meaningful sense.

From this perspective, the expression 'emo-truth' might appear problematic, since the expressive value of the statement does not pertain to its locutionary content, where its putative truth could be at stake, but to its illocutionary force and perlocutionary effects, that is, whether the statement successfully performs an *action* (pleading, demanding, requesting, promising, etc.) and achieves a desired *effect* (convincing, persuading, deceiving, cheating, frightening, etc.). It is thus more a matter of emo-*force* than emo-truth. In the final chapter we shall demonstrate how truth and force nonetheless remain intertwined in the experience of truth-telling, in which truth content in the locutionary aspect must be accompanied by a particular kind of illocutionary force to become effective. Rather than simply testify to the abandonment of the concern for truth, 'emo-truth' might well point to the way to bringing truth back into democratic politics.

REGIME: EQUIVALENCE VS EQUALITY

The expressionist logic of discourse that we have reconstituted is immediately familiar to all of us, since it functions as a spontaneous ideology in Western liberal democracies without being reducible or even traceable to any particular epistemological theory or political orientation. We encounter it in every affirmation of the *situated* character of all knowledge, which approaches all truth claims as conditioned by the situation from which they are uttered. If this situated character is understood in the reductionist manner, knowledge, which can be true or false, is *reduced to its situation*, which cannot be true or false by definition. A statement reducible to its situation (or serving as a mere 'reflection' of this situation) is no longer liable to evaluation in terms of its truth or falsity, but at most to checking whether it *expresses its situation* accurately or correctly. We thus move from analysing how a truth claim is constructed, presented, argued, proven, supported or falsified to questioning what the statement *expresses*, be it identity, culture or a political standpoint.

Since they cannot be true or false, these expressions are not different in kind from opinions or preferences; the only difference is that the latter need not express anything and as such are free to prefer anything whatsoever for no reason, while in the logic of situated knowledge statements remain *tied* to their situation, which they presumably cannot transcend. The knowledge that can be produced is therefore not unlimited. Yet, these are precisely the limits that the pursuit of knowledge has historically sought to overcome: the progress of sciences is at least partly driven by the desire to *overcome* one's present situation and the limits it imposes on our knowledge and understanding, hence the attempt to *refound* it on these very limits appears to be a curious case of self-imposed constraint.

The same applies *a fortiori* to the idea of grounding knowledge in the standpoint one adopts with regard to one's situation – the idea known as 'standpoint epistemology' in social sciences. As such, this kind of grounding does not exclude the idea of truth. On the contrary, the awareness of one's position in a social hierarchy may provide both an *impetus* to search for truth (about, for example, the origins and the contemporary persistence of that hierarchy) and the best *perspective* on its pursuit (by giving immediate access to the experiences others must first take up as the object of study). Quite simply put, one's standpoint may help one produce *better* knowledge, theories with *greater* explanatory powers, hypotheses supported by *more* evidence – in short, the knowledge that, while fallible, may be held as true, at least in the absence of the knowledge that would be better still.

However, if the knowledge thus inspired and directed by one's situation and standpoint on it ends up *reducible* to them, this adjudication between better or worse knowledge, greater and lesser explanatory power is no longer possible, since standpoints cannot be the object of true or false statements. While it is possible to argue for the superiority of the standpoint of the marginalised or the oppressed in ethico-political terms, it is much more difficult to do so in epistemic terms: if oppression is bad, in what sense is the knowledge derived from it 'good', or at least 'better' than the knowledge derived from another, presumably non-oppressed standpoint? Once knowledge is justified by the standpoint from which it originates, we are bound to adjudicate in vain between these starting points rather than the *end-points* of the journey, that is, the true or false knowledge produced by scientific methods or through deliberative discourse.

All that remains is the knowledge that is privileged because the standpoint from which it arises acquires an epistemic privilege due to its political, economic or cultural status, which may be derived from either its hegemonic or its marginalised character. While one may agree that this knowledge is good or valuable, it becomes difficult to prove that it is in any way *true* and the very question of its truth becomes irrelevant, since what matters more is the authenticity of the standpoint being expressed and the strategic function of this expression in the political field. One's knowledge ends up literally as good as one's standpoint and functions more in the mode of a 'political weapon' (Arendt 2006: 231), whose truth is entirely beside the point.

In the academic field the idea of standpoint epistemology has generated a lively debate that problematised its philosophical and political implications (Grebowicz 2007; see more generally Harding 1991; Hekman 1997; Hartsock 2004; Latour 2004). The very occurrence of this debate demonstrates, however, that we still remain in the realm of truth, precisely to the extent that its meaning continues to be contested. Yet, in the political field, the same spontaneous ideology prevails in a rather less subtle and refined manner, yielding two familiar scenarios. Firstly, we may observe the conflict around the occupation of the locus of the epistemically privileged standpoint, which today is defined by the experience of exclusion, oppression or subjugation. The entire project of the alt-right, identitarianism and 'white nationalism' is a thinly disguised attempt to apply the logic of standpoint epistemology to the position commonly held to be majoritarian or privileged, but increasingly wary of losing this status. Presenting itself as the 'new oppressed', the (soon to be former) oppressor plays the victim *in advance*, claiming for itself the privileges associated with being the opposite of privileged. While this appropriation is decried by its opponents as hypocritical, we must note that, according to the expressionist logic at work in it, it can no longer be simply refuted as false. If it is no longer a matter of knowledge, whose truth and falsity may be established by method and argument, but only a matter of (self-)expression of one's own situation and standpoint, then it is impossible to prove that whoever expresses their sense of marginalisation or oppression is not 'in fact' marginalised or oppressed, simply because we no longer know to what exactly this 'in fact' refers. It is difficult to resort to the once familiar process of accumulating facts to disprove such claims, since these facts may be dismissed as meaningful and relevant only from another standpoint and their very introduction into the debate offers yet another demonstration (but not proof!) of the marginalisation asserted in the first place.

The second scenario is a consequence of precisely this contestation and consists in attempting to resolve this conflict by splitting up the privileged position into a plurality of standpoints: if we cannot decide who is more oppressed, let us agree that we are all a bit oppressed in our own ways and endow with value every standpoint as long as it expresses something, anything at all. We thereby arrive at an *identitarian pluralism*, in which the most diverse identity

35

claims may be legitimately expressed as long as none of them claims to attain a privileged position. To recall Badiou's diagnosis, every body is entitled to expressing its grievances in its own language, yet no one's grievance is bad enough to endow their language with any privilege over others. While this approach might be preferable to the conflict over the privileged standpoint, it leaves society in a state of passive nihilism, where a plurality of positions exist with no hope of adjudicating between them, since what is expressed in them are not truth claims but identitarian predicates, the legacy of oppression or the perceptions of being marginalised.

The problem with this position is not merely that some of these claims may be indefensible, since we have abandoned the standards of argumentation and proof according to which they could be defended. Much more importantly, this pluralism entails the perpetuation of the very processes and relations that gave rise to the grievances in the first place: since there is no longer a standpoint from which the *entirety* of the system may be evaluated (or there are too many of such standpoints), the grievances in question can only be ceaselessly *communicated* but never *resolved*, since their resolution is disabled by the very logic that transformed truth claims into grievances to begin with.

Thus, the expressionist logic does not merely characterise the most evidently pathological forms of political discourse (of charlatans, cranks and conspiracy theorists) but operates in a much wider context, including rather more respectable forms of political and academic discourse. We therefore concur with Bruno Latour's claim about the uneasy resemblance of the least palatable tendencies in political discourse today to the most refined exemplars of critical discourse in social sciences:

> it worries me to detect, in those mad mixtures of knee-jerk disbelief, punctilious demands for proofs, and free use of powerful explanation from the social neverland many of the weapons of social critique. Of course conspiracy theories are an absurd deformation of our own arguments, but, like weapons smuggled through a fuzzy border to the wrong party, these are our weapons nonetheless. (Latour 2004: 230)

This evidently does not mean that critical discourse is somehow responsible for the lapse of politics into various forms of identitarianism, let alone that the two have somehow become identical, but only that a tendency towards privileging expression over argumentation is irreducible to any particular context, let alone a particular orientation within it.

It is indeed easy to see how the expressionist logic *itself* facilitates its own progressive envelopment of ever more domains or contexts: after all, if all statements do nothing other (and nothing more) than express particular standpoints or identities, they become phenomena of the same order, which may in principle be *substituted* for one another, entirely irrespective of their content. If there are only opinions to be expressed, it does not really matter whether the opinion in question concerns a work of art, a theoretical treatise, a political party, a pension fund or a new brand of toothpaste: what takes place in statements on these objects is not the questioning of their truth but the expression of the speaker's own self insofar as it relates to them.

In all these apparently different cases we are dealing with *opinions*, which, firstly, do not need to be verified or even supported by evidence; secondly, express one's inner self and hence are *worthy* of being expressed irrespective of their content with no fear of or shame about being wrong; and, thirdly, are not expressed in order to persuade others or arrive at a consensus but simply enunciated *as such*, with no discussion or deliberation to follow. While the argumentative logic implied the non-equivalence of statements in its very principle of the 'force of the better argument', which presupposed the possibility of adjudicating *which* argument is better, in the expressionist logic there is no such thing as a better or worse argument, since what is enunciated in it is not an argument at all. Instead, in the new regime all enunciations circulate as *equivalent*, no better or worse than each other. While some opinions may be more popular than others, this does not make them any better, let alone truer in any meaningful way.

There may be many reasons why we could be interested in someone's opinion on the latest musical fad, their preferred brand of toothpaste or their favourite opera singer, but they have nothing to do with truth and usually pertain to our fondness for the person in question, our flattering nature or an insidious strategy to curry favour with someone. Conversely, when someone shares with us an opinion that we are not interested in, we brush it off and say 'whatever', which is as such an ideal response to the expression of *any* opinion: whatever someone's preference is, it does not matter; there is no truth in it. Thus, while the opinions in question are certainly

37

not equal in their popularity, circulation or prestige, they nonetheless remain *equivalent* in their status as opinions that can no longer be adjudicated as to their truth or falsity. The shift from the argumentative to the expressionist logic of discourse entails the levelling of all differences in kind between the statements that are expressed, rendering them all equivalent with one another. This is why we propose to define the post-truth condition as a *regime of equivalence.*

The idea of equivalence helps us grasp what is at stake in post-truth and abandon facile misunderstandings of this condition. While it would certainly be naïve to imagine that we once lived in a 'truth era', in which our politics and ethics were safely grounded in absolute truths, it is rather less far-fetched to suggest that we have moved from a discursive regime that ventured to discriminate between statements on the basis of various contestable truth criteria to a regime that is increasingly non-discriminating on these criteria, rendering all statements equivalent as opinions.

We may elaborate this idea of equivalence with the help of Jean-Luc Nancy's recent account of important differences between equivalence and equality – two notions that are often treated as all but identical. While the idea of equivalence presupposes a common measure in terms of which different things could be rendered *commensurable*, the idea of equality rather asserts the equal dignity of all beings or things precisely insofar as they remain *incommensurable*:

> Equivalence is not equality. It is not the equality that the French Republic sets between liberty and fraternity and that can in fact be thought of as both a synthesis and a surpassing of these two notions. Equality designates here the strict equality in dignity of all living humans, not excluding other registers of dignity for all living beings, even for all things. Dignity is the name of the value that it is absolutely valid, [which means] it has no worth if to 'have worth' implies a scale of measure. (Nancy 2015: 40)

The exemplary paradigm of the logic of equivalence is of course money as the 'general equivalent' in an economy, which renders plural and incommensurable objects, forms, ends or senses substitutable and exchangeable at the cost of effacing their singularity. Incommensurable things thus become equivalent, but only by being stripped of their singularity and subjected to the evaluative regime that calculates their 'worth' in terms other than their own.

In contrast to this economic logic that is all too familiar to us, Nancy offers the idea of a 'communism of nonequivalence' (ibid.: 41) that affirms the equal dignity of singularities as such, not insofar as they are worth something in terms of a general standard or equivalent. The singularities in question are not treated as equivalent but rather as radically incommensurable:

> [Persons] and moments, places, gestures of a person, the hours of the day or night, words spoken, clouds that pass, plants that grow with a knowing slowness. Each time it is a question of a particular consideration, of attention and tension, of respect, even of what we can go so far as to call adoration, directed at singularity as such. (Ibid.: 39)

While the economic logic of equivalence proceeds through estimation or valuation of what things are worth in some extrinsic terms, the political logic of equality rather proceeds by holding in esteem all there is, thereby implying that its dignity goes beyond any possible estimation: '[Esteem] goes beyond itself and addresses something inestimable, a term used in French to designate something more precious than any price, something incalculable, so exceeding any possible calculation that one does not even try to imagine it' (ibid.: 39).

While the logic of equivalence leads to the sterile and inconsequential affirmation of atomised individuals and groups as interchangeable and substitutable, the logic of equality affirms 'absolute and irreducible singulars that are not individuals or social groups but sudden appearances, arrivals and departures, voices, tones – here and now every instant' (ibid.: 41). While he is just as opposed as Badiou to the 'democratic materialist' circulation of bodies and languages in the space of general equivalence, Nancy is not content with adding to this circulation the exceptional eruption of truths but rather affirms the equality of *all* singularities in their very incommensurability. To the extent that Nancy has a concept of truth similar to Badiou's, it pertains not to any one of these singularities but rather to their *co*-existence as both incommensurable and equal (see Nancy 2010; Prozorov 2019: ch. 4).

We shall return to the question of the applicability of this logic of equality in the post-truth context at the end of the book. For the time being, let us consider the logic of equivalence in more detail in its application to the truth content of statements. Nancy argues that 'the regime of general equivalence henceforth virtually absorbs, well beyond the monetary or financial sphere but thanks to it and with regard to it, all the spheres of existence of humans, and along with them all things that exist' (Nancy 2015: 5). Evidently, this does not mean that the humans or things in question become equal or equalised – on the contrary, their inequality now becomes measurable and they become commensurable *in their very inequality*. Equivalence does not make beings or things more or less equal, it only makes them substitutable or exchangeable.

Thus, when we speak of a regime of equivalence of statements, we do not mean that from now, in the post-truth age every statement is held to be of equal value or equal worth. On the contrary, in this regime many statements may be found to be devoid of value or worthless, yet never *on their own terms*, but in terms of their substitutability, exchangeability or convertibility. What is worthless is simply that which cannot be exchanged, something whose singularity remains resistant to conversion or substitution into exchange value. Conversely, what is valuable is what readily assumes this exchange value, shedding all its idiosyncrasy and becoming substitutable for anything else.

In our context of post-truth, the regime of equivalence asserts that a statement is admissible only insofar as it *recognises* its own substitutability for another statement, which is evidently not the same as affirming that these statements are equal. What is at stake is rather the understanding that every statement, however popular or marginal, is an opinion 'like any other'. The most widely circulated and shared view and the most marginal or extremist stance are not equal in any meaningful sense of the word but they are equivalent precisely as statements of opinion: nothing in principle precludes their changing places and if they do not, it is only for contingent reasons.

In her essay 'The Concept of History' Hannah Arendt addressed the problem of equivalence in two at first glance very different contexts. Firstly, in the course of the revolutionary changes in the natural sciences since the beginning of the twentieth century it became increasingly difficult to sustain the modern ideal of scientific theories as verified or falsified by facts:

> Almost every axiom seems to lend itself to consistent deductions and this to such an extent that it is as though men were in a position to prove almost any hypothesis they might choose to adopt, not only in the field of purely mental constructions like the various overall interpretations of history which are all equally well supported by facts, but in the natural sciences as well. (Arendt 2006: 86)

40

It is not a matter of theoretical pluralism, whereby different theories would 'reveal different but objectively true aspects of the same phenomenon' (ibid.: 87), but of a rather more disconcerting discovery that any thesis whatsoever could be consistently 'proven'. Once the meaning of a phenomenon is found in the wider process in which it figures, it becomes possible to '[impose] upon the maze of facts almost any pattern' (ibid.: 81), so that all hypotheses become in some sense equally 'true'.

Arendt then moves on to the totalitarian regimes of the twentieth century and argues that their defining feature goes one step further in this assertion of the equivalence of all hypotheses:

> action can be based on any hypothesis and [. . .] in the course of consistently guided action, the particular hypothesis will become true, will become actual, factual reality. The assumption which underlies consistent action can be as mad as it pleases; it will always end in producing facts which are then 'objectively' true. (Ibid.: 87–8)

The totalitarian conviction that 'everything is possible' paves the way for extremely arbitrary and violent action that seek to produce in the real the truth of the hypothesis these movements began with. In this manner, it is not only our knowledge of reality that ends up ultimately contingent and arbitrary but so also does in some sense reality itself, which at any point in time can be recreated in various ways on the basis of the most bizarre assumptions which nonetheless yield worlds, in which these assumptions 'become axiomatic and self-evident' (ibid.: 88). In this frightening image, anything could at any moment mean or become anything else, for no reason.

While Arendt's diagnosis may appear hyperbolic, it remains prescient and highly relevant for the contemporary post-truth condition precisely in her emphasis on the *equivalence* of all theories or ideologies, which results from their deployment as holistic frameworks, in which alone events or phenomena become intelligible. If it is possible to prove or act on any hypothesis, then not only truth but also meaning end up effaced, 'and the consistency we would be left with could just as well be the consistency of an asylum for paranoiacs or the consistency of the current demonstrations of the existence of God' (ibid.: 87). Once the question of truth gives way to the requirement of consistency, we are left with a plurality of explanatory frameworks

41

that all appear to work and between which it is impossible to adjudicate. While these frameworks could never become equal in their scope, reach or popularity, they remain equivalent *as* frameworks of interpretation or action, whose truth is no longer at issue.

In the mode of discourse that we termed argumentative, this equivalence was limited by the existence of the *hierarchy* between statements that counted as true, however provisionally or contestably, and the statements excluded as false. The hierarchy could be founded in different ways: for example, statements supported by evidence vs statements lacking evidence, statements supported by accepted scientific knowledge vs statements in contradiction with it, statements produced in accordance with certain accepted standards vs statements unacceptable in terms of these standards, and so on. In one way or another some *order* of discourse is established and maintained by separating true and false statements, excluding some statements as a priori unacceptable or inadmissible, establishing procedures for adjudicating between right and wrong, better or worse constructed statements, and so on. Foucault's famous lecture 'The Order of Discourse' (Foucault 1981) is a good example of how such an order is sustained through a series of *exclusions* (e.g. of statements considered unreasonable or false), *rarefaction* (through privileging some statements as primary and foundational, enabling subsequent secondary commentary on them) and *restrictions* (of some statements to some figures, circumstances, places, etc.).

The argumentative logic of discourse limits equivalence by these and other ordering procedures, which function as thresholds or limits to substitution or exchange. If no such limits or thresholds exist, equivalence begins to reign supreme, resulting in a *minimally ordered discourse*, in which statements circulate as undifferentiated or like units, opinions 'like any other'. While in the Foucauldian ordered discourse one could easily observe numerous *kinds* of statements: unreasonable talk, apprentice speech, foundational discourse, commentary, educational discourse, and so on, governed by different rules of formation and enjoying a different status in the discursive economy, in the equivalentially structured discourse all statements are of the same kind: opinions expressing the speaker's self.

Since there is no ordering procedure to separate true and false opinions, make some opinions more fundamental or restrict the opinions on some things to specific kinds of speakers, all opinions end up commensurable and substitutable, never as equal but only as equivalent. Precisely because of the assumption of equivalence, it is now possible to establish the *worth* of particular opinions, not in any substantive terms that would return us to evaluating these opinions on their own terms, but only in terms of their exchange value: Trump's latest tweet on the coronavirus might thus be shared a thousand times more than the latest article on the subject in the professional journal. Just like money as a general equivalent permits us to estimate greater values in terms of lesser values or the other way round, circulation, 'likes' or 'shares' permit us to render commensurable the most diverse opinions, as long as we bracket off entirely the question of their content, their meaning and, finally, their truth.

Since thousands of pages of critical theory have focused on the ordering operations of discourses, the idea of a minimally ordered or simply disordered discourse strikes us as somewhat unlikely, almost unnatural. We are more accustomed to seeing ordering operations or, when they appear invisible, simply positing them as concealed, yet still there. This is why critical theory finds it so difficult to come to terms with post-truth: if what we were trained to target was the *order* of discourse, there is little left to target in the regime of equivalence that is no longer interested in establishing lines of exclusion, rarefaction and restriction but lets things flow freely, even as there is very little freedom to be gained from this free flow.

CONTRAST: POST-TRUTH POLITICS OR TRUTH POLITICS?

We may elaborate our understanding of post-truth as a regime of equivalence by contrasting it with Ignas Kalpokas's recent political theory of post-truth, outlined in the eponymous book. We certainly share Kalpokas's basic understanding of the post-truth condition in terms of an increasing *indistinction* between truth and falsehood (as opposed to the triumph of the latter over the former). We also agree that this condition is not an attribute of particular political positions but a *universal* condition of our time, facilitated by but not reducible to the innovations in communication technologies that enable the 'collusion' between the producers of information, who find it easier to target their audiences, and its consumers, who find it easier to select the information that appeals to them (Kalpokas 2019: 11–22). Finally, we agree with Kalpokas's idea of the shift from the age of information to the age of *experience*, in which affective selection

43

criteria become more important than strictly cognitive or pragmatic ones (ibid.: 34–5).

Yet, while we agree with Kalpokas's *diagnosis* of the post-truth condition, his *interpretation* of this condition remains tied to what this condition has arguably succeeded, that is, truth. It is as if Kalpokas recoils from the radicality of his own diagnosis and renders it more bearable through an interpretation that makes it more familiar and acceptable to us. Firstly, when Kalpokas asserts that the specificity of the post-truth condition consists in the fact that phenomena now become true by virtue of their *effects*, he is arguably describing the logic of performative efficacy that characterises any 'pre-post-truth' period as well. There is nothing particularly 'post-truth' in the performative dimension of language, that is, its illocutionary force and perlocutionary effects. The capacity of statements to produce certain effects qualifies them as 'true' in such diverse settings as scientific experiments (where an expected effect may confirm a theory), ancient curses (whose successful materialisation qualifies one as a true sorcerer or witch, not a mere impostor) or weather forecasts (which are viewed as true when they successfully predict a certain state of affairs). By the same token, there is nothing particularly new about particular narratives or ideological discourses becoming 'true' in a particular context by virtue of the effects of identification, sympathy or solidarity that they produce. If the effects of an utterance or a practice make it true, this evidently must mean that truth and falsehood remain *distinct* at least to some extent, which is precisely what no longer happens in the post-truth condition, by Kalpokas's own (as well as our) definition. In contrast, as we shall discuss in detail in Chapter 2, post-truth consists precisely in the opposite tendency of the *decline* of performative efficacy of speech, which can longer produce this distinction between truth and falsity and hence remains in some sense spoken *in vain*.

The same criticism may be advanced against Kalpokas's second and related line of interpretation, which, in a play on words, views truth as a result less of its effects than of its *affects*: things become (held as) true when they please, entertain or captivate us. While the importance of the affective dimension in the rise of post-truth politics cannot be overstated, it is its linkage with truth that remains problematic, as long as post-truth is defined in terms of the indistinction between truth or falsity. If what is pleasant to us is endowed with the status of truth, however problematic the logic behind this

44

endowment might be, then truth must still be held as *distinct* from falsehood, and, moreover, must still be held in some regard, since there would otherwise be no reason whatsoever to label pleasant or entertaining statements true. Just as in the case of performative efficacy, there is little new in the tendency to elevate the opinion that pleases one to the status of truth, even though in the 'pre-post-truth' age this elevation was probably a less than lauded practice. If post-truth is to be conceptualised in its specificity, then the pleasure in question must be *dissociated* from truth and, as we shall argue in the following chapter, lie in discourse as such, entirely irrespective of its truth and even of its meaning.

Thirdly, Kalpokas's discussion of post-truth in terms of the abandonment of the demand for truth for the more modest requirement of *verisimilitude* again begs the question of whether there is anything new about this condition. As he recognises, even contemporary philosophy of science, which is quite distant from today's post-truth discourses, has long accepted verisimilitude (or the relative 'truth-likeness') of a theory as a sufficient condition for the progress of knowledge. It is enough that a theory be *more truthlike* than its predecessors for it to be accepted as truth, until a more verisimilar theory comes along. Since we are unlikely to know the (whole) truth about any given object, we must make do with getting *closer* to the truth.

For Kalpokas, this idea of verisimilitude 'opens up possibilities for post-truth to enter the fray' (ibid.: 93). Yet, unless the idea of verisimilitude is used very loosely or metaphorically, it is difficult to see how this is possible. Verisimilitude abandons the idea of finding the complete and undistorted truth but retains the *distinction* between truth (or even truthlikeness) and falsity: giving up the search for the absolutely best explanation, it nonetheless remains capable of *adjudicating* between more true and less true explanations, which is the only reason theories can be compared and found wanting in terms of their verisimilitude, and not in terms of some other criterion, such as aesthetic value, brevity, economic utility or political expediency. For Kalpokas, the danger of this notion consists in privileging explanatory power over correspondence with facts: 'if a truth-claim is well-structured and provides a compelling narrative, then it can exert a strong explanatory power and have predictive potential as a self-fulfilling prophecy' (ibid.: 93). Yet, this is only a problem if this claim is no longer evaluated in terms of its truth-*likeness*, which presupposes our capacity to evaluate whether something is at all like the truth, but *only* in terms of its coherence, clarity and predictive potential, which indeed would make any ideology or conspiracy theory appear to qualify as true, as in Arendt's frightening premonition. While certainly a weaker truth criterion than the idea of correspondence in epistemic realism, verisimilitude still belongs to the domain of truth, even if it presses onto its limits.

The final point on which we would diverge from Kalpokas concerns the question of *meaning*. For Kalpokas, the post-truth condition should be understood as a quest for meaning and meaningfulness in an age when both political tendencies and technological innovations have put meaning in peril, either by reducing politics to management and administration or by providing too much information that one struggles to make sense of. Understood in these terms, post-truth becomes something we all can easily relate to and perhaps even accept, if only because the alternative is so unappealing. Thus, at the end of the book, Kalpokas explicitly rejects the snobbish and patronising discourse of its critics who file under post-truth any idea that conflicts with the current mainstream or expert consensus (ibid.: 127–30).

Yet, the question remains of whether this quest for meaning is really the defining feature of what we have come to call the post-truth condition. It is somewhat counter-intuitive to view Trump, Farage, or, on the other side of the ideological spectrum, Macron or Kurz as offering a pathway out of the meaningless into the meaningful, providing a sense of orientation about where we are and where we are going. If anything, these and other figures of our age are usually criticised for reducing political discourse to meaningless staple phrases or soundbites, which could be flamboyant or vapid but are rarely meaningful. It appears that the quest for meaning rather belongs to the period *preceding* post-truth: perhaps the entire modernity, from the Renaissance onwards, could be viewed as the quest for meaning after the decline of the symbolic efficacy of religion that previously took care of that need. Modern science, grand political ideologies, popular culture are all answers to this desire for meaning. Yet, if this is the case, the phenomenon of post-truth appears to elude us, becoming all but indistinct from whatever age preceded it. Kalpokas recognises this in the final chapter of the book:

> [There] seems to be no room for the difference between pleasure excited by truth and one caused by post-truth. The only difference there is seems to be that of meaning, created within the broader cultural and societal

context, and the meaning of truth seems to be changing from one based on strict correspondence with facts to a more verisimilitudinal one, in which the most important thing is that a proposition makes sense in the environment within which it is uttered. Or, to put it in a different way, the meaning of truth is that the statement has meaning for the audience, the meaning being collusively co-constructed by both the communicators and the audiences. (Ibid.: 115)

Kalpokas appears to argue that the pleasure formerly provided by truths in the more narrow sense of correspondence to facts has given way to the pleasure provided by context-dependent, affective and verisimilar 'truths'. Yet, if we take into account our claims above about the belonging of contextual, verisimilar and affective truths to the 'truth' era, then the difference appears to vanish altogether. Just as it is difficult to see how sheer 'correspondence to facts' could yield any kind of pleasure, it is difficult to see how this restrictive truth could fail to have 'meaning for the audience', which is the criterion that he reserves for the post-truth era.

It is as if Kalpokas begins with post-truth only to end up explaining the desire for and attraction to *truth*, which he finds, in a diluted and compromised form, even in the post-truth condition. As a result, the post-truth condition ends up more *familiar* (since we know it from the 'truth era' that preceded it) and less *dangerous* (since we are accustomed to political projects defined in terms of the quest for meaning). It is not a coincidence that in his political interpretation of post-truth Kalpokas relies on Ernesto Laclau's theory of hegemony, which was developed to account for the paradigmatically modern political phenomena or events, from class struggle (Laclau and Mouffe 1985) to populism (Laclau 2005). In Laclau's approach, articulatory practices ensure that the desire for meaning is always satisfied, in a fragile and tentative way, through the institution of a certain *hegemonic order*, whose particularistic, context-specific and affective truths claim the universality they can never possess. Laclau's hegemony thus accords with Foucault's idea of a *regime of truth*, in which truth functions as the product of contingent practices of ordering the production of statements, the practices that are themselves neither true nor false. In both approaches, social or scientific discourses are held together by a particular 'truth' ascending to the status of the universal: there is truth, only and insofar as there is *one* truth, clearly contrasted with falsity. It is easy to see how both these approaches are perfectly adequate for describing the era of mass politics, grand ideologies, national public spheres – the era whose *passing* arguably brought us into the post-truth condition. Neither Laclau's hegemony nor Foucault's regime of truth appears to fare very well in describing societies in which political discourses are increasingly devoid of even a partial fixation of meaning, where floating signifiers continue to float, as master signifiers become increasingly incapable of mastery.

Of course, Kalpokas realises that the post-truth condition does not really follow Laclau's logic of hegemonic articulations, yet he seems to view it more as a radicalised extension of the same logic than as a break with it. That way he is able to conclude, somewhat too optimistically, that the post-truth condition remains a matter of a search for meaning in a world where former grand narratives of meaning no longer work. Yet, if that were so, we could not really speak of *indifference* that defines post-truth: a search for meaning, however understood, must presuppose some discrimination between better and worse meanings, things that are more or less meaningful. It is precisely this discrimination that the regime of equivalence that characterises post-truth no longer requires, instead producing a flurry of opinions that can be used to construct individually tailored 'meanings', whose very plurality and interchangeability ensures their ultimate meaninglessness.

In our view, it is the dispensation not merely with truth (and the desire for truth) but also with meaning (and the desire for meaning) that permits us to distinguish the post-truth age from the preceding era, in which truths were contested and meanings challenged precisely because they *mattered*, both to their producers and to their audiences. The novelty of the post-truth condition is that with the increasing indistinction of truth and falsity, formerly stable meanings also tend to dissolve, paving the way for numerous combinations of freely floating elements that never amount to meaningful articulations but retain their fragmentary and transient nature. In contrast to a hegemonic order or a regime of truth, such a setting produces a surplus of possibilities yet none of them acquires the status of truth. We may thus fully appreciate the diagnosis offered in the title of Peter Pomerantsev's (2015) celebrated book on post-truth politics in Russia: *nothing is true and everything is possible*. If nothing is true (if there is no regime of truth or no hegemonic articulation), then the elements of discourse float freely, entering into the most diverse combinations, hence the range of possibilities is much expanded. Conversely, if everything is possible, if nothing is proscribed or excluded as false or nonsensical, then not a single statement can be qualified as true any more.

PARADIGM: THE SPREAD

We shall conclude our diagnosis of the post-truth condition by addressing Ben Lerner's novel *The Topeca School*, which may be read as a fictional genealogy of our present predicament. Set around the time of the 1996 US presidential election, the novel focuses on Adam (a character loosely based on the author), a high school student taking part in national forensics and debating championships. While the original intention of debating championships was for young people to become trained in a variety of fields to be able to speak competently and confidently on different subjects, the sheer competitiveness of the debates soon led to the overshadowing of any substantive competences by purely formal ones. 'Much of the coaching and practice focused on how to use one's body to lend a speech structure, when and where to step to mark transitions, when and how to gesture, opera without music' (Lerner 2019: 135–6).

There were two kinds of debates in these championships: 'extemp' debates, which were largely improvised and required rhetorical prowess, and policy debates, which demanded background research and were less concerned with the niceties of speech. While policy debates were originally viewed as more substantive than the ornamental extemps, the competition in this form of debating eventually led to the disappearance of all meaningful content from them as well. The novel focuses on a particular technique called the *spread*, in which the debater seeks to damage or defeat their opponent by producing an overwhelming number of quasi-arguments at high speed, 'make more arguments, marshal more evidence than the other team can respond to within the allotted time, the rule among serious debaters being that a "dropped argument", no matter its quality, its content, is conceded' (ibid.: 22). Accordingly, training in policy debates became increasingly focused on speaking as quickly as possible: 'holding a pen in the teeth while reading, which forces the tongue to work harder, the mouth to over-enunciate; reading evidence backward so as to uncouple the physical act of vocalization from the effort to comprehend, which slows one down' (ibid.). An unprepared audience could not possibly follow, let alone understand, the arguments made in the spread, which made it controversial for 'lay judges' and older debaters. 'To an anthropologist or ghost wandering the halls of Russel Hugh School, interscholastic debate would appear less competitive speech than glossolalic ritual' (ibid.: 23). When delivering his arguments, Adam himself would feel

> less like he was delivering a speech and more like a speech delivering him, that the rhythm and intonation of his presentation were beginning to dictate its content, that he no longer had to organize his arguments so much as let them flow through him. [He] was more in the realm of poetry than of prose, his speech stretched by speed and intensity until he felt its referential meaning dissolve into pure form. (Ibid.: 25)

Yet, the young debaters knew that it was unfair to say that no one, 'save perhaps the auctioneers', actually used language that way. On the contrary, the spread had already become remarkably widespread in everyday life:

> [They] heard the spoken warnings at the end of the increasingly common television commercials for prescription drugs, when risk information was disclosed at a speed designed to make it difficult to comprehend; they heard the list of rules and caveats read rapidly at the end of promotions on the radio; the last thing one was supposed to do with those was comprehend them. Even before the twenty-four hour news cycle, Twitter storms, algorithmic trading, spreadsheets, the DDos attack, Americans were getting 'spread' in their daily lives; meanwhile, their politicians went on speaking slowly, slowly about values utterly disconnected from their policies. (Ibid.: 24)

Adam himself appears to have been practising the spread in his daily life when arguing with his parents: 'out of him would issue an overwhelming barrage of ridiculous but somehow irrefutable arguments' (ibid.: 28–9). He is also not averse to speed-talking, participating in freestyle rap battles with his high school friends, which make his otherwise uncool activities more palatable to teenagers:

> [The] key was to narrate participation in debate as a form of linguistic combat; the key was to be a bully, quick and vicious and ready to spread an interlocutor with insults at the smallest provocation. Poetry could be excused if it upped your game, became cipher and flow. If linguistic prowess could do damage and get you laid, then it could be integrated into the adolescent social realm. This shifting of aggression to

the domain of language was sanctioned by one of the practices the types have appropriated: freestyling. It was socially essential for him: the rap battle transmuted his prowess as a public speaker and aspiring poet into something cool. (Ibid.: 127)

As he prepares for a championship, Adam is coached by Peter Evanson, an erstwhile national champion in extemp and eventual 'architect of the most right-wing government Kansas has ever known, overseeing radical cuts to social services, ending all funding for the arts, privatising Medicaid, implementing one of the most disastrous tax cuts in America's history, an important model for the Trump administration' (ibid.: 143). When training Adam, Evanson exhibits particular skills in what we will come to know as *trolling*, 'committing the plausibly deniable outrage, then taking tactical umbrage, claiming the higher ground' (ibid.: 142). To Adam's mother, 'Evanson embodied what disturbed us – the choreographed spontaneity, all in the service of manipulation, of winning' (ibid.: 209). Adam's parents, both trained as psychologists, observe with disdain this 'linguistic overkill' (ibid.: 214) that deprives speech of all meaning as it continues to endow it with power: Evanson's future career in Kansas ominously prefigures the current post-truth era, and the spread serves as the paradigmatic example of the contemporary weaponisation of language.

As Adam's mother Jane listens to Adam's opponent trying to spread him, she fails to understand much of the language but knows it was 'the shadow of speech, of reason' (ibid.: 211). Adam's father Jonathan studies a phenomenon called *speech shadowing*, in which the patients, asked to repeat sequences of speech that they have just heard, lapse into senseless babble, leading Jonathan to a 'theory' that 'under conditions of information overload, speech mechanisms collapse' (ibid.: 44). Jane is the author of a famous and controversial book about toxic masculinity, addressing the very process of the shifting of *aggression* to the domain of language that makes Adam acceptable to his teenage peers. Aggressive men also make their appearance by repeatedly calling Adam's mother on the phone to whisper obscenities that Jane easily deflates by asking them to speak louder and more articulately. The entire family seems to exist in the midst of language accelerating beyond meaning, slipping away or breaking down, yet somehow still retaining its power. The novel also features a character Darren, a teenager with speech difficulties who is half-jokingly accepted into Adam's social circle with eventually disastrous results as he acts out his rage in a violent attack against a young woman in the group. It is as if the sole alternative to aggression entering and taking over language was non-linguistic physical violence. The outside of language turns out to be nothing other than what its inside sublimates, pure force merging with pure form in the triumph of the senseless.

CHAPTER TWO

Subject to truth

POSTMODERNISM AND THE CONCERN FOR TRUTH

In the previous chapter we defined the contemporary post-truth condition as a regime of equivalence, in which statements are no longer discriminated as to their truth and falsity but rather circulate freely as expressions of the self, and cannot be either true or false and for this reason no longer need to be supported by proofs and evidence.

While the descent of this disposition is traced back to a variety of events, from the innovations in information technology to the crisis of neoliberal hegemony, one of the more controversial claims links the emergence of post-truth politics to the post-structuralist or postmodernist philosophy of the 1960s and 1970s. Postmodernist thought is held to be directly or indirectly responsible for the advent of post-truth, because of its anti-foundationalist approach that undermines both the truth claims of modern science and the legitimacy of liberal-democratic regimes (Andersen 2017; Williams 2017). These accusations invoke the familiar themes of the 'science wars' of the 1980s and early 1990s (Walzer 1986; Wolin 1994; Fraser 1995), in which the variably defined 'post-structuralism' and 'postmodernism' were routinely accused of undermining the very foundations of Western politics and culture, particularly the authority of truth and the scientific method.

In this chapter we shall briefly revisit some of these accusations in the contemporary discussion of post-truth, critically engaging with perhaps the most sustained critique of postmodernist complicity in post-truth in the work of Michiko Kakutani. Yet, instead of rehashing the rather worn attacks and defences in this debate, we shall venture to offer a different perspective on the question. Rather than merely defend post-structuralist philosophers from facile misreadings and false associations, we shall highlight the contribution some of these philosophers actually make to understanding the post-truth disposition, particularly in its relation to biopolitics and democracy, which is the main focus of this book. We shall therefore focus on the two leading theorists of biopolitics, Foucault and Agamben, who, in their different ways, pose the question of the function of truth in the *subjectivation* of living beings. Both Foucault and Agamben displace the question of truth from the inquiry into its essence (what truth is) into its function in social praxis (what truth does). This shift also permits us to understand what is at stake in the condition marked by the decline of the efficacy of truth. If truth constitutes subjects, what happens to the subject in the post-truth age? By reframing the question of truth in these terms, these authors not merely offer us a perspicacious diagnosis of our predicament, which should not be confused with any complicity in its advent, but also permit us to find a way out of it.

In her *Death of Truth*, Kakutani includes 'postmodernism' as a philosophical orientation among the factors leading to the present 'death of truth'. In fact, it is posited as a *key* factor, discussed already in chapter 2, after the introductory chapter of a more historical nature, and repeatedly returned to throughout the book. Her diagnosis is as follows:

> [Very] broadly speaking, postmodernist arguments deny an objective reality existing independently from human perception, contending that knowledge is filtered through the prisms of class, race, gender and other variables. In rejecting the possibility of an objective reality and substituting the notions of perspectives and positioning for the idea of truth, postmodernism enshrined the principle of subjectivity. Language is seen as unreliable and unstable (part of an unbridgeable gap between what is said and what is meant), and even the notion of people acting as fully rational, autonomous individuals is discounted, as each of us is shaped, consciously or unconsciously, by a particular time and culture. (Kakutani 2018: 48)

Rather than identify any specific 'postmodern' author or theory as a culprit, this diagnosis lumps together a certain *relativism* (dependence of knowledge on a particular perspective) and a certain *historicism* (being shaped by a particular time and culture) – the positions that are as old as philosophy itself. Moreover, neither of these approaches suffices to reject the idea of truth as such, but only a truth *independent* from perspectives and socio-historical factors – a notion that is hardly defensible, at least in the social sciences and the political realm that interest us here. Furthermore, these two philosophical positions are not entirely compatible with what she calls 'the principle of subjectivity', as the subjectivity in question is no longer *free* to construct its truths but is rather shaped by perspectives, history and culture that precede and exceed it. In fact, Kakutani's presentation recalls less any philosophical doctrine, modern or postmodern, than what we have called a spontaneous ideology of situated knowledge, which is indeed at work in the post-truth disposition, but can hardly be shown to have originated in the theories Kakutani discusses.

Nonetheless, Kakutani quickly moves from this still rather moderate diagnosis towards inferring more extreme conclusions from it:

> Science, too, came under attack by radical postmodernists, who argued that scientific theories are socially constructed: they are informed by the identity of the person positing the theory and the values of the culture in which they are formed; therefore, science cannot possibly make claims to neutrality or universal truths. (Ibid.: 54)

This statement brings together a number of problematic points. Firstly, the fact that scientific theories are socially constructed (as opposed to what? Given in nature or innate in our minds?) does not lead to their *dependence* on personal identity (which could well be bracketed off in the process of social construction) or even on the values of the culture (since social construction may take place in the more restricted, yet still social, communities of scientists). Secondly, science does not and should not make claims to neutrality: on the contrary, it should *discriminate* between true and false explanations, the latter discarded mercilessly and without regret. Thirdly, science rarely makes claims to *universal* truths, yet not because it is hopelessly contaminated by the identities or values of its practitioners, but because it knows that its truths are fallible and hence subject to revision or abandonment in future research. Indeed, the only reason why it is necessary to undertake this future research is that the current truths are neither universal nor absolute but liable to revision in the light of new knowledge. Thus, this depiction of the alleged attack of postmodernists on science ignores the fact that this attack, if it ever took place, would miss its target entirely, because it ignores how science actually works (see Latour 1993). We end up with two incorrect portrayals: firstly, of postmodernists themselves, who hardly ever said anything attributed to them, and secondly, of the scientists, who are defended from postmodern attacks in a way that utterly distorts the very nature of their activity.

A particularly illuminating example of the problematic nature of the argument is Kakutani's treatment of Jacques Derrida, the favourite object of attack in the 1980s culture wars:

> Deconstruction posited that all texts are unstable and irreducibly complex and that ever variable meanings are imputed by readers and observers. In focusing on the possible contradictions and ambiguities of a text (and articulating such arguments in deliberately tangled and pretentious prose), it promulgated an extreme relativism that was ultimately nihilistic in its implications: anything could mean anything; an author's intent did not matter, could not in fact be discerned; there was no such thing as an obvious or common-sense reading, because everything had an infinitude of meanings. In short, there was no such thing as truth. (Kakutani 2018: 56–7)

The problem is that even if we accept this rather tendentious description of Derrida's method (and concede the point about his style), it simply does not follow from the preceding sentences that there is 'no such thing as truth'. Yes, the meaning of the text is unstable and complex, and additional meanings emerge in the course of reading that go beyond the author's intent. While obvious or common-sense meanings might indeed exist, they are in no way privileged in relation to the meanings that require hermeneutic effort to unravel. Yet, all that follows from this is *not* the non-existence of truth, but the difficulty of reading, analysis or any other activity that aims to arrive at it, the fallibility of claims about truth or even meaning and the consequent need to remain open to the possibility of the falsification of such claims. This does not, however, mean that anything can mean anything: Derrida would evidently object to the argument that his *Of Grammatology* was actually a cookbook or that deconstruction was a ball game. In fact, even a cursory reading of Derrida would show that rather than give licence to making blanket claims to truth or meaning, Derrida's work rather emphasises the utmost difficulty and the need for utmost methodological rigour to make even *one* such claim. This again only makes sense when truth is presupposed to exist: after all, if it does not, why bother with the painstaking critical enterprise of deconstruction?

On the basis of this problematic account, Kakutani concludes the chapter by associating deconstructionism with the discourse of Trump and his aides:

> Though deconstructionists are fond of employing jargon-filled prose and perversely acrobatic syntax, some of the terms they use – like the 'indeterminacy of texts,' 'alternative ways of knowing,' and the 'linguistic instability' of language feel like pretentious versions of phrases recently used by Trump aides to explain away his lies, flip-flops, and bad-faith promises. For instance, a Trump representative telling an adviser to the Japanese prime minister, Shinzo Abe, that they didn't 'have to take each word that Mr. Trump said publicly literally'; and a former campaign manager, Corey Lewandowski, asserting that the problem with the media is: 'You guys took everything Donald Trump said so literally. The American people didn't. (Ibid.: 59–60)

It is difficult to see how the distinction between literal and figurative speech can be traced back to deconstructionist doctrines of indeterminacy of texts or linguistic instability. What is more interesting is that this distinction may be usefully deconstructed with the help of none other than Derrida himself, whose work, rather than give Trump's aides their talking points, may actually be deployed to criticise the possibility of ever speaking strictly literally or merely figuratively, which would in turn problematise the use of this distinction to legitimise political decisions or statements of the kind Kakutani discusses (see Derrida 1988).

Derrida is certainly not the only author blamed for the advent of post-truth: Foucault, Lyotard and Baudrillard are frequently mentioned as well, while Nietzsche assumes a special place on the list since he is often viewed as the forefather of 'postmodernism' (see Andersen 2017; Williams 2017). Such abridged quotations from Nietzsche as 'no facts, only interpretations' (Nietzsche 1977: 485) and 'truth is a kind of error' (ibid.: 493) are offered as evidence for the complicity of Nietzsche and the Nietzscheans of the twentieth and the twenty-first centuries in our present predicament. Yet, just as in the case of Derrida, neither of these two soundbites implies the *non-existence* of truth. To say that there are no facts but only interpretations is simply to say that our truths are attained by interpretive activity and not simply *read off* already given facts. In contrast to what we have called the regime of equivalence, Nietzsche did not assert the equivalence of all interpretations: on the contrary, the fundamental motif of his entire philosophy is the *evaluation* of interpretations by their *value for life*, that is, whether they are life-affirming or life-negating. It is precisely as a matter of such evaluation that he is able to say that 'truth is a kind of error without which a certain species of life could not live. The value for life is ultimately decisive' (ibid.: 493) Moreover, the notion of error in this statement does not connote *untruth* or falsity but rather refers to the process of *errancy*, wandering around without a clear direction or map, which is how some twentieth-century philosophers of science actually described the scientific search for truth (Feyerabend 2010).

Rather than prefigure the post-truth disposition, Nietzsche's perspectivism questions less the truth claims themselves than their claims to universality or absoluteness. In particular, it targets the disposition of what Nietzsche called 'unscientific man', 'who takes his opinion for truth, if it flatters him and makes him look good' (Nietzsche cited in Heit 2018: 44). This wariness about taking a mere opinion for the absolute truth does not contradict and may in fact coexist perfectly well with a wariness about reducing truths to mere opinions. Nietzsche opposed both dogmatic scientism and dogmatic relativism, opting instead for a 'cautious reserve' with regard to truth claims that views them as fallible and contestable but not for that reason dispensable: 'Lack of certainty and cautious reserve is liberating and advantageous for educated, strong, cultured people' (Heit 2018: 59).

From this perspective, even Nietzsche's criticism of the will to truth must be read as targeting less the truth than the *concealment* of the will to it, which presents itself as mere registration of the 'objective reality out there' (Gemes 1992: 64). For Nietzsche truth is the product of active experimentation, trial and error, errancy and wandering. This is why he opposed the attitude of 'reverence' for truth as 'already the consequence of an illusion. [One] should value more than truth the force that forms, simplifies, shapes, invents' (Nietzsche 1977: 602). Yet, this force is nothing but the will to truth as such, since in its absence no one would be bothered to form, simplify, shape or invent anything. In Kojève's words, 'being would be *there*, but it would not be *true*' (Kojève 1969: 186). Truth is thus both the source and the product of the active furnishing of the world, and its subsequent conversion to something simply existing 'out there' cannot but betray this activist spirit, without which nothing would be true.

On this cursory reading, it is evident that rather than negate truth, Nietzsche's philosophy is rather animated by the *concern* for truth, wariness about its betrayal or abuse, the questioning of its limits and the search for what drives our pursuit of it. The same attitude characterises the work of Nietzsche's French readers, often too hurriedly lumped together under the category of post-structuralism or postmodernism. We need only recall Foucault's (1981, 1989) investigations of *regimes of truth*, constituted by operations of exclusion, rarefaction and restriction, Lyotard's (1988) deconstruction of Holocaust revisionism, which was the most infamous case of post-truth *avant la lettre*, or Derrida's (1998) demonstration of the deconstructibility of claims about the foundational status of truths, their completeness or closure. All these studies are marked by a truly Nietzschean concern for truth, awareness of its admixture with relations of power, scepticism about its absolutisation or universalisation, and the desire to navigate between competing and incommensurable truth claims, adjudicating between them in the absence of any rule for judgement. Just as for Nietzsche, for these authors truth may be *problematic*, which evidently presupposes that it must *exist* in the first place. It is problematic because of the effects of power it produces, the will it is both animated by and tends to suppress, the tendency to overstep its limits in a quest for absolutes and universals, and so on. Yet, it does not mean that 'anything can mean anything' or that 'there is no such thing as truth'; what these latter statements rather imply is precisely that truth is *not a problem*, because it does not exist or, which amounts to the same, that it is indistinct from falsity.

It should be quite evident that insofar as these authors belong to the genre of philosophy, their discourse unfolds entirely *outside* the horizon of post-truth, which we have defined as constituted by the indifference towards the true–false distinction and the consequent assertion of the equivalence of all statements. While different philosophical schools and orientations certainly disagree about what constitutes truth and how it should be attained, we would struggle to recall a single one of them that would proclaim indistinction between truth and falsity. As Badiou has argued at length, philosophy is distinguished from both sophistry and anti-philosophy precisely by its being concerned with (and concerned about) truth (Badiou 1999, 2011a). Even anti-philosophical discourse (from St Paul to Lacan) does not abandon truth but rather approaches it as ineffable, unfigurable or otherwise unpresentable. It is only sophistry that denies the existence of truth as such, opting instead for the idea of multiplicity of discursive games and rhetorical strategies between which there is no possibility of adjudication.

It is sophistry rather than philosophy, however bombastic or arcane its style might be, that might serve as the true precursor of post-truth. Even if pays lip service to a certain philosophical author, idea or school, post-truth discourse is not merely not postmodern or post-structuralist, but simply not philosophical at all. While philosophy takes up truth as a problem of inquiry, the post-truth indifference to the very categories of true and false makes philosophical discourse superfluous and ludicrous, since it takes seriously what the champion of post-truth denies. A painstaking investigation into different truth conditions in different genres of discourse or the historical transformation of the meaning of truth within the same genre is of no interest to a discourse that has dispensed with truth as such. It is therefore not surprising that governments associated with post-truth politics tend to be particularly hostile to philosophy as an academic discipline: if there is no truth, philosophy literally has nothing to study and could therefore be defunded without any regret. Rather than bring about the reign of post-truth, philosophy appears to be among its main enemies and hence one of its first victims (see Weinberg 2019).

This brings us to a key point we shall demonstrate below: rather than bringing about the reign of post-truth, postmodernists and post-structuralists (whatever these terms mean today) are best at *diagnosing* it, precisely insofar as they are more attentive to what is at stake in true discourses and truth denialism than the more conventional approaches. If the authors lumped together as postmodern or post-structuralist have a lot to say about the post-truth condition and how we have ended up in it, this is no reason to blame them for it. As Kalpokas argues (2019: 127), 'such attributions of guilt amount to blaming a diagnosis for having caused the diagnosed condition'.

In the remainder of this chapter we shall focus on two continental philosophers that have been most influential in theorising biopolitics, Foucault and Agamben, and outline their less widely discussed approaches to truth, its origin and functions as well a possible diagnosis of how we have come to live in the post-truth condition. We shall first address Foucault's response to the question of *why* discourses of truth emerge, what function they serve and how they relate to the rise of subjectivity. This will permit us to critically re-engage with Badiou's claim, discussed at the beginning of Chapter 1, about Foucault's theory as being complicit in the 'truthless' age of democratic materialism. Instead, we shall demonstrate that Foucault's account of the subjectifying function of truth is quite close to Badiou's own theory of truth procedures, which, in turn, cannot break with the biopolitical mode of subjectivation. We shall then proceed to Agamben's elaboration of the subjectifying function of truths and the possible eclipse of this function in the contemporary devaluation of the performative *efficacy* of speech. In this manner, we shall not merely exonerate these theorists of biopolitics from any complicity in the post-truth condition but also demonstrate how they also help us formulate a critical theory of post-truth.

FOUCAULT: WHY IS THERE TRUTH?

Foucault's 1980–1 course *Subjectivity and Truth* (Foucault 2017) is the first of his late lecture courses at the Collège de France to deal with Greek and Roman Antiquity. The course of the previous year, *On the Government of the Living* (Foucault 2014), marked a transition between Foucault's work on governmentality and biopolitics and his turn towards the techniques of the self and aesthetics of existence. In that course Foucault addressed the regulation of truth-telling in early Christian practices of baptism, penance and spiritual direction. In *Subjectivity and Truth* he maintains the focus on truth-telling but extends the temporal context back into Antiquity to focus on Greek, Hellenistic and Roman techniques of the self, particularly with regard to the problematics of sexuality and matrimony. The field of what we now call sexual behaviours becomes for Foucault a fruitful site for inquiring into the relationship between discourses of truth and the constitution of the subject, which we shall discuss in this section.

The object of Foucault's investigation is the philosophical discourse on marriage in the Hellenistic period, in particular such Stoic authors as Musonius Rufus, Hierocles and Antipater of Tarsus (Foucault 2017: 123–203). These texts, which prescribe the restriction of sexual relations to the married couple, modified the earlier Greek ethics of *aphrodisia*, which did not privilege any particular type or setting for sexual practices. Instead, the Greeks of the classical period affirmed two principles regulating the 'use of pleasures': the principle of *activity* that discredited any passive position in a sexual relation and the principle of socio-sexual *isomorphism* that required a proper sexual act to respect the partners' social standing and roles. Without prohibiting any particular type of sexual act, this ethics of *aphrodisia* could nonetheless adjudicate between proper and improper acts (ibid.: 75–93). For instance, a sexual act between a free man and a male slave was proper as long the free man was in the active position and turned improper when he assumed a passive position. On the other hand, a sexual act of a free man with a married woman conformed to the principle of activity but violated the principle of isomorphism insofar as it encroached on the rights of one's neighbour. In contrast to this ethics of activity and isomorphism the approach to sexuality in the Stoic discourse increasingly privileges the family as the sole legitimate locus of sexual activity, limits sexual relations to the function of procreation and transforms marriage from an economic relation into an affective bond that goes beyond mere carnal pleasure.

After addressing this transformation in a series of Stoic texts, in the lecture of 11 March 1981 Foucault raises the methodological question of the relation of this new discourse on marriage to the social practices of the Hellenistic period. This question becomes so important that Foucault devotes almost three entire lectures to its discussion under the aegis of the 'problem of redundant discourse' (*discours en trop*). Is the Stoic discourse on marriage merely a redundant transcription of the existing judicial code and the actual practices that correspond to it? If philosophy merely expressed the practices that were already established, what was the point of this expression?

> Why was it necessary to say it, and to say it in a prescriptive form? Why transform into a rule of conduct, why present as advice for living well something that would have effectively already been established at the level of real behaviour? Why would philosophers have been led to reproduce in the form of injunctions what was already given in reality? (Ibid.: 220)

Foucault's first step in unravelling this puzzle is to reject the explanation of discourses of truth by the reality of which they speak: 'a reality to which a discourse refers, whatever it may be, cannot be the *raison d'être* of that discourse itself' (ibid.). This does not merely pertain to prescriptive discourse, which, insofar as it prescribes something, presupposes that it is not yet practised widely enough, but also to the 'veridical discourses' in general, that is, discourses that purport to tell the truth about what is:

> [There] is no fundamental ontological affiliation between the reality of a discourse, its very existence as discourse that claims to tell the truth, and the reality of which it speaks. In relation to the domain in which it is exercised, the game of truth is always a singular historical event, an ultimately improbable event in relation to that of which it speaks. (Ibid.: 221)

It is therefore never sufficient to explain the discourse of truth by the truth of this discourse in the sense of its correspondence to reality:

> [The] fact that the sky is blue will never be able to account for the fact that I say that the sky is blue. Reality will never account for that particular, singular and improbable reality of the game of truth in reality. (Ibid.: 222)

Instead, Foucault argues that one must pose the question of the 'improbable conditions' that made it possible for the 'game of truth' to emerge in this domain: 'why was it necessary to speak about marriage so much and at such length, if in actual fact marriage was in reality what the philosophers said it ought to be?' (ibid.). While philosophy begins with the ontological astonishment about being (that there is being and not nothing), it must, according to Foucault, also traverse the experience of *epistemic surprise*:

> [Why], then, in addition to reality, is there truth? What is this supplement that reality in itself can never entirely account for, which is that truth comes into play on the surface of reality, in reality, right in the depths of reality? The reality of the world is not its own truth to itself. (Ibid.: 237)

It is easy to see that this disposition of epistemic surprise clearly separates Foucault from the truth denialism with which he is still often mistakenly associated. Foucault's wonder and amazement at the existence of truth, which is never necessitated or reducible to the reality of which it speaks, could hardly be reconciled with the indifferent disposition that posits the equivalence of all statements as opinions. In contrast, for Foucault the puzzle of truth consists precisely in its *non-equivalence*, the privileged character of this discourse, which cannot simply be read off its semantic content.

There is nothing in the reality of sexuality and marriage that would make the appearance of the game of truth and error necessary: it might just as well be regulated by games of 'desire and aversion, of love and hate, of the useful and the harmful, the effective and the ineffective' (ibid.: 236 fn.). There are fields of practice regulated by rather more implicit and ambiguous criteria, such as taste, or left virtually unregulated and open to the free play of opinions. Conversely, nothing excludes the possibility of discourses of truth arising in these fields as well. This means that discourses of truths can only emerge out of and on the basis of their non-necessity or *contingency*, as something that did not have to be and could have been otherwise. We must be particularly careful in distinguishing this contingency from any claim about the *non-existence* of truths. The non-necessity of truths does not in any way undermine their existence, but on the contrary renders it more valuable, insofar as something comes into existence which might as well *not* have existed. Truth is not something that is always there, as a necessary attribute of every existing entity. In themselves, entities are neither true nor false and it is only the contingent emergence of a discourse of truth around these entities that makes it possible to attribute truth or falsity to them.

Thus, contrary to the accusations, Foucault's emphasis on contingency does not invalidate truths in general or debunk some truths in particular but rather raises the question of their emergence and purpose, detrivialising them and making them interesting and problematic at once. On the basis of this principle of contingency Foucault proceeds to identify four characteristics of discourses of truth. The first is their *supplementary* character. While Foucault makes no reference to Derrida's (1998: 141–52) notion of supplementarity, there is an evident resonance with Derrida's use of the notion to designate something that is at once essential and extraneous, constitutive and external to that which it supplements. Truth arises 'in the depths' of reality, yet it is not in any way necessary from the standpoint of this reality itself. Truth merely adds something to reality, but what it adds is something essential to this reality, which it nonetheless cannot formulate without being supplemented by a specific discourse.

The second characteristic of the discourse of truth is that it is *unprofitable*, 'in that one cannot deduce this game from a simple economy that would make it effective in relation to the domain on which it operates' (Foucault 2017: 238). Historically, discourses of truth have been remarkably costly in every sense without bringing many political or economic benefits to their practitioners. Despite all the 'dogmas, sciences, opinion, institutions' (ibid.: 236 fn.), there has been rather little truth produced throughout history: 'On the scale of human history the game of veridiction has cost much more than it has yielded' (ibid.: 238).

The third characteristic of truth is its *polymorphous* nature: there is not one game of truth (e.g. the scientific one) but rather a multiplicity of possibly incommensurable games, not all of them having the same degree of scientificity or even claiming to be scientific at all. Moreover, even within the domain of science, 'the games of truths of genetics cannot be superimposed on those of algebra or particle physics' (ibid.: 237 fn.). The ascent of science to the status of the privileged game of truth in Western societies is a contingent historical event that, just like the truths of science themselves, was not necessitated by the reality of these societies themselves.

The fourth and final characteristic is the *efficacy* of true discourse. Even as supplementary, unprofitable and polymorphous, it is capable of producing effects in the reality in which it is deployed. Yet, these effects are not limited to merely restating as true that which takes place in this reality, but also *modify* the reality itself by virtue of having the *authority* of truth. In the section of the manuscript not enunciated in the lecture Foucault gives the example of economics, a science whose 'truth status' may be dubious but which is nonetheless capable of producing multiple effects in many spheres of existence (ibid.: 236 fn.). The relationship between truth and politics that concerns Foucault in these lectures pertains precisely to the investigation of these effects. To speak of a 'political history of truth' is not to dissolve discourses of truth in prior relations of power or rationalities of government, thereby depriving them of their consistency and autonomy, but, on the contrary, to demonstrate the effects of these discourses on social practices or the constitution of the subject's relationship to itself (ibid.: 239).

It is from this perspective on truth as a supplementary, polymorphous and unprofitable discourse with transformative and subjectivising effects that Foucault returns to the Stoic texts on marriage and ventures to resolve the enigma of their superfluous character. He considers three explanations for this apparently redundant discourse before advancing his own. In the first approach this redundancy is assumed and even valorised as the proof of the limits of philosophy in determining reality. 'If something in the real world corresponds to the Stoic model it is quite simply because this model only follows that reality' (ibid.: 234). Yet, as we have already seen, the real existence of discourse cannot be explained by the reality of what it says. This first approach thus merely returns us to the question of why this discourse was necessary in the first place.

The second approach offers a diametrically opposed answer: discourses of truth do not reflect reality, but, on the contrary, obscure, distort or conceal it. This is the explanation offered by the *critique of ideology* that was the object of Foucault's criticism throughout his work. In this approach, the reality of discourse consists precisely in 'what it does not express of reality, or in what it denies of it' (ibid.: 240). The discourse of truth represents reality in such a way that the real itself is evaded. In the case of the Stoic discourse on marriage, the evasion would concern the process of the dissolution of all societal institutions in the Hellenistic world that left marriage as the sole stable social form. Representing marriage as an ethical duty as opposed to the result of a 'real break up of social structures', the Stoic philosophers concealed the reality of sociopolitical dislocations by presenting their result as an ideal bond (ibid.: 240–1). Foucault objects to this approach for two reasons. Firstly, there is no evidence of the Stoic discourse on marriage concealing any aspect of the reality it addressed. Secondly, there is no reference in this discourse to what the critique of ideology considers to be the cause of the events or phenomena in question,

> [the] cause that the ideological analysis attributes retrospectively and hypothetically to reality. In the analysis that denounces the unspoken of a discourse, one recognizes that a discourse is ideological in the fact that it does not speak of the same causes as the one analysing the discourse. (Ibid.: 242)

Ideological analysis thus negates the truth status of the discourse it analyses while claiming this very status for its own analysis of it.

The third approach views the relationship between discourse and reality neither in terms of reflection nor in terms of ideological obfuscation but in terms of *rationalisation*. Discourse neither represents nor conceals reality but rather transforms it through its own *logos*, recomposing discontinuous and diverse practices into a coherent system. In their discourse on marriage the Stoics '[generalized] local phenomena, systematized dispersed phenomena, radicalized underlying movements' (ibid.: 243). This approach that Foucault terms 'Weberian' (ibid.: 244) is problematic because it operates with an 'arbitrary' notion of reason or rationality. There is nothing inherently more rational in prescribing absolute rather than relative conjugal fidelity, in making marriage obligatory for everyone rather than a pragmatic choice, and so on. More generally, there remains the question of the rationality of rationalisation itself: '[is] wanting to rationalize reality not the most absurd undertaking? If things really have come about, it is not because orders and advice were given. Procedures of rationalization have a very weak index of effectiveness' (ibid.).

Having dispensed with these three problematic explanations, Foucault finally advances his own interpretation of the emergence of the discourse of truth in the domain of sexuality during the Hellenistic period. In Foucault's argument, this discourse was neither an expression of the moral code nor a purely theoretical treatise on marriage but rather belonged to the genre of 'techniques of living' (*tekhnai peri ton bion*), by which one analyses, evaluates and transforms one's existence. These techniques did not produce any break with the existing moral code of the time or the fundamental values of the period but rather permitted to *reconcile* the emerging Hellenistic code of behaviour that valorised marriage with the fundamental values of the Greek ethics of *aphrodisia*. The valorisation of marriage as a singular relation distinct from the wider field of social practices appears to exclude the principles of socio-sexual isomorphism and male activity. Nonetheless, the Stoic discourse brought the two together by transforming the relationship to the self at work in sexual practices. Instituting the division between private and public life, making sexual desire the privileged object of the relation to oneself and linking sexual pleasure with the affective domain, the Stoic philosophers made it possible to continue to *affirm* male activity and socio-sexual isomorphism while at the same time *abiding* by the strict rules of conjugal fidelity and the prescription of the affective bond with one's spouse. It was precisely the inequality between husband and wife that now obliged the husband to guide and direct the wife by his own example, thereby proscribing all extramarital sexual relations that this inequality previously allowed and instituting the principle of reciprocity between spouses.

The isolation of conjugal sexuality as a privileged domain permit-ted to reinscribe the Greek principle of activity and the prescription of self-control it entailed in terms of the principle of self-mastery and the renunciation of extramarital desire (ibid.: 275–6). The valorisa-tion of activity exercised on the other was thus converted into an active domination of oneself. Thus, Foucault is able to conclude that the Stoic discourse on sexuality neither reflected nor prescribed a new moral code or a system of values but rather enabled the subject to '[be] transformed in such a way that he can live in this code of conju-gality while still maintaining the value of socio-sexual continuity and the principle of activity' (ibid.: 267), In this manner, the old Greek aristocracy could maintain its traditional values in the condition of social and political transformations in the Hellenistic monarchies, marked by the rise of new elites and the weakening of traditional aristocratic privileges. '[Philosophical] discourse was proposing, was conveying techniques, precisely in order to be able to live, to accept the modes of behaviour proposed and imposed from outside, tech-niques that literally rendered them livable' (ibid.: 275).

It is easy to see that these effects of discourse had nothing to do with reflection, obfuscation or rationalisation of reality. Instead, they *transformed* the subject's relationship to itself, making it possible for him (exclusively him!) to *subjectivise* the emerging moral code in a specific manner that would also permit upholding traditional values that nominally conflicted with it. We may clearly observe all of Fou-cault's four characteristics of the discourse of truth in this example. It is definitely supplementary in relation to the reality it describes: targeting a small aristocratic audience, resolving a tactical problem of making the new moral code liveable, intricately reinscribing tra-ditional values into it clearly point to the non-necessity of this dis-course from the standpoint of reality itself. These factors also point to its unprofitable nature: nothing in this discourse could be praised as revelation or discovery and the sheer volume of this discourse stands in marked contrast with its rather modest tactical objective. Thirdly, the discourse in question is polymorphous in the sense of combining highly diverse modes of reasoning, including parables and the inter-pretation of dreams (ibid.: 1–9, 51–8). Finally, we may observe the effectivity of this discourse, which, in Foucault's reading, had thor-oughgoing implications for Western culture: the shift in the percep-tion of sexuality from action on others to the mastery of oneself, from pleasure to desire, was subsequently taken up and transformed by

Christianity and arguably also defines our contemporary experience in a secularised and liberalised manner.

TRUTH AS A PROCEDURE OF SUBJECTIVATION: FOUCAULT AND BADIOU

Foucault's account of the non-necessity of truth in the *Subjectivity and Truth* lectures parallels the argument advanced in the previous year's course in relation to power. In *On the Government of the Living* Foucault half-jokingly described his overall approach as 'anarchaeology' (Foucault 2014: 79), whose fundamental principle is the affirmation of the 'non-necessity of all power of whatever kind' (ibid.). Rather than imagine or construct a model of a legitimate power and then use it to judge actual power relations, Foucault's anarchaeology begins with the non-necessity of government as such and then traces the ways in which various rationalities of government claim their own legitimacy in a contingent and unfounded manner.

The discussion of discourses of truth in *Subjectivity and Truth* similarly begins from the non-necessity of truth, demonstrating once again the centrality of the co-implication of power and knowledge to Foucault's thought. Power and knowledge do not merely depend on each other, providing each other with the objects they constitute, but also share a fundamentally contingent character in relation to the reality in which they appear. Reality demands neither to be known nor to be governed, hence both of these practices are supplementary and cannot derive their justification from the domain in which they unfold. At the same time, they are not extraneous to this domain and are able to produce effects within it that need not be restricted to either restating or maintaining what already exists. Just as power relations produce and transform subjectivities, discourses of truth intervene and transform the relationship of the subjects to themselves and to others, thereby altering the way we experience our existence in the most diverse spheres. By the same token, just as we can always contest particular forms of power by asserting their non-necessity and demanding their justification, so we can always contest discourses of truth by demonstrating that their emergence can never be justified by the way things are in reality and that their effects go beyond merely reflecting what is already the case.

Thus, Foucault proposes a highly intricate relationship between truth and the subject that is reducible neither to the *domination* of the subject by discourses of truth nor to the *production* of the subject in these discourses. While the first approach views the operation of true discourse as negative and repressive, the second posits the subject as entirely produced in discourse without remainder. In both cases, there is no subject *outside* the discourses of truth, either because it is their product or because it is their victim. In contrast to these two approaches, in *Subjectivity and Truth* Foucault introduces a *gap* between the subject and discourse that permits the former to *make use* of the latter without being entirely subsumed by it or experiencing its statements as a matter of necessity. While Foucault has been and is often still read as highlighting the oppressive effects of truth, be they ordering, homogenising or levelling, in the *Subjectivity and Truth* lectures we rather observe a facilitating, enabling or even emancipatory function of true discourse. Rather than repress the pre-existing subject or produce the subject out of nothing, this discourse offered the subject the possibility of *living* in the new conditions while maintaining its old values. For this reason, the non-necessity of truth does not only mean that the truth in question may or must be abandoned, but can also be understood in the more positive sense of offering to the subject the possibility of being otherwise than one is.

It is notable that throughout this extensive analysis Foucault never once addresses the question of whether the discourse in question is *actually* true or not. It evidently is *not* true within *our* contemporary regime of truth and some of its truth claims cannot but appear quaint or ludicrous. Yet, Foucault appears entirely uninterested in the question of what the truth (of sexuality) *is* and remains focused on what this set of truth claims *does*, or what it achieves in the wider domain of social practices and power relations. And yet, Foucault's relative lack of interest in the *essence* of truth does not entail his belonging to the post-truth camp, since it is compensated by his attitude of epistemic surprise before the *existence* of truth discourses throughout history, his marvel at the sheer amount of effort involved in verifying and fortifying statements that at first glance might appear to be simple redescriptions of what is.

We may now revisit Badiou's somewhat ungenerous affiliation of Foucault with the democratic-materialist disposition that defines the post-truth era. Badiou viewed Foucault's philosophy as a mere 'linguistic anthropology' that addresses the ways in which bodies and languages are regulated in different historical periods (Badiou 2009a: 35, 527). For Badiou, Foucault's history of the regimes of truth could only describe the regimes themselves while bracketing off the question of their truth. And yet, despite this stringent criticism, there are important parallels between the ways the two authors construct the very concept of truth (see Gillespie 2008: 89–90). While Badiou's set-theoretical account of the truth procedure is exceedingly complex and Foucault's line of reasoning in *Subjectivity and Truth* may appear deceptively simple, the relation between truth and reality that they chart is surprisingly similar, which suggests that Badiou's critique of Foucault must be revaluated.

For Badiou, truth is a technical term, designating the effects of *fidelity* to the event. It is strictly all that is *true to* the event that erupts in the situation. Since the event is undecidable from an ontological perspective and almost imperceptible from within the situation, the elements of the situation that are connected to it form a subset that is similarly impossible to identify in terms of the positive language of the situation that Badiou calls its 'encyclopedia'. The truth is thus an indiscernible or generic subset that evades all identifying predicates; it

> contains a little bit of everything [but] *only* possesses the properties necessary to its existence as multiple in its material. It does not possess any particular, discerning, separative property. At base, its sole property is that of consisting as pure multiple, of being. Subtracted from language, it makes do with its being. (Badiou 2005: 371, emphasis original)

It follows from this description that truth is necessarily infinite, since any finite subset of the situation could logically be discerned by the predicates of the encyclopedia. It also follows that the truth as a generic subset is manifestly universal, that is, 'it is the truth of the entire situation, truth of the being of the situation' (ibid.: 525; 2009a: 33–4). Since the truth is infinite, its process is never complete but exists in fragments, for Badiou reserves the name of the *subject* (Badiou 2005: 392–3). Badiou's subject is simply a finite subset of a truth, that is, a set of statements, practices or organisational forms that have been produced in a certain concrete context of the unfolding of the truth of the situation. It is evident that this subject transcends the boundaries of any initially given subsets of the situation and for this reason is capable of transforming it in its entirety. Badiou defines this transformation as the *generic extension* of the situation (ibid.: 381–5), which *adds* the generic subset of the truth to the initial situation, thereby making the indiscernible intrinsic to it.

At first glance this complex account of the truth procedure is furthest away from Foucault's rather more straightforward argument. In Badiou's own interpretation, Foucault's approach ventures to describe the *specificity* of discourses in different historical periods while subtracting their possible *genericity* or truth content. In contrast, Badiou attempts to do the reverse: seize in historical discourses *only* that which is generic, that is, properly universal about them. As a result, the two authors' assessments of the same historical period could be strikingly different: while Foucault would focus on the discourses of truth that dominated that period irrespective of their generic universality, Badiou would focus on the generic truths even if they were exceptional or even marginal during the period in question.

Nonetheless, the relation between truth and reality that Badiou outlines remains strikingly similar to Foucault's fourfold definition. Firstly, Badiou's truth is clearly *supplementary* in relation to the reality of the situation. Contrary to frequent misreadings, the event to which truth is faithful to is *not* external to the situation but manifests its very being as inconsistent multiplicity (ibid.: 327–53). The truth does not transcend the bodies and languages given in the situation but is the truth *of* these bodies and languages themselves. If it were otherwise, if the truth manifested some novel content arising from the event or arose from some particular body or language, it could never have universal consequences for the situation. At the same time, this immanent truth is in no way determined by the situation itself. If there were no event that erupted in the situation in a contingent manner, no truth would be able to arise at all. Even though the truth reveals nothing other than the being of the situation itself, such a revelation is not at all necessary from the perspective of the situation. There are indeed only bodies and languages, yet truths may also exceptionally erupt in their midst.

This brings us to the second of Foucault's characteristics: the *unprofitability* of truth. In Badiou's approach, truth is not merely unprofitable but also risky and dangerous for the subjects involved in its pursuit. The faithful subject that undertakes a truth procedure confronts at every point the resistance from *reactive* subjects that deny the occurrence of the event and hence the possibility to generate any truths from it and *obscure* subjects that seek to destroy the truths already produced as traces of the event within the situation (Badiou 2009a: 50–61). Truth appears to be its own reward, as its subject forces it within the situation that remains indifferent or even hostile to it.

Let us now consider the principle of *effectivity*. Both Foucault and Badiou argue that the effects of truth do not consist in its reflection or obfuscation of reality but in its transformation through the subjectivation of those who faithfully affirm it. Just as Stoic discourses on sexuality in Foucault's reading produced subjects that related to themselves and to others in a different way, Badiou's faithful subjects both transform their own existence, embarking on a 'life in truth' irreducible to particular needs or interests, and transform their situation or world by forcing the truth in it and bringing what 'inexists' in it to appearance (ibid.: 321–4, 507–14). Badiou's truths also produce subjectivating effects when they are not upheld faithfully, namely reactive and obscure subjects. The effects of truth thus spread even beyond its immediate adherents.

Finally, Badiou's truth also has a *polymorphous* character, but in contrast to Foucault this polymorphism is limited to four types of procedures that Badiou specifies as science, art, politics and love (Badiou 2005: 339–42). While all these truths function in a similar way by manifesting the very being of the situation, they do so in different ways: while political truths are addressed to every member of the situation, amorous truths only concern the couple in question, even as the truth itself remains universal. Scientific and artistic truths appear to take a middle path: while they are produced by particular individuals and groups, they remain non-exclusive and available to all.

While there is no hierarchy between different truths (Meillassoux 2014: 34), there certainly remains a hierarchy between the four truth procedures and *other* domains of existence, in which no event can apparently take place and which therefore can produce no truths but merely a free play of opinions. There is no truth in religion, economy, sports, sexuality and innumerable other fields of experience, in which there are only 'bodies and languages', 'individuals and communities' and no possibility of faithful subjectivation. This restriction of the polymorphism of truths separates Badiou from Foucault, for whom it is entirely possible that a discourse of truth could emerge in any domain whatsoever, even though it might not necessarily be very successful and effective there.

This difference between the two authors may be explained by their different approach to the *universality* of truths. For Badiou, universality follows by definition from the understanding of truth in generic terms as comprising 'a little bit of everything' from the situation without being determined by any particular predicate. The four procedures of art, science, love and politics differ from the procedures of yoga, religion, sports and sex precisely because they are capable of producing such generic subsets, irreducible to any particular determinants. For this reason, Badiou's truths are endowed with a clear privilege over other procedures. This is not the case for Foucault, for whom discourses of truth can be produced in any domain whatsoever precisely because they need not be universal in any rigorous sense. The Stoic discourse on marriage did of course universalise marriage as the sole legitimate context for sexual activity, yet, as Foucault demonstrated, it was hardly universal in either its intention or its audience, since it served a highly particular purpose of reconciling the values of aristocratic families with the new moral code. Other discourses of truth analysed by Foucault, from judicial psychiatry to Christian confession, are even less universal.

In the absence of a strict criterion of universality Foucault was able to investigate a wider array of discourses that at least claimed to be true without himself adjudicating whether or not they are true. It is this non-committal and almost agnostic attitude that led Badiou to somewhat dismissively characterise Foucault's approach as a merely empiricist project of retracing historical patterns of ordering bodies and languages. Nonetheless, in his 1984 eulogy for Foucault Badiou was rather more circumspect about Foucault's approach, arguing that 'despite what one read here and there, it was indeed the universal that made him so self-assured' (Badiou 2009b: 123). He also singled out Foucault's turn to the question of subjectivation in his final work as particularly and personally 'touching' (ibid.: 124). While the concern with the universal may be found in many of Foucault's works despite his own apparent distaste for the concept (Foucault 2014: 79–80), we may suggest that the universal that Badiou referred to pertained precisely to the understanding of truth as a contingent procedure of subjectivation. While Foucault did not adjudicate the universality of the contents of the discourses that he analysed, a certain sense of universality could be traced in the formal concept of truth, which we have reconstituted above. Although the true discourses of Antiquity, the Middle Ages or early modernity may appear to us as lacking any credibility or even meaning, they operate in much the same way across these different periods: as non-necessary, unprofitable, polymorphous procedures of subjectivation. While Foucault and Badiou clearly differ on the question of the genericity of truths, they at least have this formal concept of the truth in common.

Yet, our reading of Foucault's interpretation of the Stoic discourse on marriage also suggests another affinity between the two authors that goes beyond the formal structure of the concept of truth and rather pertains to that which truth is for, namely *life*. As we recall, in Foucault's analysis of the Stoics, the function of truth made it possible to *live* in the new conditions, reconciling one's values with new moral and legal codes. In Badiou's approach, truth serves a similar function, though its description is rather more elevated than in Foucault's account: 'to live as an Immortal'. For all his dismay about life as the central category of democratic materialism, Badiou himself cannot avoid recourse to the notion of life when presenting his alternative, a life lived by participating in the 'subjectivizable body' of truth. He redefines life as 'participation, point by point, in the organization of a new body, in which a faithful subjective formalism comes to take root' (Badiou 2009a: 35). There are of course other possibilities, that is, the already mentioned obscure and reactive subjects, whose lives are defined respectively in terms of conservation and mortification:

> [Life] is a subjective category. A body is the materiality that life requires, but the becoming of the present depends on the disposition of this body in a subjective formalism. To live is thus an incorporation into the present under the faithful form of a subject. If the incorporation is dominated by the reactive form, one will not speak of life but of mere *conservation*. It is a question of protecting oneself from the consequences of a birth, of not relaunching existence beyond itself. If incorporation is dominated by the obscure formalism, one will instead speak of *mortification*. (Ibid.: 508–9, emphasis original)

Thus, Badiou is neither willing nor able to abandon the very terms that define the biopolitical regime that he criticises. Firstly, the 'intra-worldly' advance of the truth procedure requires material support in the living *body*, without which it remains abstract and impotent. The transworldly body of truth is ultimately composed of the worldly physical bodies, even as it aspires to transcend their particularity: 'The Immortal exists only in and by the mortal animal' (Badiou 2001a: 84). We may speak either of the *incarnation* of the truth in the body of the human animal or the *incorporation* of this animal into a new, subjective 'body of truth' – either way, the truth procedure cannot proceed without latching on to the bodies it desires to transcend.

Secondly, the result of incorporation into the body of truth is nothing other than life and, moreover, 'living as such' (Badiou 2009a: 514). The setting aside of the mere life of the subhuman animal leads to a true life, which 'gets the better' of bio-psychological drives and makes it possible to live 'as an Immortal'. There is certainly a difference between the two notions of life at work here, the sub- and the super-human ones, but life itself remains the sole horizon of politics. In fact, it is precisely the move from one notion of life to another, from one body to another, that defines biopolitics in Giorgio Agamben's famous interpretation. For Agamben biopolitics begins with the 'inclusive exclusion' of *zoe* (unqualified life that we share with both animals and gods) into *bios* (a qualified form of life in the polis) (Agamben 1998: 6). The constitution of *bios* as the political form of life presupposes the entry of *zoe* into this realm in the marginalised, subordinated or suppressed position: it is included in the polis, but solely in the mode of its exclusion from it, as a negative foundation, 'as if politics were the place in which life had to transform itself into good life and in which what had to be politicized were always already bare life' (ibid.: 7).

It is easy to see that this logic is at work in the constitution of Badiou's 'body of truth'. As Agamben himself argued, '[Badiou] still conceives of the subject on the basis of a contingent encounter with truth, leaving aside the living being as the "animal of the human species" as a mere support for this encounter' (Agamben 1999b: 221). Incorporating itself into the eventual present, the human animal sets aside its animality or *zoe* in order to constitute a new form of life (*bios*) in the body of truth. The finite body of the human animal that Badiou derisively dismisses as a charmless 'biped without feathers' (Badiou 2001a: 12) is absolutely necessary for the new body of truth to be possible, yet in this new body it no longer plays an important role, its particular interests and desires set aside in favour of the universal content of the truths. Moreover, the human animal also ends up 'disciplined' for the purposes of the more effective unfolding of the truth procedure:

I place heroism on the side of discipline, the only weapon both of the True and of peoples, against power and wealth, against the insignificance and the dissipation of the mind. But this discipline demands to be invented, as the coherence of a subjectivizable body. Then it can no longer be distinguished from our own desire to live. (Badiou 2009a: 514)

76

At this point, we can raise the question of what, if anything, separates Badiou's *askesis* of truth from the Stoic regimen of care of the self, whose self-disciplining in the discourses of truth was, in Foucault's reading, also in some sense indistinguishable from one's desire to live in a changing environment, though perhaps not necessarily as 'immortals'. Of course, the truths of the Stoics appear rather more worldly than Badiou's, insofar as they did not transcend the proverbial 'bodies and languages' but rather pertained precisely to devising a new language to address certain relations between living and speaking bodies. Yet, as Foucault demonstrated, this did not prevent the Stoic discourse from becoming a discourse of *truth* rather than a mere redescription of the real, its ideological obfuscation or rationalisation. Badiou's formula 'there are only bodies and languages except there are also truths' must therefore be qualified further: there are only bodies and languages, except there are also truths, which can only be the truths *of* these bodies and languages.

We end up with an image that is rather different from the initial stark contrast between the biopolitics of democratic materialism, analysed by Foucault's linguistic anthropology, and the politics of truth prescribed by Badiou's own materialist dialectics. Instead, both of these forms of politics exemplify the operation of the biopolitical logic of the inclusive exclusion of 'mere life' as the negative foundation of 'good life' (or 'true life'). In itself, the statement 'there are only bodies and languages' does not authorise any biopolitics (or any other kind of politics, for that matter). It is a strictly ontological claim that is politically indifferent: there is no reason why these bodies and languages should be privileged objects of politics, its material supports or serve any other function. In order to make this formula biopolitical we must add to it the specification of the form of life (*bios*) that these bodies are to be inclusively excluded from or, in Badiou's lexicon, of the body of truth into which they should be negatively incorporated. This specification is necessary even if the truth in question consists precisely in the affirmation of a particular relation between the speaking bodies as was the case with Foucault's Stoics.

This evidently does not invalidate Badiou's criticism of democratic materialism as a particular mode of biopolitics, but only his attempt to transcend biopolitics *altogether*. To be against 'democratic materialism' is not to oppose biopolitics as such. There is no idea without a relation to life, hence Badiou's truth procedure remains biopolitical, but there is also no politics without ideas, hence democratic materialism is not without a certain 'truth content' of its own, however modest. Ultimately, both Badiou and Foucault answer the question 'why is there truth?' in the same way: truth is a matter of forming and transforming one's life, including one's body and one's language, and a politics of truth is consequently *always* a biopolitics, insofar as it takes these bodies and languages as its object in order to produce a new form of subject.

AGAMBEN: FROM OATHS TO TWEETS

We have seen how Foucault and Badiou transform the question of truth from an epistemological question into an existential one, demonstrating how we have come to rely on truth, which in itself is neither given nor necessary, for our very existence as subjects. Irreducible to, yet still dependent on bodies and languages, discourses of truth permit us to adopt a free relation to them and to furnish subjective forms of life out of them. In this section we shall address Agamben's work on the decline of the oath in contemporary culture, which both elaborates the argument of Foucault and Badiou and inverts it, addressing the implications of the loss of the subjectivating efficacy of truth.

Agamben's point of departure in *The Sacrament of Language* is similar to Foucault's approach to truth, even though his archaeological perspective casts a longer shadow into the past, ultimately finding the source of truth in the very experience of becoming human. If Foucault's subject of truth becomes such in the effort of reconciling its old values with new rules and Badiou's subject of truth becomes such in the effort of fidelity to the evanescent event that sets it on the path of affirmation of generic truths, Agamben's subject is bound to the truth by virtue of the very experience of anthropogenesis, becoming human by 'entering' language, abandoning infancy and beginning to speak.

In this 'anthropogenetic' experience, human beings establish a relationship between themselves and language, assuming responsibility for what they say: '[The] living being, who has discovered itself speaking, has decided to be responsible for his words, and, devoting himself to the *logos*, to constitute himself as the "living being who has language"' (Agamben 2009a: 69). Just as the old Greek nobility found in the discourses of truth concerning sexuality a way to maintain themselves as active subjects, the hypothetical early humans in Agamben's analysis found a way to affirm their own trustworthiness through binding themselves to the content of their enunciations:

> [For] the living human being, who found himself speaking, what must have been decisive is the problem of the efficacy and truthfulness of his word, that is, of what can guarantee the original connection between names and things, and between the subject who has become a speaker – and thus capable of asserting and promising – and his actions. (Ibid.: 68)

Properly human language can only exist when the living being 'committed itself to respond with its life for its words, to testify in the first person for them' (ibid.: 69).

In Agamben's argument, *oath* and its attendant, *curse*, are two of the earliest modalities of the affirmation of the truth of one's discourse. An oath establishes a connection between words and things, language and reality, affirming that what is said is indeed (or will indeed be) so and sometimes also specifying the sanction to take place if one does not act as one said, that is, the curse that accompanies a broken oath (ibid.: 65). This is why for Agamben every saying is either a blessing or a curse, a benediction or a malediction: oath is a blessing when its fulfilment confirms the positive force of language and a curse when it is violated, destroying the link between words and things or actions (ibid.: 36).

For an oath to be possible in the first place,

> [it] is necessary to be able to distinguish and articulate together in some way, life and language, actions and words, and this is precisely what the animal, for which language is still an integral part of its vital practice, cannot do. The first promise is produced by means of this division, in which man, opposing his language to his actions, can put himself at stake in language, can promise himself to the *logos*. (Ibid.: 69)

The first, or proto-oath is thus an act in which the speaker affirms that it is serious about its use of language, that its words will be linked to actions and that what is said is not in vain. Every actual oath, promise, guarantee, commitment and other countless performative speech acts are, in Agamben's view, 'the relics in language of this constitutive experience of speech – veridiction – that exhausts itself with its utterance, since the speaking subject neither pre-exists it nor is subsequently linked to it but coincides integrally with the act of speech' (ibid.: 58). It is not a coincidence that all these performative formulae must be uttered in first person and lose their performative efficacy when used in reporting on the activities of others. One can report on the oaths made by others, but one can only make an oath in one's own name. Truth is thus a way to make language *work* for a living being and a way to make living beings *responsible* for their use of language. The human is not simply a speaking being, but a being whose speech may be true or false.

In Agamben's reading, religion and law subsequently 'technical-ize this anthropogenic experience of the word in the oath and curse as historical institutions, separating and opposing point by point truth and lie, true name and false name, efficacious formula and incorrect formula' (ibid.: 70). The performative force of language is thus ordered and routinised in familiar formulae, reserved for spe-cific speakers endowed with particular authority. What began as the establishment of a relation between living beings and their acts of speech ends up split into a myriad of institutions and authorities, dogmata and rituals, ceremonies and routines that all seek to stabi-lise 'the originary performative force of the anthropogenic experi-ence' (ibid.: 70).

At the end of the book, having offered a lengthy genealogy that traces our current experience of the performative force of language back to ancient oaths and even further to the first human experience of language, Agamben makes a somewhat startling conclusion that throws a different light on the entire preceding discourse:

> [We] are today the first generations to live our collective life without the bond of the oath. Humanity finds itself today before a disjunction or at least a loosening of the bond that, by means of the oath, united the living being to its language. On the one hand, there is the living being, more and more reduced to a purely biological reality and to bare life. On the other hand, there is the speaking being, artificially divided from the former, through a multiplicity of technico-mediatic apparatuses, in an experience of the word that grows ever more vain, for which it is impos-sible to be responsible, and in which anything like a political experience becomes more and more precarious. When the ethical – and not simply cognitive – connection that unites words, things and human actions is broken, this in fact promotes a spectacular and unprecedented prolif-eration of vain words on the one hand and on the other, of legislative apparatuses that seek obstinately to legislate on every aspect of that life on which they seem no longer to have any hold. The age of the eclipse of the oath is also the age of blasphemy, in which the name of God breaks

away from its living connection with language and can only be uttered 'in vain'. (Ibid.: 71)

At first glance, Agamben's claim is rather self-evident. Oaths and especially curses certainly appear in decline in contemporary culture, reduced to official rituals devoid of any meaning. Yet, if we agree with Agamben's genealogy, then the decline of the oath has far-reaching consequences for the very experience of *being human*. If the living being and the speaking being no longer coincide in the oath but dwell in the separate dimensions of bare life and communication technology, then it is no longer possible for the human being to place itself at stake in language and speak either truly or falsely. The result is the proliferation of 'vain words' and, what amounts to the same, *blasphemy*.

Blasphemy is traditionally understood as uttering the name of God in vain, for example saying 'Oh my God!', 'Gosh!' or 'Jesus Christ!' in trivial settings without actually appealing to the deity in question in a petition or a prayer. It is therefore a diametrical opposite of the oath, in which the name of God is relied on to produce the sought performative effect:

> Blasphemy presents us with a phenomenon that is perfectly symmetrical to the oath. Blasphemy is an oath, in which the name of a god is extracted from the assertorial or promissory context and is uttered in itself, in vain, irrespectively of a semantic content. The name, which in the oath expresses and guarantees the connection between words and things and which defines the truthfulness and force of the *logos*, in blasphemy expresses the breakdown of this connection and the vanity of human language. (Ibid.: 40–1)

Contrary to the misperception we shall encounter in the following chapter, there is no 'injury' done to God in blasphemy – if injury is done to anything, it is to language *itself*, which loses its performative efficacy. Yet, if this performative efficacy functions in the process of anthropogenesis to subjectivise the living being as human by putting its life at stake in its discourse, what happens when oaths and curses lose their efficacy and all that remains is blasphemy, which is no longer even recognised as such, precisely because there presumably is no longer any *other* way to speak than in vain?

This is as good a description of the post-truth predicament as any we are aware of. Yet, Agamben does not proceed to advocate to resolve this crisis by restoring the oath as the apparatus of the articulation of words and reality. Doing so would amount to bringing back or propping up the remaining apparatuses of religion and law, whose prior technicalisation and routinisation of the oath may have been the primary causes of its decline. Instead, Agamben argues, quite provocatively, that

> it is perhaps time to call into question the prestige that language has enjoyed and continues to enjoy in our culture, as a tool of incomparable potency, efficacy and beauty. And yet, considered in itself, it is no more beautiful than birdsong, no more efficacious than the signals insects exchange, no more powerful than the roar with which the lion asserts his dominion. (Ibid.: 71)

What separates human language from the languages of animals is not its inherent properties but rather the possibility for subjectivation that it offers:

> The decisive element that confers on human language its peculiar virtue is not in the tool itself but in the place it leaves to the speaker, in the fact it prepares within itself a hollowed out form that the speaker must always assume in order to speak. (Ibid.)

While one might have expected the theme of vanity of speech and generalised blasphemy to continue along the familiar narrative of the cultural criticism of late modernity, Agamben does not pursue this direction. Instead, his argument carries a strong and quite unexpected resonance with his earlier work, especially *Language and Death*, whose affirmative intention consists in overcoming the negativity at work in the human experience of language, the negation of the (animal) voice that is the presupposed foundation of language as the system of signification. In *Language and Death*, the process of entering language is approached less from the ethico-political perspective of *The Sacrament of Language* than from an ontological perspective that highlights the negation of the living being in the constitution of the speaking being. 'Man is the living being who removes himself and preserves himself at the same time – as unspeakable – in language; negativity is the human means of *having* language' (Agamben 1991: 85, emphasis original). We may easily note the parallels between this negative foundation of language by the removal of animal voice and the negative foundation of political forms of life (*bios*) by the 'inclusive exclusion' of unqualified life (*zoe*) that Agamben would develop in his later *Homo Sacer* series.

The removal of the animal voice leaves the human being in a purely negative, 'hollowed out' structure that Agamben terms Voice, a presupposition that can never be itself brought to language, but only indicated through linguistic markers, known in linguistics as *shifters*, that refer to the taking place of discourse: 'I', 'this', 'here'. It is only by virtue of the negativity of the Voice that human beings can enter language and begin to speak, as opposed to animals that are always already within language:

> If language were immediately the voice of man, as braying is the voice of the ass and chirping the voice of the cicada, man could not experience the taking place of language or the disclosure of being. But if, on the other hand, man radically possessed no voice (not even a negative Voice), every shifter and every possibility of indicating the event of language would disappear equally. (Agamben 1991: 84–5)

Agamben's affirmative project in *Language and Death* unfolds between these two extremes. Severing the link between language and death must proceed through the liquidation of the figure of the Voice. 'Only if language no longer refers to any Voice [. . .], is it possible for man to experience a language that is not marked by negativity and death' (ibid.: 95). But what sort of language would it be? If the negative foundation of the Voice is produced by the 'removal' or negation of the 'animal voice' or natural sound, then a self-evident 'solution' would be to refrain from this negation and return to the natural immediacy of language, akin to the braying of the ass or the chirping of the cricket. In his frequently used examples of the braying of the donkey or the chirping of the cricket Agamben seeks to describe precisely such an immediate experience of language devoid of any split, discontinuity or difference:

> [It] is not language in general that marks out the human from other living beings, but the split between language and speech, between semiotic and semantic (in Benveniste's sense), between sign system and discourse. Animals are not in fact denied language; on the contrary, the are always and totally language. Animals do not enter language, they are already inside it. Man, instead, by having an infancy, by preceding speech, splits this single language, and, in order to speak, has to constitute himself as the subject of language – he has to say 'I'. (Agamben 2007a: 59)

It is important to stress that we are not dealing here with a naïve desire for the return to a presumably natural origin. Firstly, entering language *is* the origin of being human and whatever being preceded it was not properly human on Agamben's definition. Secondly, and more importantly, in Agamben's understanding the origin in question is not an event in the distant past but something that remains at work in contemporary practices. The proto-oath is not something that was done and over with forty millennia ago but keeps happening over and over again in every act of speech, just like the 'big bang which is supposed to have given rise to the universe but continues to send toward us its fossil radiation' (Agamben 2009b: 109).

Yet, if this originary experience never ceased to take place in the here and now, its deactivation or reversal also remains a permanently available possibility. Thus, Agamben finds the possibility of redemption at the very site of the contemporary degradation of language:

> Perhaps in the age of absolutely speakable things, whose extreme nihilistic furor we are experiencing today, the age in which all the figures of the Unspeakable and all the masks of ontotheology have been *liquidated*, or released or spent in words that merely show the nothingness of their foundation; the age in which all human experience of language has been redirected to the final negative reality of a willing that means nothing – perhaps this age is also the age of man's in-fantile dwelling in language. (Agamben 1991: 92, emphasis original)

In other words, the contemporary decline of the performative efficacy of language illuminates the problematic nature of the original anthropogenetic experiment that ties human beings to their enunciations and makes it possible to rethink our relationship to language as such:

> [is] it possible that being is not up to the level of the simple mystery of humans' having, of their habitations or their habits? And what if the dwelling to which we return beyond being were neither a supercelestial place nor a Voice but simply the *trite* words that we *have*? (Ibid.: 94, emphasis original)

What are these *trite words*? In the final pages of *Language and Death* Agamben speaks of a 'language without Voice, a word that is not grounded in any meaning' (ibid.: 95) as something that 'we must still learn to think', which suggests that this vision of language is something esoteric, akin to Benjamin's pure language that, in Agamben's reading, 'does not mean anything, but simply speaks' (Agamben 1999b: 54). Alternatively, Agamben might be interpreted as talking about a particular use of language, for example in (modernist) poetry, which he extensively analysed as a mode of discourse that bears within itself the deactivation and profanation of the signifying function (Agamben 1999a: 62–75, 87–101).

We suggest another, rather more literal reading. What we must still learn to think is not some new idea or concept, yet to be invented or discovered, but rather the fact that what we have been looking for as something new is in fact something that we had all along. It is not a matter of the introduction of a new idea but of a shift in perspective that reveals the importance of something we tended to dismiss: our 'habits' and 'trite words'. In other words, what we must still learn to think is not some very difficult thought but the disappearance of the very *object* of thought:

> [We] can cease to hold language, the voice, in suspense. If thought is thought in the voice, it no longer has *anything* to think. Once completed, thought has no more thought. We came as close as possible to language, we almost brushed against it, held it in suspense: but we never reached our encounter and now we turn back, untroubled, toward home. So, language is our voice, our language. As you now speak, that is ethics. (Agamben 1991: 108)

What does this enigmatic passage mean? Earlier in the text, Agamben remarks in parentheses that 'the cricket, clearly, cannot think in its chirping' (ibid.: 107). Thought is only possible by virtue of the negative structure of human language, in which the living being is at once negated and conserved, elevated to the status of the subject by placing its life at stake in its words. If this negative structure is itself negated, and thought has nothing left to think, we end up with nothing other than the habitual use of language that no longer means anything but 'simply speaks', the trite words that we have, that we have always had but vainly hoped to replace by words that would be more meaningful or powerful because they were true.

The capture of speaking beings in negativity and death is thereby reversed into a plenitude of speech that, however, no longer has anything *at stake* in it, that does not *think* while it speaks, just like the cricket that does not think in its chirping but simply chirps away. To speak that way is to speak vainly and haphazardly, and even to speak blasphemously, with a caveat that there is no longer any authority that could accuse us of blasphemy. Rather than return to the origin, we arrive at a place *before* the origin, before any scission and any articulation between the living and the speaking. The reversal of the anthropogenetic apparatus of language leaves us with a language that is strictly equivalent to that of the cicada or the donkey.

On the final page of *The Sacrament of Language* Agamben appears to backtrack a little from the radical nature of his own conclusions by isolating another possible experience of language, in which it would retain its performative efficacy without, however, being reducible to the ordering formulae of religion and law. This experience of speech 'abid[es] in the risk of truth as much as of error, forcefully pronounced, without either swearing or cursing, its yes to language, to the human being, as speaking and political animal' (Agamben 2009a: 72). This experience is of course philosophy, which is 'constitutively a critique of the oath', ceaselessly questioning the very link between words and actions that constitutes both religion and law without abrogating it entirely. It thereby 'puts in question the sacramental bond that links the human being to language, without for that reason simply speaking haphazardly, falling into the vanity of speech' (ibid.).

While it is perfectly understandable that a philosopher would seek to elevate the status of their own discourse, this otherwise elegant solution does not really work, especially in the light of the concluding claims of *Language and Death*. The critique of the oath, taken to its logical conclusion, cannot but end in the taking leave of language and thought and the return to purely habitual, trite speech, akin to the braying of the donkey. The theme of the 'end of philosophy' in Agamben's work must be taken seriously and literally: this is not the end that somehow befalls philosophy as an external shock or disaster, but the end of the philosophical project as such, the accomplishment of the critique of the oath, which at once deprives the oath of its efficacy and *itself* of any meaning. In the language, where an oath is no longer possible, where everything is speakable without effect, philosophy has nothing to say and can only *retrace* its history, the history of its own arriving at an end. Similarly to the famous examples of ritualised arts in Kojève's (1969: 158–62) account of the end of history (Japanese theatre, bouquets, tea ceremonies, etc.), we would be dealing with a purely ritualised discourse that has long lost its meaning but *whose reproduction may still be enjoyable*. Words that have ceased to be meaningful or effective may nonetheless remain *pleasant* and this pleasure is in fact the only reason to *go on* speaking when nothing is any longer at stake in speech. It is no coincidence that the prime site of vain speech in the world today is named after the sound made by birds.

A language in which an oath is impossible, which is no longer characterised by the disjunctive articulation of words and things, only offers the experience of enjoyment of word *as* thing, of speech *as* action. If the apparatus of the oath posited truth as a connector between words and things, the identity of word and thing, speech and action, simply leaves no place for truth because the 'hollowed out' space where the human being could emerge as a subject of true and false discourse is now definitively closed.

This reading of Agamben permits us to re-engage with Kalpokas's argument about the enjoyment that sustains post-truth. Kalpokas understands post-truth as a radicalisation of Romantic *escapism*, which imagines social reality to be the object of the self's enjoyment of itself as it perceives itself to be omnipotent. 'In a true romantic fashion, the individual takes center stage, becoming the criterion of truth and existence, pitting facts and "alternative" facts against one another and creating their own version of reality as a piece of art or escapist fiction' (Kalpokas 2018: 1143). This escapist tendency is enabled by innovations in media and communication, particularly the rise of social media that enable the selection of information and the emergence of filter bubbles, isolated from the information one considers unpleasant.

While certainly suggestive, Kalpokas's argument about romantic escapism does not explain the proliferation of discourse in the post-truth era. Why are the self-aggrandising individuals not content with escaping into the imaginary worlds of television series, video games or pornography, but insist on writing and commenting on Facebook posts, debunking mainstream media reports and constructing most intricate conspiracy theories, all the while undermining their own claims to be true by negating the existence of truth as such?

The pleasure in question cannot simply be the pleasure of escape, since one remains resolutely *in the midst* of social reality. Yet, neither can it be the pleasure of meaningful *engagement* with this reality through social praxis or critical discourse, since both would presuppose the true–false distinction that is no longer there. Instead, it can only be the pleasure of speaking *as such*, which alone permits to understand why one would *go on* speaking in the absence of any truth claims, without seeking adherence or aiming at eliciting other effects in the real. This pleasure of speech, expressed so clearly in the braying of the donkey and the chirping of the cricket, goes beyond the enjoyment of any particular content or effect, its object being language *as such* in its sheer materiality.

Similarly, the ease of oscillation between contrary or contradictory positions that has so much shocked the observers of 'populist' movements and leaders since 2016 is only explicable if we approach their discourse as something more, less or simply *other* than argumentation, a rhetorical practice aimed at convincing an audience – namely, as the use of language for pure enjoyment. Donald Trump tweets not because he is eager to communicate a message to his followers, nor because he considers this mode of communication effective, nor because he wishes his tweets to be admired for their rhetorical virtuosity. He tweets because he *likes to tweet* – anything whatsoever. When Trump detractors worldwide laughed at his tweet containing a meaningless word *covfefe*, presumably as a result of a typographical error, they missed the point of tweeting entirely. There is pleasure involved in tweeting and retweeting that has nothing to do with meaning or thought and is easily attained in its absence. Just ask the braying donkey.

If this rather unorthodox diagnosis is taken seriously, we may also pose the question of a possible cure. If anthropogenesis was not a singular event in the past but the transcendental origin that is both presupposed and produced in the present, then it could be both reversed and restarted, at any time and for any number of times. The age of 'absolutely speakable things' is not some new age that succeeds the age of the oath but rather the extreme point of the *pendulum* that can always swing to the other extreme without, however, necessarily ending up in the ritualised and technicalised normativity of oaths and curses. The pathway out of the post-truth condition rather lies in grafting onto the transcendental origin of every possible oath in the experience of language that Foucault and Agamben call 'veridiction' or truth-telling.

Understanding truth in its relation to subjectivation, as the process of binding the speaker to its enunciations and thereby forming and transforming its subjectivity, permits us to approach post-truth not merely in its technological or mediatic dimensions but as an *ethico-political predicament*, in which more is at stake than the increased circulation of inanities and falsehoods. Instead, post-truth marks a critical moment in our historical existence as political subjects. If subjectivation by truth has defined us from Antiquity or even the earliest stages of human history, how can a subject emerge and exist in the post-truth era? What is an ethics and a politics that would define such a subject?

In Chapter 3 we shall address the genealogy of the contemporary 'age of absolutely speakable things', focusing on postcommunist Russia, the homeland of many of the post-truth practices and technologies that are now widespread globally. Since we do not approach post-truth as the inexorable outcome of a historical process but rather as a pendulum swing away from subjectivation by truth, we will analyse the Russian postcommunist experience as an outcome of a series of contingent events that led the Russian society towards accepting and even asserting the equivalence of all things. In Chapter 4 we shall attempt to isolate a practice that would enable the pendulum swing into the opposite direction – not 'back to truth', since one never really goes back to anything, but rather *towards* it.

CHAPTER THREE

The Russification of the West

VLADIMIR ZHIRINOVSKY:
THE BIRTH OF POSTCOMMUNIST TROLLING

Our discussion of post-truth politics in the first two chapters largely focused on contemporary Western democracies, which remain the prime site of inquiry into the post-truth condition. Yet, this focus may lead to a distorted perception of the post-truth condition as a problem internal to liberal-democratic politics, perhaps a symptom of its crisis but still belonging to its horizon. Nonetheless, a quick glance beyond Western democracies reveals that post-truth politics operates in the regimes that are distant from conventional understandings of democracy: Turkey, Philippines, Russia, and so on. Peter Pomerantsev's *This is Not Propaganda* (2019b) offers a chilling description of the quick worldwide spread of post-truth phenomena, from troll farms and fake news to anti-vaccination and climate change denialism. In this chapter we shall therefore extend our focus beyond Western democracies and address the emergence and transformation of post-truth politics in postcommunist Russia.

The focus on Russia is particularly pertinent, since the rise of post-truth to the top of the political agenda in the West coincided with the crisis in Russia–West relations after the 2014 annexation of Crimea and Russia's intervention in the Donbass region of Ukraine. Both of the key events that made 'post-truth' the catchword of 2016 and beyond, that is, the Brexit referendum and the US presidential election resulting in Trump's victory, were marked by Russia's attempts at influencing the outcome, in both cases successfully. Moreover, in these attempts Russia deployed the kind of campaigning and communication techniques that later became associated with the victors of the two campaigns, Johnson and Trump. Thus, Russia successfully used post-truth methods to elect post-truth candidates, which certainly warrants a more detailed consideration of post-truth in the context of a non-democratic regime such as Putin's Russia.

Yet, an even more important reason to focus on Russia is that the phenomena and processes usually subsumed under the rubric of post-truth actually preceded Putin's ascendance as president in 2000 and indeed, as we shall see, made it possible. Thus, in this chapter we shall forgo retelling the by now familiar story of Russia's interference in Western politics and focus instead on what made this interference possible and almost inevitable, that is, the prior domestic success of post-truth strategies in the establishment and maintenance of the Putin regime. Rather than view post-truth interventions as some new method of foreign policy (e.g. 'hybrid' or 'non-linear' war), we shall approach it as an extension into the international domain of an already established domestic *technology of governance*. Our analysis will demonstrate that rather than function as an internal mutation of Western liberal democracies, post-truth serves as an effective strategy of de-democratisation, enabling the formation and consolidation of authoritarian regimes. Moreover, these regimes appear very difficult to criticise and confront, once such critique can no longer be a matter of telling truth to power but is only an opinion among others, an opinion defenceless before the power which claims to do nothing more than act on the opinion of its own, to which it is entitled by the laws of the very democracy that it seeks to undermine.

Our analysis below is therefore intended less as a case study in Russian postcommunism, which we attempted elsewhere (Prozorov 2009), than a genealogical investigation of the descent of the mode of politics that no longer appears exclusively Russian at all. In fact, one of the more uncanny and disconcerting aspects of the Brexit- and Trump-era politics in Europe and the USA is the similarity between the discourses of alt-right or far-right politicians, commentators and online trolls and the Russian political discourse of the early 1990s, similarly characterised by the harassment of 'libtards' (called 'liberasts' in Russian), the spread of outlandish conspiracies and obscene rumours, utter indifference to fact-checking, evidence and even basic logic, not to speak of elementary decency. What at the time appeared as the 'infantile illness' of an emergent democracy, to be gradually

91

outgrown in the course of the 'Westernisation' of Russia, has reappeared in full force in the very West that, having failed to Westernise Russia, now appears itself progressively Russified. From this perspective, Trump's true precursor is neither Mussolini nor Hitler, but Vladimir Zhirinovsky, whom Trump uncannily resembles even in his gesticulation and the pitch of his voice. It is only too fitting, therefore, if we begin our genealogy of postcommunist post-truth with the rise of Zhirinovsky's Liberal Democratic Party.

The Liberal Democratic Party (LDPR) was founded in 1990 and in spring 1991 became the first officially registered non-communist party in the USSR, which led to rumours that it was a pet project of the KGB designed in order to discredit and possibly hijack the emerging multi-party democratic system. Its leader, Vladimir Zhirinovsky, received 8 per cent of the votes in the first Russian presidential elections in June 1991 on an ultra-populist and nationalist platform. In the first democratic parliamentary elections in Russia in December 1993, LDPR came first in the party vote gaining 23 per cent, yet struggled to replicate this success in single-member districts, since it lacked public figures aside from its flamboyant leader. While the party never repeated this success and its popularity ebbed in the late 1990s, it quickly re-established itself as a permanent feature of the Russian political landscape in the Putin era, polling respectably at 12–16 per cent for over twenty years. The accusations of the party's associations with the regime continued to plague it in the Putin period, as the party has tended to vote in favour of almost all government proposals in the parliament while still proclaiming itself oppositional. Yet, this contradiction was merely one among many in the party's programme and rhetoric, which did not seem to hamper its electoral fortunes.

From the beginning of Zhirinovsky's career, observers have noted that his party could not be identified with any ideological orientation. Its name is an obvious misnomer, as the party is neither liberal nor democratic in any meaningful way, nor is it much of a party either, the entire party structure serving more like Zhirinovsky's personal fan club. The very choice of the name may be seen as the example of trolling *avant la lettre*: at the time when the multi-party system was about to be introduced in the USSR, the name 'Liberal Democratic Party' was reserved by the Soviet authorities for the party that had nothing but contempt for liberalism and democracy, so that much more deserving candidates for this name had to be content with less attractive alternatives. Even more interestingly, the party stuck with its name in the 1990s, when the words 'liberalism' and 'democracy' lost much of their allure by being associated with the chaotic and inept reforms of the Yeltsin presidency, and even in the late Putin era, when these words carried the risk of being branded unpatriotic or even a 'foreign agent'. The continuity of LDPR's name since 1990 suggests that this name functions more like a *logo*, devoid of any semantic content.

The same goes for the party's ideological programme and rhetoric, which is driven towards adopting the most extreme position on any issue, frequently bordering on the absurd and occasionally stepping over that border. In the early 1990s, Zhirinovsky became famous because of his flamboyant and vaudeville style, which contrasted with both the worn-out ideological dogmata of the communists and the overly earnest and moralising discourse of the democratic opposition. Instead, Zhirinovsky's public appearances featured endless monologue rants, in which he would promise free vodka for all men, a husband for every woman and, famously yet inexplicably, that Russian soldiers would soon wash their boots in the Indian Ocean. These rants would habitually use expletives and often contain threats of physical violence to journalists, politicians and even foreign heads of state. Appearing on every television programme where he could get invited, from cooking to relationship advice shows, he would use every opportunity to provoke a scandal and turn the attention onto himself. Zhirinovsky seems to have violated every possible taboo in Russian politics, yet his popularity does not seem to have suffered much. Even the 2018 accusations of sexual harassment by a male journalist that would easily derail a political career in the still strongly homophobic Russia did not really stick or were shrugged off as merely confirming what one knew all along but could not be bothered to say in public.

LDPR's lead in the 1993 parliamentary election was perceived as a shock to the newly emerged Russian political system. The election itself, which followed almost two years of conflict between Yeltsin and the Supreme Soviet dominated by communists and nationalists, was widely expected to lead to a pro-Yeltsin majority that would finally enable the pursuit of economic reforms allegedly resisted by the previous parliament. The fact that this majority did not materialise and the pro-Yeltsin Russia's Choice party only came second after Zhirinovsky's LDPR led a well-known commentator, Yuri Karyakin, to utter what has become an infamous judgement on election night: 'Russia, you've gone mad!'

LDPR's triumph was interpreted by many Western analysts as the sign of Russia's looming relapse into authoritarianism, and Zhirinovsky was routinely compared to Mussolini, Hitler and other notorious totalitarian leaders. Yet, this was hardly the perception inside Russia, where the threat of relapse into totalitarianism was rather associated with the 'red–brown' union of orthodox Stalinists and Russian nationalists that led the resistance to Yeltsin in the Supreme Soviet (see Prozorov 2009: 171–5; Ostrovsky 2017: 151–63). Instead, for all his verbal attacks on democracy, Zhirinovsky's rise would be entirely unthinkable outside the democratic political system. Street rallies, political advertising on television, reliance on volunteer activists – all of these familiar features of liberal-democratic systems that were still so novel for the post-Soviet society were instrumental in Zhirinovsky's rise. Of course, dependence on democracy is not always translated into loyalty to it, and in his vitriolic soliloquies Zhirinovsky continued to praise the virtues of dictatorship, promising to do away with elections as soon as he managed to win one.

This combination of dependence on and derision of democracy is merely one more contradiction that did not hamper but rather enabled LDPR's successful presence in the Russian political landscape for over thirty years. Zhirinovsky's triumph in the 1993 election took place in the aftermath of the violent struggles of 1993, which gave the electorate a taste of civil war that most wished to avoid. Yet, rather than consolidate Yeltsin's victory in these struggles by giving pro-government parties a solid majority, a plurality of the voters sought to support a demagogue who predictably cursed both sides and presented himself as an alternative to this debilitating conflict: neither communist nor liberal, neither pro- nor anti-Soviet, neither pro-government nor oppositional. In a certain sense, Zhirinovsky's entire subsequent career enacted this alternative: a party that endlessly rants against the government yet always votes in favour of its proposals, a leader who behaves like an extremist yet proves remarkably conciliatory in informal deals, a hope for Russia's imperial resurgence and a permanent fixture of lowbrow daytime television. With Zhirinovsky, it seemed that postcommunist Russians could have their cake and eat it, its enjoyment in no way hampered by its progressive derealisation.

Para-Soviet practices in the post-Soviet era

Embodying contradictions without ever resolving them, lying with impunity and threatening in a non-threatening way, Zhirinovsky's LDPR was a paradigmatic precursor to post-truth politics. It is not a coincidence that its triumph occurred in the first free parliamentary election in Russia, when the demise of the ideocratic project of the Soviet Union appeared to finally open the space for the free circulation and competition of alternative ideas, ideologies and projects. Nonetheless, this competition never really materialised after the demise of the Soviet Union, as the post-Soviet society quickly lost interest in political participation after a few years of mobilisation against the regime in 1988–91.

What explains this quick demobilisation of the post-Soviet society? In order to understand this process, we need to pay attention to the patterns of the societal coexistence with the regime in the late-Soviet period. The long decline of the Soviet ideocracy, progressively ritualised after the death of Stalin and increasingly dissociated from the lived experience of the Soviet citizens, entailed a devaluation of the ideological dimension of politics as such (Yurchak 2006). In an earlier book (Prozorov 2009) we have analysed this process in terms of the emergence of a 'para-Soviet' *ethos of disengagement*, cultivated by the diverse groups of Soviet citizens, who, faced with a regime that forcefully crushed every open expression of dissent, chose to withdraw from the public sphere entirely into a variety of private lifestyles and hobbies (rock music, Orthodox Christianity, yoga, fishing, Satanism, kung fu, etc.), stylising their lives in such a way that nothing recognisably Soviet remained in them, yet nothing anti-Soviet was expressed either.

Rather than confront the regime explicitly and from an alternative ideological standpoint, which would certainly invite a repressive response, these para-Soviet subjects chose to withdraw from the official rituals of the regime or, when that was impossible, participate in them with an exaggerated enthusiasm that was a thin disguise for utter contempt. In the late-Soviet period this latter attitude received the name *'styob'* (literally, 'jibe'). *Styob* is usually understood in terms of the ironic distancing from the structures of authority and the subjection of the official discourse to a desublimating *parody* that deprives it of both sense and force. In this manner, *styob* carries a certain liberating effect for its subject despite leaving the parodied phenomenon strictly intact. By making the maxims of the Soviet ideology meaningless, the practitioners of *styob* also sought to render them powerless with regard to their hold on one's existence (see Yurchak 2006: 127–30; Groys 2003: 212; Prozorov 2009: 107–12).

As a result, by the late 1970s it was possible to dwell in the Soviet society in the para-Soviet mode, becoming indifferent to its ideological rituals while not affirming any alternative ideological content. While the liberating effects of this disposition are indisputable, they have come at the price of a thoroughgoing *depoliticisation* of the late-Soviet society, which postcommunist Russia inherited. The more Soviet citizens excelled at *styob*, the less they were capable of taking and upholding a serious political stand. Thus, while *styob* certainly contributed to the degradation of the Soviet order by desublimating its ideological maxims, its empowering effects should not be overestimated. Indeed, the very appeal of the *para*-Soviet ethos is conditioned by the impossibility or extreme danger of assuming an explicitly *anti*-Soviet position. It was only because the Soviet system was deemed to be here to stay that it made sense to cultivate liveable spaces in its interstices, furnishing them through alternative cultural practices that deactivated the official discourse through ironic parody of its maxims.

Conversely, the relative decline of *styob* under the late Gorbachev testified to the weakening of ideological hegemony and the newly gained possibility to challenge the state frontally on the terrain of ideology and not beside it in the practice of parodic displacement. And yet, after a brief surge of political activity in 1988–91, the Russian society again retreated into a para-political space beside the new system, passively observing the conflicts in the postcommunist political elite without participating in them. It is as if the brief period of political activity in the perestroika era only sought to do away with a system already on its knees, rather than construct any alternative to it. The true victor in the process of the demise of the Soviet Union was not some anti-Soviet alternative ideological project but the para-Soviet ethos of disengagement.

This permits us to understand the universalisation of scepticism and ironic detachment in the postcommunist period, when no ideological orientation was able to attain any degree of hegemony. The long decline of the Soviet ideocratic project revealed the utter contingency at the heart of ideological order, especially when observed from a para-Soviet position of being beside but not wholly outside the system. This revelation did not pertain merely to the Soviet ideology but to *all* hegemonic orders: the para-Soviet society was not merely uninterested in mobilising in order to 'build communism', but was also equally disdainful about any rival projects of 'building capitalism', (re)building the nation-state, restoring the Russian Empire or what not. Just as the architectural design of a building is fully revealed when it is on fire, the slow demise of the Soviet order revealed the mechanics of ideological construction that sustained it, with the effect of a profound disenchantment that disabled in advance any new construction of a positive order. When society as a whole becomes a critic of ideology, it finds false consciousness everywhere in the social order and can only embark on a new ideocratic project in bad faith.

As a result, the demise of the Soviet ideological edifice in 1989–91 was followed not by any new ideological hegemony (e.g. of liberalism, nationalism or social democracy) but by the continuation of disengagement and depoliticisation within the notionally liberal-democratic constitutional order (see Kharkhordin 1997; Holmes 1997). This depoliticisation was manifested in different ways throughout the 1990s: the quick distancing of perestroika-era pro-democracy activists by 'reformist' *technocrats* entrusted with economic reforms, the subsequent rise of late-Soviet era industrial *managers* (*khozyaistvenniki*) as an alternative to the discredited technocrats, and the eventual eclipse of the inept managers by *security officials* at the end of the decade (Gudkov 2001; Illarionov 2007; Kryshtanovskaya 2005). While at first glance Zhirinovsky's sheer flamboyance makes him stand out from this rather dreary series, the phenomenon of LDPR merely confirms the depoliticising tendency by offering a politics so devoid of any demand for engagement that one would never have to disengage oneself from it. While numerous political figures tried their luck with aggressive populist nationalism in the early 1990s, they usually failed miserably to attract any support, not simply because they lacked Zhirinovsky's somewhat elusive charisma, but because unlike them Zhirinovsky did not demand anything but the enjoyment of this charisma and an occasional vote in favour of LDPR in exchange for this enjoyment.

Understanding the fundamentally depoliticised nature of post-communist society, which would only support a political project on the condition of *not* participating in it, Zhirinovsky devised the first successful strategy of postcommunist politics: a paradoxically safe extremism that simultaneously satisfies and exhausts the desire to do away with things as they are and thereby ensures that things will stay the same. The success of Zhirinovsky in 1993 had important implications for the subsequent developments in Russian politics. LDPR demonstrated how ideological omnivorosity, devoid of any principles and openly manifesting contradictions, could enable a lasting presence in the political system. While attempts to imitate Zhirinovsky paled before the original, the overall logic underlying his approach became widespread in the politics of the 1990s and beyond.

Particularly important in this process was the new orientation to the Soviet past, especially its historical symbols and cultural tropes. During the political struggles of the perestroika period and the immediate aftermath of the dissolution of the USSR, the pro-democratic forces and the Yeltsin presidency initially sought to delimit the emergent Russian state from the USSR as the ideocratic project. The day of the adoption of Russia's declaration of sovereignty in 1990 (12 June) was briefly and informally called Independence Day, the day Russia presumably became independent from the Soviet Union. In this logic, the emergence of the Russian Federation in December 1991 could be viewed in terms of the *restitution* of statehood, whereby the new democratic republic could establish historical continuity with the republic proclaimed after the February revolution of 1917 but soon destroyed by the Bolsheviks. This restitutionist approach to history, which was partly realised in the Baltic states after their regaining independence in 1991, would have entailed dispensing with or at least devaluing much of the Soviet symbolic legacy, particularly that of a more ideological nature.

As is well known, this restitutionist approach did not prevail and instead Russia proclaimed itself the *successor state* to the Soviet Union. This decision was far more fateful than it might appear at first glance. By casting itself as 'USSR minus', as that which *remains* from the USSR, Russia not merely tied itself in its very self-definition to what it wanted to separate from (thus becoming a 'post-Soviet' country in perpetuity) but also legitimised in advance all revanchist projects of the reintegration of the Soviet Union. Understandably, in this successor logic, Soviet cultural legacy became not something to be discarded but rather something to be cherished and promoted as the common cultural basis that serves as the foundation for reintegration. It is notable that much of the culture promoted in the framework of the so-called 'Russian World' initiatives that have become infamous since 2014 is not classical let alone ancient Russian culture but rather specifically Soviet mass culture, which Russia shares with other post-Soviet states and on which it relies to promote their reintegration and undermine the more nationalist or Western-oriented political forces. Thus, the Soviet symbolic edifice, once ready to be discarded without regret, became the most important tool of Russian 'soft power'.

Yet, this reappropriation of the Soviet cultural legacy faced the obvious problem of reconciling this often highly ideologically charged legacy with the new realities of capitalism. While some of this content could be rendered ideologically neutral, it was not easy to claim as one's own the anti-bourgeois bombasts of early-Soviet film, song or literature while at the same time extolling 'bourgeois' values in socio-economic policy. It is here that Zhirinovsky's neutralisation of all semantic content and his indifference to contradictions proved useful.

On New Year's Eve in 1995 the nationwide TV channel ORT (subsequently renamed Channel 1) aired a musical film called *Old Songs about What Matters Most*, whose script was co-written by the celebrated television journalist Leonid Parfenov and the future head of Channel 1 and the key figure in the Putin regime Konstantin Ernst (see Ostrovsky 2017: 218–27). The film featured vignettes from different periods of Soviet history, soundtracked by new versions of the Soviet songs of the period, performed either by surviving Soviet superstars or by contemporary Russian pop musicians. The film enjoyed unprecedented success and its soundtrack sold millions of copies. Three sequels were made, all equally popular, and these films continue to be broadcast every year during New Year and Christmas holidays. The secret of their success consists in their successful transformation of the Soviet period into a 'usable past', which may be reappropriated in a novel ideological context through the neutralisation of its own ideological valence. The vignettes from Soviet life (set in collective farms, factories or 'houses of culture') were conventionally comical, devoid of ideological connotations and, aside from a few recognisable landmarks, might as well have taken place in medieval Europe or contemporary Latin America. The familiar Soviet songs were usually remixed in accordance with the fashions of the time and often performed by currently popular singers, attracting a younger audience to the show whose content would otherwise be unintelligible for it.

The success of *Old Songs* was replicated in other artistic fields, ushering in a veritable avalanche of remakes, sequels and prequels of Soviet classic films, albums of cover versions of Soviet standards by contemporary pop stars, and TV series set during the Soviet period. Even more important was the replication of this strategy on the political level, which was not coincidental, given Konstantin Ernst's move in 1999 from entertainment television to heading Channel 1 and masterminding the careful construction of Putin's television image during his ascendance to the presidency (see Ostrovsky 2017: 297–303). Along with Vladislav Surkov, who moved to the presidential administration from advertising and marketing jobs in the banking sector, Ernst became a key figure in micromanaging Putin's public relations (see Pomerantsev 2015: 72–6).

The first major controversy of the Putin presidency pertained to a series of acts on the national flag and anthem. Throughout the Yeltsin period the president faced an oppositional parliament dominated by the Communist Party that refused to officialise the *de facto* national flag (the tricolour) and the anthem (the instrumental 'Patriotic Song' by Glinka) that were only adopted by presidential decree as provisional state symbols. In 2000, enabled by the first pro-presidential majority in postcommunist history, Putin sought to pass new laws on state symbols, enshrining the tricolour flag by law. Yet, rather than adopt the Glinka anthem, he surprisingly opted for returning to the old Soviet anthem originally adopted under Stalin, with new lyrics written by Sergei Mikhalkov who also penned the original Stalin-era version in 1944 and then rewrote the lyrics in 1970 (Ostrovsky 2017: 267–70). The tricolour, which was banned in the USSR due to its use in World War II by the collaborationist Russian Liberation Army of General Andrei Vlasov and which became the symbol of the anti-Soviet democratic movement of the perestroika era, now coexisted side by side with the anthem of the Stalin era, whose new lyrics were so inane that one involuntarily recalled the old ones.

In much the same manner, the Putin presidency was able to reappropriate the key figures from both the Red and White sides in the Russian Civil War, to glorify the Soviet Union as a great power and to ridicule socialism as an ineffective economic model, to celebrate the anniversary of the Bolshevik secret police *Cheka* and denounce the Bolshevik Revolution as the betrayal of the nation at war. And yet, the price of this omnivorous appropriation is the proliferation of meaninglessness: when popular culture fails to respond to the post-Soviet transformation other than by replaying Soviet-era cultural tropes that no longer have a meaningful referent, the lesson learned is that content does not matter as long as the form continues to serve well.

We may also observe this privilege granted to form over content in the early postcommunist journalism, exemplified by the first privately owned newspapers *Kommersant* (established in 1990) and *Segodnya* (established in 1993). Explicitly positing themselves as the voices of a new postcommunist elite, these papers cultivated a somewhat aloof and ironic stance towards the emerging political regime. Journalists such as Maxim Sokolov are often credited with inventing a particular style of reporting, in which the author's conspicuous erudition and skilful wordplay produced a playful reception of the less than palatable realities of early postcommunism (Schwartzbaum 2018; see also Ostrovsky 2017: 120–39). The new reality became acceptable only as derealised, becoming less traumatic when wrapped in an aestheticist discourse full of allusions, citations and inside jokes that one could enjoy on its own terms while forgetting entirely the contents allegedly reported in it (Timofeevsky 1991). If the 'meaning' of the early postcommunist period consisted in the looting of state property by the coalition of communist nomenklatura and organised crime (Reddaway and Glinski 2001; Volkov 2002), then it was probably for the best to dwell in meaninglessness, especially if the latter was presented in such a stylish and trendy manner. Much like the braying donkey or the chirping cricket in Agamben's theory, the journalism of *Kommersant* and *Segodnya* communicated little more than its enjoyment of its own discourse.

From this perspective, the entirety of postcommunist culture may be viewed as a series of sequels to the *Old Songs about What Matters Most*, where everyone has long forgotten what it was that mattered most and is simply content with singing the old songs, sometimes with new lyrics and sometimes with old ones – after all, the old and the new have now become entirely equivalent.

WHERE MEANING RUNS DEEP

Yet, meaninglessness is not a sustainable condition in the long run. If meaning cannot be found on the surface, it will have to be found *behind* or *beneath* the surface. From the absence of explicit meaning one infers the presence of implicit meanings, even if they remain entirely obscure. Thus, the increasing disappearance of meaningful

101

distinctions in the postcommunist public sphere, where former communists fought other former communists about how better to build capitalism, gave rise to the increased search for the hidden meaning of this apparently meaningless chain of events. The 1990s were the high point of conspiracy theorising, from the more predictable and worn, such as the republication of the Protocols of the Elders of Zion to support the presentation of the Yeltsin administration as a plutocratic Jewish conspiracy, to the ironic deployment of conspiracies by contemporary artists. The popularity of conspiracy theories in the post-Soviet period is easily explained by the foundational nature of such theories for the Soviet regime itself, which, particularly in the Stalin period, was looking for and inevitably found conspiracies everywhere, partly because of the originally conspiratorial nature of the Bolshevik party: 'in worldview and practice it was a conspiracy that perceived conspiracy everywhere and in everything, gaslighting itself' (Kotkin 2017: 902; see more generally ibid.: 306–9, 332–3, 439–40). Having come to power as a result of a series of conspiracies, the victorious Bolsheviks knew all too well how easily their own regime might fall as a result of a conspiracy and feared nothing more than a conspiracy within their own ranks. After decades of being governed by a conspiratorial regime that viewed itself as surrounded by conspiracies, it is hardly surprising that the conspiracist disposition survived the dissolution of the Soviet order, which itself was interpreted by its dwindling supporters as a gigantic conspiracy, and became the main instrument of orientation in the new postcommunist reality.

In 1992 Sergei Kurekhin, a famous avant-garde musician and performance artist, appeared on national television with a ninety-minute-long programme about an alternative history of the Soviet Union that revealed that Vladimir Lenin was in fact nothing other than a hallucinogenic mushroom. Basing the story on the popular myth of widespread drug addiction among the leaders of the Revolution, Kurekhin argued that Lenin's addiction to such mind-altering mushrooms as amanita eventually reached such an extent that his consciousness was gradually displaced by that of the mushroom. Thus, a series of biographical events in Lenin's life, known to every Soviet citizen since childhood, were reinterpreted in a new light. For instance, Lenin's famous armoured car, on top of which he allegedly recited his April Theses in 1917, was revealed by Kurekhin to be identical in its cross-section to the rhizome of the amanita mushroom, while the famous lines from Lenin's political writings ('less is better', 'one step forward, two steps back') were shown to be direct quotations from some mushroom-picking manual. A small number of television viewers were offended by the programme, some were successfully duped by it, while many who were not actually convinced by its claims easily believed that this was a genuine historical programme, albeit a very bad one. After all, the early 1990s was the period of numerous historical revelations about the Soviet past, usually of a rather unpalatable nature, and the Russian society was already used to the pattern of having its beliefs shattered, its truths debunked and its symbols profaned time and again. Nothing was any longer what it seemed, so what exactly is so strange about Lenin, whom official propaganda had already turned into something less or more, but definitely other than merely human, actually being a mushroom? Worse things have happened, including by Lenin's orders.

Kurekhin's performance revealed a paradox of the newly won freedoms of speech and expression. In the Soviet period, official propaganda provided Soviet individuals with one authoritative truth, which these individuals had to obediently repeat but usually found ways not to abide by, given the excessive, unreasonable or simply absurd demands it made of them. Soviet citizens knew by heart the official claims about the advantages of Soviet collectivised agriculture over private farming, but living through a perennial shortage of foodstuffs taught them not to lend these truths much credence. The Soviet subject thus gradually came to know two things: what the truth *is* and *that it is untrue*.

What happens when the official ideological edifice tumbles down? In the absence of official ideology the subject is no longer obliged to obey any official truth, hence their knowledge of what the truth is is no longer valid and they remain lost and disoriented in the plurality of competing truth claims. Yet, what helps them survive this disorientation is the *other* thing they learned under Soviet indoctrination, namely that the truth, whatever it is on the surface of the discourse, is *in fact untrue*. In a manner reminiscent of negative theology, the post-Soviet subject responds to the plurality of truth claims with an affirmation that truth is always *elsewhere*, always hidden and never uttered just like that. Whatever truth claim is made in the public sphere, it is not true since truth is necessarily something ineffable. Of course, in this shrewd attempt not to be duped, the subject unwittingly attunes itself precisely to the kind of discourse that aims to bring the ineffable to speech, to go beneath the surface reality to arrive at the hidden meaning of what is.

This must be the secret of the immense popularity of the novels of Victor Pelevin, perhaps the best-known contemporary Russian author. From his earliest works that date back to the collapse of the Soviet Union, Pelevin sought to come to terms with the new post-communist reality through an idiosyncratic admixture of satire and esotericism that relies heavily on the tropes of conspiracy theory. In Pelevin's debut novel *Omon Ra* (1992) the protagonist, obsessed with space travel, enlists in a military academy where he undergoes preparations for a mission to the Moon. The mission would be officially 'unmanned', yet, because of the numerous deficiencies in Soviet technology, the tasks reserved for the machines would actually be performed by human pilots, who would not be able to survive the return journey and hence would sacrifice their lives for the prestige of the Soviet project of space exploration by shooting themselves after completing their missions. The Soviet technological breakthrough is thus a result of unspeakable human sacrifice. Yet, this is only the first step in Pelevin's deconstruction of Soviet ideology. After being launched to the Moon, Omon successfully performs his mission, but the gun he should use to kill himself misfires and he eventually finds out that he is actually in a subway tunnel outside Moscow and that the entire Soviet space programme has been a gigantic hoax. While the novel primarily targets both the Soviet propaganda with its claims of the technological superiority of socialism as well as the underlying ideology of patriotic sacrifice, the novel's revelation also uncannily resonates with the Moon-landing denialism discourse in the USA, which could perhaps be dated as the first major post-truth narrative.

In 2005 Alexei Fedorchenko made a mockumentary that offered another take on the Moon landing discourse. The film, called *The First on the Moon*, presents found footage that suggests that the first attempt to fly a manned capsule to the moon was actually undertaken by the Soviet Union in 1938. The pilot, Captain Ivan Kharlamov, manages to return to Earth, his capsule landing in Chile. He then makes his way to the Soviet Union via Polynesia and China before eventually being found by Soviet troops in Mongolia during the Battle of Khalkin-Gol, having suffered a brain injury. He is committed to a psychiatric hospital and eventually disappears, most probably perishing in the Stalinist purges of the period. The film won the award for best documentary at the Venice Film Festival despite being entirely fictitious, and numerous viewers in Russia were duped by the film, seeing it as a revelation of newly available historical facts. The enunciated content of the film corresponds to the first reversal in Pelevin's novel, which reveals that Soviet space travel is really possible, if only as a matter of enormous individual sacrifice. Yet, the enunciative position of the film itself, as an elaborate quasi-documentary hoax, performs the reversal akin to the one Pelevin practises at the end of his novel, when even this heroic and sacrificial project is revealed to be a hoax, which ridicules the Soviet and post-Soviet patriotism that demands to be the 'first' in everything, including trips to the Moon, be it at the cost of enormous sacrifice or elaborate deceit.

In May 1999, three months before Putin's appointment as prime minister and Yeltsin's designated successor, Pelevin published perhaps his most famous novel, *Generation P*, which both succinctly summed up the chaos and disorientation of the 1990s and prefigured the line of exit from this period that the Putin presidency would soon undertake. The novel's protagonist, Vavilen Tatarsky, a polytechnic dropout and an unsuccessful poet, ends up working as a salesperson at a commercial kiosk of the type that began popping up all over Russia with the liberalisation of trade in 1992. He meets a former classmate who helps him land a job in an advertising agency where his task is to invent 'authentically' Russian-style ads for Western consumer products. As Tatarsky is making a successful career in the advertising business, he gradually comes to understand that the entire Russian political elite, from the president to every member of parliament, are nothing other than 3D projections, existing only on television screens and manipulated by advertising agencies. A special corporate unit called 'People's Will' (the name of a populist terrorist group from the nineteenth century) employs individuals who travel around the country to talk to people in bars and at railway stations, pretending to have seen these politicians in person and thus fortifying the perception of their reality.

This first twist in the novel exploits the tendency in the postcommunist society, which had only begun to discover marketing and advertising, to endow these exotic spheres and their practitioners, including the so-called 'political technologists', with almost magical powers. Yet, Pelevin does not stop there. In the course of his many drug trips Tatarsky also discovers that the advertising industry is itself working in the service of none other than ancient Mesopotamian goddess Ishtar. By keeping the people fixated on the objects of consumption, advertising wards off the coming of the goddess's death, which takes the form of a five-legged dog affectionately named Fuckup (*Pizdets*). Having been thus enlightened, Tatarsky becomes the new 'earthly husband' of Ishtar, his 3D copy appearing in almost every television commercial. The first level of conspiracy, where politics is run by advertising executives, is thus complemented and subverted by an even deeper and more esoteric level as the petty world of advertising executives is revealed to be part of a centuries-old struggle for the salvation of a goddess.

The same structure can be observed in most of Pelevin's subsequent novels, which have become increasingly formulaic. The main protagonist (usually a younger member of the 'creative class' of journalists, copywriters or sales managers) accidentally discovers that the world of business, politics, advertising or high culture is not what it seems and that in reality it is run by creatures either criminal or supernatural or sometimes both (vampires, werewolves, etc.). It is the struggles between these creatures that explain, that is, endow with meaning, the phenomena of our surface reality that are otherwise inexplicable. Postcommunist politics, economy, culture merely reflect the underlying reality of the conspiracy of vampires or other supernatural creatures. And yet, Pelevin does not stop at this first level of conspiracy theorising, since this concealed reality ends up in turn concealing something even more fundamental, usually described in mystical, esoteric, New Age or Buddhist terms. In short, in the course of the novels the protagonist travels from the meaninglessness of superficial reality to the conspiratorial reality beneath it, which in the end also ends up dissolved as s/he advances further towards the more enlightened knowledge of the nullity of all things worldly and, in the quasi-Buddhist version that is increasingly prominent in his works, the nullity of all things period.

Pelevin's narrative strategy thus proceeds through a double negation. Firstly, the immediate reality of post-Soviet political and social life, which is presented as drab and meaningless, is negated by a conspiratorial narrative that explains it away as a mere illusion or projection, generated on a more fundamental level populated by powerful media, security service and underworld figures. Yet, this negation is in turn itself negated by another, esoteric explanation that introduces an even deeper level to this reality, in which it is hard to recognise any of the contemporary events and phenomena. The outcome of this double negation appears to be one's return to this surface reality but now fully aware of its superficial nature that enables one to take a certain distance from it while continuing to live in it.

There nonetheless remains a question of whether this distance is in any way liberating. The ongoing popularity of Pelevin's novels, published once every year since 2009, appears to be based on a curious parallel between his double negation strategy and the disposition of the postcommunist society under an increasingly authoritarian regime. Most ordinary Russians do not have much credence or interest in the surface reality utterly suffused by official propaganda. Despite media censorship, there still remain ample possibilities to negate this image of Russia 'getting up from its knees' by observing the unprecedented corruption, grotesque illegality and rampant violence that have become the norm in Putin's Russia (Dawisha 2015; Belton 2020). There is no shortage of investigations of the kind undertaken, for example, by Alexei Navalny's Foundation for the Struggle against Corruption that demonstrate the obscene underside of the official propaganda of Russia's revival. Yet, so far these revelations have failed to translate into any significant protest movement. In our view, this is because they merely confirm the structure of reality that constitutes the conspiracist mindset. If the surface is *never all there is* and there are always ulterior forces and interests at work, then it is hardly surprising when such forces and interests come to be revealed. In fact, what would be truly scandalous and perhaps fateful for the regime would be the revelation that there is *no underside* to it, that what we observe is *all there is*, and there is nothing at all going on behind the scenes.

The second reason why the revelations of corruption, illegality and violence are politically ineffective is that this first negation is all too quickly followed by the second negation. Just as in Pelevin's novels, this second negation is usually framed in mystical or esoteric terms, ranging from the invocation of the mysterious and ineffable 'Russian soul' that separates Russia from the rest of the world and apparently explains a wide range of contemporary phenomena, from the lack of indoor toilets to the penchant of the police for the gang rape of detainees. Alternatively, the esoteric interpretation may posit a hidden struggle on the global level (e.g. between the Rothschild and Rockefeller families, which has been a popular explanation of nearly everything since the early 2000s), which both explains and justifies the problems revealed in the first negation.

The unpalatable realities revealed by the first negation are in this second negation at once conserved (since there is no sense in trying to change this reality, given its dependence on a more fundamental one) and displaced, or at least placed at a distance from oneself, since they are not what is ultimately most important. As a result of this double negation, one is able to dwell in the society, fully aware of the gap between the official propaganda and the obscene reality, yet also distancing oneself *from this very gap* as no longer intolerable, since both the shiny surface and the dirty depths ultimately arise from a more fundamental depth, the awareness of which is both enlightening and disempowering, since it is not accessible in everyday experience but only presupposed as the ultimate explanation of the otherwise inexplicable. Such a disposition may relieve the stress of living under Putinism but it does little to empower one to even venture to transform it – how would one even go about such a project, if we are at once assured of both the underlying conspiracy behind the veneer of the political system and the deeper mystical meaning of this very conspiracy, which is accessible only at a level entirely foreclosed from human action?

The disempowering nature of Pelevin's discourse is also assured by the very rhythm of the release of his books: every year, usually in late autumn, Pelevin's readers purchase what is by and large the same book, telling the same story all over again. It is as if the enlightenment reached at the end of every novel is ultimately transient, and by starting the next one we are back to the meaningless and dreary everydayness, which we will submit to a double negation all over again. Perhaps, this then is the ultimate truth of Pelevin's texts, so esoteric that it cannot be attained by reading only one of his books but only reveals itself to those who brave the tedium of reading him repeatedly: the enlightenment attained by mystical, esoteric or Buddhist insights is as false as the surface story we began with. As the famous singer-songwriter Boris Grebenshikov put it in a song from 1995, 'you can either vote or join the Buddhists, but when you wake up in the morning, it is emptiness all around' ('Don't Scythe', *Navigator*, 1995).

THE EPISTEMOLOGY OF CONSPIRACISM

Let us now address the way the Putin regime constituted itself in and out of this emptiness. Whereas Yeltsin's reform project was hampered and ultimately defeated by ten years of cohabitation with an oppositional parliament and increasingly disobedient regional leaders, the Putin presidency sought to remove all possible challengers to its political predominance from the outset (Shevtsova 2001, 2002; Baker and Glasser 2005). The 2000 election of Putin as president led to a realignment in the Duma, whereby the formerly oppositional Fatherland-All Russia joined the hastily formed and unexpectedly victorious Unity bloc in the new ruling party United Russia, giving the presidency a secure majority that subsequent elections only fortified. While in 1999–2003 the opposition was still represented in parliament by the strong Communist Party (CPRF) and the two liberal parties Yabloko and Union of Right Forces, in the 2003 elections the representation of the CPRF more than halved, leading it to adopt a much tamer and conciliatory stance, while the liberal parties failed to cross the 5 per cent threshold. Since then, the parliament has featured only the ruling party with a secure majority and the 'systemic opposition' (CPRF, Zhirinovsky's LDPR, and a nondescript clone of United Russia called Just Russia), whose 'oppositional' character consists in their occasional voting against select economic measures of the government, largely for symbolic value.

Similarly, the regional elites, highly influential in the Yeltsin period also on the federal level (since governors and regional parliament speakers were also members of the Federation Council, the upper chamber of the parliament), were gradually reduced to an insignificant status through a series of measures (see Bunin 2001; Fedorov 2001). In 2000 the parliament passed a series of laws, amending the composition of the Federation Council, depriving regional leaders of representation on the federal level and making it possible for the president to fire regional governors. In 2004, in the aftermath of the Beslan massacre (Ostrovsky 2017: 295–6), direct election of governors was abolished as such, replaced by their appointment by the president with subsequent confirmation by regional parliaments, all controlled by United Russia. In 2011–12 governor elections were restored, as part of a minor concession to the opposition protesting the falsification of parliamentary elections, yet in order to become a candidate in these elections one now needs to pass the so-called 'municipal filter' by collecting signatures in one's support from members of municipal councils, which has made it all but impossible for any oppositional candidate to run.

The final obstacle to Putin's supremacy came from the business elite, called 'oligarchs' in popular parlance – a term first used in

1996 by Boris Nemtsov, a liberal politician assassinated in 2015 (see Nemtsov 2000). These oligarchs, particularly media tycoons such as Boris Berezovsky and Vladimir Gusinsky, became highly influential in the second term of the Yeltsin presidency, periodically bringing down government ministers or entire cabinets when their interests were not taken into consideration. During Putin's first term the oligarchs were subjected to the policy of 'equal distancing' from the emerging regime, even though many were quick to point out that some were distanced much more than others and new oligarchs from Putin's inner circle were emerging to take the place of the distanced ones (see Gaman-Golutvina 2000, 2001; Shevtsova 2002). One of the latter, Mikhail Khodorkovsky, was arrested in 2003 on the eve of the parliamentary election and eventually served over ten years in prison for fraud and tax evasion before being released in 2013 on condition of immediate emigration. His arrest and the defeat of the liberal parties he supported led to the consolidation of presidential power to the extreme degree: after 2003 Putin's hegemony was unchallengeable (Dawisha 2015; Anderson 2007). Even when his popularity appeared to be waning, as in the protest sequence of 2011–12, the societal opposition, excluded from every branch of power, soon discovered that street protests were of limited efficacy and could easily be suppressed by the authorities.

How did the Putin regime achieve all this? Putin's initial victory and the subsequent consolidation of his power were evidently helped by his starting position as prime minister and Yeltsin's anointed successor as well as his former role as head of FSB and Secretary of the Security Council (the two most powerful positions in the security field, which Putin held simultaneously in 1999). Yet, they were also aided by the media campaign led by the political technologists of the presidential administration, the already mentioned Ernst and Surkov, as well as Gleb Pavlovsky, a Soviet-era dissident who became a key Kremlin advisor in the second term of the Yeltsin presidency and was instrumental in managing Putin's ascendancy before eventually being kicked out of the Kremlin in 2011, allegedly because he supported Medvedev's running for the second term as president.

These political technologists knew all too well that any attempt to impose a new ideology from above would be futile and counterproductive, given the post-Soviet society's skills in disengagement and dissimulation. Instead, they sought to establish the dominance of the presidency by grafting onto and strengthening the conspiracist disposition already at work in post-Soviet society and culture (Pavlovsky 2000; see also Pavlovsky 2014, 2019) The new postcommunist order would not derive its legitimacy from any ideological content of its own, but, paradoxically at first glance, from radicalising to the point of absurdity the ideology critique that weakened and eventually doomed the Soviet order. While the Soviet ideological discourse fell victim to the para-Soviet disposition that upheld its maxims while convinced of its untruth, the Putin regime would found itself on the untruth of each and every ideology, inciting the subject to suspect and ultimately reject every ideological maxim. The motto of Russia Today (RT), the official propaganda television channel launched in 2005, is 'Question more'. This has been the adage of the Putin regime from its very inception: since the ruins of Soviet socialism were populated by subjects who remained convinced that every truth is untrue, that every claim to truth conceals ulterior interests, surely the most economical way to govern these subjects was not to try, vainly, to deny their beliefs in the untruth of truth, but to affirm them to the maximal extent. Thus, the regime would deride and ridicule all those who claim to speak the truth as at best naïve dupes and at worst cunning conspirators.

If the Soviet order sought to replace the true statement '2 + 2 = 4' with an ideological distortion of '2 + 2 = 5', which the Soviet citizens learnt to uphold and reproduce while being convinced of its untruth, the Putin regime refrained from imposing any official answer to the question, opting instead for uncertainty (2 + 2 equals 3 or 4, but most probably less than 6), augmented by attribution of ulterior motives to all those offering a determinate answer (what does this speaker stand to *gain* by insisting that 2 + 2 is 4?).

The first test of this strategy came with the attempt of the state to take over NTV and Media-Most empire of Vladimir Gusinsky. While NTV, the first private television channel in Russia established in 1992, supported Yeltsin in the 1996 presidential election, it became more oppositional after the 1997 Comm-Invest auction, in which Gusinsky was a losing party despite allegedly being promised the ownership of the company. In 1999 Gusinsky miscalculated badly by throwing his weight behind Fatherland-All Russia, the bloc headed by Yevgeni Primakov and Yuri Luzhkov, which was expected to beat the CPRF to the first place in the parliamentary election, but ended up a distant third, behind the communists and the pro-Putin Unity.

Soon after Putin's election as president, Gusinsky was arrested and released after three days on condition he sell all his media assets to the state-owned Gazprom-Media, effectively handing control of all his media assets to the Kremlin, which eventually took full control of the channel and quickly transformed it into yet another pro-regime outlet. While the NTV affair was unfolding, the official government spokespersons sought to present the conflict as, in a widely ridiculed expression, 'a dispute between business subjects', Media-Most and its creditor Gazprom, which took over the media assets as collateral for the loans Gusinsky allegedly could not pay back (see Ostrovsky 2017: 175–7, 273–5).

Yet, the spin doctors of the regime also engaged in a more active attempt to legitimise the regime's actions. Eager to neutralise the liberal opposition's claim that the takeover of NTV was an attack on the freedom of speech, the regime's apologists retorted that 'independent' or 'free' media was an illusion, since all media merely served the interests of their owners. The oppositional orientation of NTV had nothing to do with its journalists' liberal or other convictions, but was determined solely by Gusinsky's business interests that happened to be at odds with the interests of the state. In this interpretation, mass media does not simply report the news, but always offers a particular interpretation determined by the hidden interests of its owners. It was therefore only to be expected that once the ownership of the channel moved from Gusinsky to Gazprom, the editorial policy would change quite significantly. Yet, since NTV was never free to begin with, it could not have lost any freedom, hence the entire affair was indeed wholly economic and not political.

The same argumentation was reprised in numerous eventual hostile takeovers of TV channels (TV 6), newspapers and magazines (*Segodnya*, *Itogi*) and internet portals (Lenta.ru, Gazeta.ru). If the media outlet was never free or independent, its takeover is not a question of freedom of speech and, since all media only report what is in the interest of their owners, it is not a question of true or objective reporting, since no such thing exists anyway. Any belief in the truth claims of independent media is at best an illusion and at worst a hostile act in the 'information war' against Russia. What one should do instead is 'question more', including of course the questioner's own questioning. And yet, when the questioning of the governmental takeover of independent media is held to be equivalent to the questioning of the ulterior motives of such questioning, the act of questioning loses any critical or emancipatory content, merely contributing to the progressive disempowerment of civil society, which renders itself suspect by any critical statement it makes. The injunction to question has thus largely served to legitimise acts of hostile takeover of civil society by the regime: it empowers only those *already* in power who can now practise such takeovers without concern for either truth or freedom and respond to any criticism by questioning the motives of the critics.

Thus, rather than impose any official version of the truth, the Putin regime consolidated itself by grounding itself in the conspiracist disposition that affirms that every truth claim is ultimately a lie. Every discourse *is not what it says it is*. Behind every statement there are hidden interests and ulterior motives that remain unsaid in the discourse yet still determine what is said in it. This is why one should never be satisfied with the truth claims made in the statement itself – instead, one must literally *undermine* it, that is, *mine under* it in search of the hidden agenda that determines it. This conspiracist logic generalises the ancient rhetorical question 'Cui bono?': one only says or does something because they (or someone else) expect to benefit from it. This is why all universal truths are suspect: since we cannot all benefit or at least not benefit equally, every invocation of the universal (be it freedom of speech, human rights, rule of law, etc.) only masks the particular interests that stand to benefit from this invocation.

This disposition is clearly not unique to Putinism but resonates clearly, if uncannily, with the strategies of critical discourse in social sciences that reduce events or phenomena to their situation of origin and view them as expressions of particular interests, sometimes unbeknownst to the speakers themselves:

> [What's] the real difference between conspiracists and a popularized, that is, a teachable version of social critique inspired by a too quick reading of, let's say, a sociologist as eminent as Pierre Bourdieu? In both cases, you have to learn to become suspicious of everything people say because of course we all know that they live in the thralls of a complete illusion of their real motives. Then, after disbelief has struck and an explanation is requested for what is really going on, in both cases again it is the same appeal to powerful agents hidden in the dark acting always consistently, continuously, relentlessly. (Latour 2004: 228–9)

By the same token, the Putinite propaganda discourse dismisses the truth claims of its critics as mere illusions or misconceptions, arising from their particular identities or circumstances in the manner that is entirely inaccessible to them but perfectly transparent to the questioning minds of the regime apologists. Against all protestations to the contrary, these apologists easily demonstrate that their interlocutors' 'behaviour is entirely determined by the action of powerful causalities coming from the objective reality they don't see' (ibid.: 239). As a result, the manifest contest of discourse is a priori declared radically insufficient: everything must be explained and the explanation is never found on the same level but always *beneath* the statement itself.

This approach entails a notable downgrading of the semantic content of discourse. *What* is said now begins to appear less important than *why* it is said. This is one more reason why one should always 'question more': to any statement whatsoever we can and must pose the questions of why it has been uttered, whose interests it serves, what agenda it conceals, why it has been made here and now. Evidently, the answers to these questions cannot be deduced from the content of the statement but rather involve the *attributes* of the speaker: X criticises the human rights record of the president because he is Jewish, has a permanent residence permit in the US, plays the shakuhachi, or what not. In a cruel inversion of the progressive intentions of the champions of situated knowledge, the speaker's situation here usually functions as the ground for devaluing and dispensing with their knowledge claims. This leaves the interpretive discourse free to decide on which real or even imaginary features of the speaker should be mobilised in explaining the statement. It also leaves open the possibility of contesting any such interpretation with an alternative structured along the same lines. After all, the advantage of explaining observable practices by hidden motives and interests is that one will never run out of possible explanations: who knows what kind of things might remain hidden?

In the Russian context the logic has given rise to two complementary strategies of conspiracy theorising (see Yablokov 2018). Firstly, it is possible to interpret the weakest correlations between phenomena as indicators of a *causal relationship*, the actual cause remaining hidden and its operation impossible to demonstrate by definition. Even when no correlation can be observed, apparently unrelated events can be articulated by postulating a causal mechanism that remains entirely non-transparent. As Dmitry Kiselev, the Russia Channel propagandist sanctioned by the EU and the USA, tends to say, 'Coincidence? I don't think so.' As the possibility of coincidence is negated, causation is *postulated* without being *explicated*, leaving open the possibility of the most outrageous hypotheses except for the one that would assert the relation in question to be purely accidental.

Secondly, since there is *no limit* to the number of possible explanations, it is frequently more advantageous for the propaganda apparatus not to stick to any one of them but simply to dump them *all* into the public discourse to see which one might stick, or, in case none does, to confuse the audience by exposing it to contradictory explanations at the same time. In this manner, the most straightforward occurrences become confusing and murky, while every determinate stance on any issue is drowned out by a dual objection that 'nothing is a coincidence' and 'nothing can be excluded'. While the first strategy is more applicable domestically due to the regime control over the media that permits it to deploy false causalities without any resistance, the second features more prominently in the international domain, where such control is lacking and the objective is to prevent the consolidation of a determined critical stance on the regime by throwing up a dozen 'alternative explanations' complementing it.

As a result of this conspiracist logic, politics becomes *epistemically weak*: there is no truth on its surface and the knowledge of its depths is scant and precarious. The enunciated content of any statement is a priori suspect and rendered conditioned by the attributes and motives of the enunciating subject. At first glance, this should preclude any hegemony or predominance of the ruling regime, which can no longer ground itself in truth. Yet, by denouncing truth the regime simultaneously undermines every position from which the *criticism* of its policies can be advanced. To begin with, since there is no truth on the surface of discourse, the semantic content of criticism can always be dismissed as irrelevant and deflected by pointing to the hidden agenda of the critic in question: what or who is behind this criticism, since there *always* is someone or something behind every speech act. Moreover, since the agenda we question is hidden by definition, it could not and need not be demonstrated by any evidence or proof. Instead, it is merely alluded to in a purposefully vague and ominous manner, invoking allusions to foreign interference, oligarchic intrigues, eternal rivalries, and so on. The injunction to 'question more' does not empower the questioner but only reminds them that their own discourse can always be questioned too. In this manner, an authoritarian regime may easily disarm its critics without bothering

115

to refute the actual contents of their discourse but simply by questioning its 'true' meaning, which is by (their) definition necessarily concealed in it.

The disempowering effects of the 'question more' disposition may be clarified by revisiting Hans Christian Andersen's 'Emperor's New Clothes'. While the standard reading suggests that the adults in the tale are simply afraid to contradict the emperor for fear of being imprisoned or executed, our analysis of the postcommunist slide towards post-truth authoritarianism permits to complicate the story. Perhaps, the adults in question are not particularly afraid of the emperor's wrath: after all, a leader walking around stark naked does not really arouse much fear. Instead, having been exposed to media coverage of the new clothes for weeks, the people got somewhat confused and do not know how to react when they observe the emperor in the nude. Having been trained to question every truth claim, they easily suppressed their first impulse to declare that the emperor has no clothes. Surely, it is not as simple as that. Perhaps, this is a cunning test of the subjects' loyalty to the emperor, which makes perfect sense given the complex international situation and the intrigues of our geopolitical rivals. By not publicly remarking on the emperor's being naked, the subjects would then demonstrate that they would remain loyal to the emperor in the hypothetical event of invasion or attack. Or perhaps, the emperor's current predicament is a result of a domestic conspiracy involving the political establishment that seeks to undermine the emperor's position by making him a laughingstock. In this case, again, it is best not to say anything, because it might only make the emperor's position worse. Alternatively, it might be that the emperor is simply being progressive, and nudity is, so to speak, the new clothes – in this case, publicly saying that the emperor is naked would amount to revealing oneself as an uncultured swine, ignorant of the recent trends in the world of fashion. Finally, since no one else in the audience seems to be saying anything, perhaps it is only I that cannot see the emperor's clothes, because my eyesight is weakening and I really need to see an ophthalmologist urgently: if I cannot even see the emperor's clothes, what would I fail to see next? In short, this is just all too complicated – who knows what is going on: is it a test of our loyalty, an elite coup to be resisted, a new fashion to admire, a problem with eyesight to address? One can never be sure, can one? And if not, then the best thing to do is surely to keep questioning while keeping silent, as the others do. Ultimately, does it really matter if the emperor is naked or not? There is frankly nothing here that we have not seen before and, after all, who can really tell what is clothing and what is nudity? Did not some French philosopher say that binary oppositions should be deconstructed?

We may easily see how this questioning disposition can lead to the acceptance of any statement whatsoever or of any two contradictory statements at once. Once the atmosphere of conspiracist complexity has set in, everything exists in an indeterminate state of being affirmed and denied, present and absent, true and false at the same time. Stating and restating the obvious fact of the emperor's nudity may hardly rupture this indeterminacy, as it would be immediately incorporated into the regime of equivalence as *yet another* particular opinion, serving ulterior interests of someone 'behind' the speaker, a hidden agenda of the concealed 'elite', or, less ominously, only expressing the speaker's private quirks, which are as charming as they are insignificant. It is no wonder that the only one who bothered to remark on the emperor's new clothes was a child who in all likelihood still remained under the illusion that his opinion mattered.

WHY SO SERIOUS?

The conspiracist strategy was employed by the Putin regime repeatedly after the Gusinsky affair. The suspicions or accusations of the regime's involvement in the assassinations of political opponents, from Anna Politkovskaya in 2006 and Boris Nemtsov in 2015 to the attempted poisoning of Alexei Navalny in 2020 with many in between, were habitually deflected by suggesting that the killings in question did not 'benefit' Putin (the infamous *cui bono?*) and that it was the opposition *itself* and its foreign puppet-masters that actually benefited from the killing of its leaders that could now be blamed on Putin (EUvsDisinfo 2020). Since benefit or profit can be denied without any substantiation or proof, this denial serves to remove the regime from the list of suspects. Yet, since this benefit and profit can at the same time be imputed to anyone whosoever, in the form of a conspiratorial 'hidden agenda', the list of suspects is potentially infinite, excluding only the most obvious culprit. In this manner, all accusations against the regime have been dismissed as merely part of a grand Western conspiracy against Russia, which dated back to the mythical Cold War-era Dulles Plan or, why not?, the Protocols of the Elders of Zion. Any demonstration of evidence pointing to the involvement of regime associates in the attacks or killings was no longer even considered, since the entire discourse revolved around a conspiracy that could only be concealed and hence never proven by any evidence.

In a similar fashion, all expressions of dissent against the regime, from the 2011–12 protests against election fraud to the 2019 demonstrations in Moscow demanding the registration of oppositional candidates for the city council elections, were interpreted as mere surface manifestations of a more fundamental conflict between Russia and the West, in which the opposition played the role of at best unwitting dupes and at worst the 'fifth column', assisting the West in its centuries-long attempt to dominate and dismember Russia. It no longer mattered that what motivated the protests were rather less elevated and sometimes decidedly illegal activities of ballot-stuffing, vote buying and voter intimidation. These accusations were not addressed in substance but simply referred to the attributes of the critics (hipsters, homosexuals, Jews, holders of dual citizenship, etc.), which explained away their critical disposition entirely irrespective of what ostensibly motivated it. Once the discourse is framed in this manner, every individual instance of protest serves as the vindication of the conspiracy theory and the legitimisation of the continuing suppression of the protest movement.

The same logic was deployed in legitimising Russia's invasions of Georgia in 2008 and Ukraine in 2014, which were justified with reference to a perennial conflict between Russia and the West (Lucas 2008; King 2008; Prozorov 2010). Russia's actions were held to be opposed by the West not because they violated Georgia's and Ukraine's territorial integrity, but because the West had *always* opposed Russia and sought to contain its inevitable rise. In this framing, criticism from the West merely confirmed that Putin was doing the right thing. It is rather Western praise that would be suspect, since it would presumably mean that Russia's leadership was acting against its own interests, the accusation ceaselessly made against both Gorbachev and Yeltsin.

The reference to a perennial anti-Russian conspiracy permitted the regime to legitimise, for example, the annexation of Crimea by referring to purely hypothetical alternatives: 'if we did not incorporate Crimea, NATO warships would be there now', or 'the Russian-speaking population would be exterminated by Ukrainian fascists'. It also permitted the official line to vacillate endlessly between contradictory and mutually exclusive statements, since they were no longer perceived as lies and falsehoods but as part of 'special operations' in the grand existential conflict with the West (Kalb 2015; Grant 2015; Pynnöniemi and Racz 2016). These statements are not meant to be assessed on their face value, but approached as 'moves' in the perennial conflict, hence the contradictions between them no longer even need to be addressed – what matters is their effectiveness in disorienting the enemy. This effectiveness may retroactively validate the most outrageous lies, as if the inner truth of the conspiracy theory somehow washed away the falsity of individual statements. And yet, this inner truth can never be adjudicated by evidence but only alluded to, hinted at, whispered or winked. It is as if, just like in Pelevin's novels, the truth of the real was too obscene to be rendered into public discourse without distorting it into acceptable statements that are nonetheless not really true.

If this is the case, then the periodic relapses of the discourse of power into obscenity attain added value as giving us a glimpse of the real and the true, otherwise concealed by euphemisms that divert us from the truth. It is in this context that we should approach Putin's periodic obscene quips that date back to his immortal promise as prime minister in 1999 to 'whack [Chechen militants] in their outhouses'. We may also recall the 2002 invitation to a French journalist to visit Chechnya to undergo circumcision 'after which nothing will grow back', or the comparison of the white ribbons adopted as a symbol of 2011–12 protestors to used condoms.

Scholars of populism have noted how the same periodic relapse into obscenity or vulgarity also characterises the discourses of Western populist politicians, for whom this profane language testifies to their folksy authenticity in contrast to the metropolitan elites with their politically correct, regulated speech (Fieschi 2019: 36–9). The more this obscenity violates the existing rules, the more it demonstrates that the speaker in question is indeed 'for real'. This is why these instances of obscene discourse so easily shock the opponents of the politicians in question but only serve to mobilise their supporters: the sheer revulsion of others at these statements, for example Trump's infamous genital-grabbing comments, shows those already supportive of the speaker that he is authentic simply because those others are not.

As we have argued above, when the argumentative logic of political discourse gives way to the expressionist logic that defines the post-truth disposition, the vulgarity of the claim does indeed serve to establish its authenticity and hence becomes something to be admired. This explains why obscene quips that cannot be true or false in any meaningful sense (e.g. the comparison of protestors' ribbons to condoms) may elicit a 'So true!' response among the speaker's followers: what is 'true' in this case is not the comparison itself but the speaker's passage beyond the regulated surface of discourse towards the ineffable real. If Trump, Putin, Salvini and others 'tell it like it is', this is only because 'like it is', that is, the true presentation of the real, has already become understood in terms of an underlying conspiracy about which one can only speak by violating the rules of political discourse. From that moment on, obscene discourse functions in a self-validating and self-reinforcing manner: the more vulgar a quip, the more it shows that the speaker is 'for real' and the cultivation of this reality requires endlessly repeating and even escalating this recourse to obscenity.

The recourse to the obscene in opposition to the overly regulated speech of the 'elite' does not merely transgress these regulations, for better or worse, but also consolidates and augments the power of the speaker *as long as he gets away with it*. Getting away with this transgression means being powerful enough to ignore the rules of discourse and access the real beneath its surface of discourse. This is why Trump's genital-grabbing comments or Putin's threaten to whack the militants in the outhouse tend to be admired by those who manifestly *lack* such power and resent the rules they must abide by. It is particularly notable that in these two cases the statements are obscene both in their enunciated content (describing respectively sexual assault and extrajudicial killing – both strictly illegal) and in the mode of their enunciation (spoken 'as it is', without concealment, embellishment or euphemism). It is not merely a matter of doing something obscene in secret, protected by the veil of civility and legality, but of also doing it in the most obscene way imaginable, throwing away the veil and flouting the rules as no longer applicable to oneself. Rather than serve as tools of destabilisation of some elitist consensus, these quips serve as markers of authoritative *privilege* that separate (would be) authoritarian leaders from the contemptible (if largely imaginary) elite at the same time as they distance them even further from the people, whose enjoyment of vulgar jokes is accompanied by the loss of the last vestiges of popular sovereignty.

The recourse of the Putin regime to obscene discourse presents an interesting contrast to the Soviet period, many of whose features the regime ventured to rehabilitate. The Soviet system was characterised by a rigid and monolithic ideological edifice, which underwent almost no transformation since the death of Stalin and prescribed in detail the rules for practising discourse from various enunciative positions: the party leadership, party members among the working class, scientists, intelligentsia, and so on. As these rules of discursive practice became sedimented and rigidified, the response of the practitioners was the above-discussed parodic *styob*, which applied these rules to decidedly inappropriate content or used them to produce entirely meaningless content. In this manner, the Soviet society began to unravel when it became evident that it no longer believed in its own maxims and instead subjected them to ridicule. Founded on the exaggerated commitment to serious speech, the Soviet system was doomed when its speech rituals became laughable.

In contrast, the Putin regime has from the outset sought to eschew any form of ideological identification in favour of a thinly disguised nihilism, which has no qualms about borrowing elements from the most disparate ideological orientations, combining them in a logically inconsistent manner and discarding them after use without any regret (see Prozorov 2009: 69–74, 203–9). Learning from the Soviet experience the dangers of failing to keep up appearances, the Putin regime has dispensed with ideology even as a matter of appearance and does not even *pretend* to believe in itself, always appearing on the verge of laughing out loud in the midst of its solemn speeches (Mikhailova 2013: 76–8; see also Žižek 1989: 28–30). To laugh *at* such a system is always already to laugh *with* it.

This is why one would try in vain to deduce a coherent ideological orientation of the regime from its official self-presentation in state media, ceremonial speeches and pompous rituals. The Soviet Union possessed such an ideological orientation and fell victim to its utter dissociation from any lived reality that made it laughable, even as the fear of state oppression led the subjects to faithfully reproduce it for decades. The advantage of the Putin regime is that it *includes* this very dissociation into its ideology, which entails that not a single official statement can be taken at face value and reproduced by obedient subjects as a truth. Since, as we have argued, the conspiracist disposition devalues the contents of statements and instead focuses on what is concealed beneath them, the official discourse can hardly be questioned as to what it says but only as to why it says it, what necessarily hidden considerations led to this or that discursive shift, which in itself is entirely meaningless. Yet, this search for the hidden truth of the apparent untruth is *ipso facto* endless and, rather than enhance our understanding of the regime's ideology, only adds to confusion and disorientation. As a result, the regime can combine the most disparate and contradictory elements in its rhetoric, while keeping everyone guessing what, if anything, all this might mean. Rather than sticking to its ideological maxims in all seriousness and thereby inviting the ridicule of society, the Putin regime ensures that it will always have the last laugh by investing even the most solemn discourse with an element of irony: farce here does not follow tragedy but is entirely coextensive with it.

The spread of irony, sarcasm and travesty during the Putin period is thus different from the Soviet era in that it carries little or no emancipatory potential. On the contrary, when deployed by the regime itself, it serves to soften the impact of authoritarian rule by suggesting that it is all somehow not serious, an ironic citation from the 'black books' of the twentieth century with an obligatory wink at the end. This reign of non-serious, parodic discourse recalls Agamben's diagnosis, discussed in the previous chapter, of the reign of *vain speech* that has lost all performative efficacy and is now incapable of either oaths or curses. This devaluation of speech may be observed on numerous levels in the official discourse, which pays lip service to values and institutions that no longer have any meaning or function and tells repeated lies while smirkingly sending the signals that they are not meant to be taken seriously.

Yet, this devaluation is also observable in the discourse of the opposition, which, due to the repressive sanctions for critical views, increasingly resorts to a 'between the lines' discourse that avoids calling things by their name but reiterates the maxims of the official discourse while demonstrating, through winks, smirks and gestures, one's distance from and contempt for it. Both the regime and the opposition seek to separate themselves as much as possible from their enunciations, thus performing the operation strictly *opposed* to the subjectivation through the oath that we discussed above with reference to Agamben. If all that is said is said in a 'quote unquote' manner, the subject does not put itself at stake in its discourse but rather seeks to *estrange* itself from it, preparing to deny what one has said even before saying it. The only thing one can swear to in this discourse is that one *did not mean it*. In this manner, *styob* has arguably become the true ideology of postcommunist Russia, whose function is to make laughable *everything*, including the ruling regime but also every instance of resistance and dissent, which find each other acceptable only insofar as neither of them lays a claim to truth (see Cassiday and Johnson 2013). The catchword of the regime might be borrowed from Heath Ledger's Joker in the *Dark Knight*: 'Why so serious?'

The other side of this estrangement from discourse is the occasional relapse of the regime into an almost archaic and mystical approach to language that is wary of its performative powers and wishes to keep them at bay. It has been noted that neither Putin himself nor his press secretary has *ever* used the name of Alexei Navalny, the anticorruption activist that is Putin's best-known critic. Whenever asked about Navalny within or outside Russia, they phrase their replies in such a way as to avoid naming him at all cost, instead speaking of 'that person', 'the above-mentioned citizen', and so on. Even when Navalny was poisoned by the Novichok nerve agent in Tomsk in August 2020, becoming the subject of headline news worldwide, Putin continued to refer to him as the 'ill person', or, literally adding insult to injury, 'the Berlin patient'. Combined with the ban on mentioning Navalny's name on state television, this approach appears to attribute to his name some mystical powers that can be kept in check only if the name is never uttered in public. No longer capable of making oaths, the regime treats the very name of its critic as a possible *curse*.

At first glance, this regime is far away from twentieth-century totalitarian movements, which at least appeared to take themselves and their ideological discourse very seriously. And yet, we should recall Hannah Arendt's incisive dissociation of totalitarian *ideology* from anything like a political *idea*, which could have adherents and opponents, whom it could mobilise for political action, where it could be affirmed or denied, enacted in new forms of life or mobilised against old ones. It would therefore be entirely incorrect to oppose the totalitarian movements' fanatical commitment to a certain idea to the contemporary post-ideological cynicism. In Arendt's famous expression, 'the aim of totalitarian education has never been to instil convictions but to destroy the capacity to form any' (Arendt 1973: 468). It appears that at least in this aspect Putinism is clearly a successor to these regimes, insofar as it scorns and ridicules all ideological convictions, except for the conviction that truth is always elsewhere and any claim to truth is nothing but an expression of particular interests. The world presupposed and produced in today's post-truth politics is not an ordered domain endowed with sense by a ruling ideology. It is rather what Arendt called a 'Protean universe where everything at any moment can become almost anything else' (Arendt 2006: 95). The difference of Putinism from its Soviet predecessor and other totalitarian systems lies not in the degree of ideological commitment but in the strategies deployed to compensate for its absence. While the twentieth-century regimes sought to destroy capacity for conviction through demanding and enforcing obedience to the endlessly shifting and contradictory party line, contemporary Russian authoritarianism is content with cultivating disorientation, in which every conviction is suspect and all that one can say about anything is that 'it's not as simple as that', followed by a conspiratorial wink. As we shall demonstrate in the following section, this strategy has been highly effective not merely domestically but also internationally.

GLOBALISING POST-TRUTH:
HOW TO WASH IT ALL AWAY IN THE WEST

The discussion of Russia's interference in Western elections and politics more generally since 2014 often views it as a separate strategy adopted in foreign and security policy at a particular point in time to achieve particular goals. This strategy is sometimes named after General Valery Gerasimov, who discussed hybrid methods of warfare in his 2013 speech, even though the object of his discussion was *not* Russian policy but alleged Western strategies of pursuing their interests by covert interventions in domestic regimes or inciting 'colour revolutions' (Gerasimov 2013; see Galeotti 2014). Relying on the familiar Soviet propaganda method of accusing the adversary of what one does themselves, the 'doctrine' was successfully applied less than a year after in the annexation of Crimea and the intervention in East Ukraine (Kalb 2015; Grant 2015; Bertelsen 2017; Pynnöniemi and Racz 2016).

The reduction of post-truth politics to an instrument of war, however hybrid, unfortunately serves to mystify the problem by making it appear both more ominous than it is and less widespread than it is. In fact, what we have observed since 2008, the year of the Georgia war and the attendant global misinformation campaign (see Allison 2008; Asmus 2010; Prozorov 2010) is merely an extension into foreign policy of the strategy that, as we have seen, has been constitutive of the Putin regime and in some respects even predates it. When Russian foreign policy was relatively passive and status quo based during 1991–2004, this strategy remained peripheral. However, after the pro-Western colour revolutions in the post-Soviet states in 2003–4 and the international criticism of Putin's increasingly evident turn towards authoritarianism, Russia's foreign policy turned explicitly revisionist and bent on undermining the post-Cold War order, in which it apparently had no worthy place. Just as the Putin administration used post-truth strategies to undermine the Yeltsin-era influence of media tycoons and regional leaders, it relied on them after 2014 to destabilise Western political systems, undermine the European and NATO consensus on Russia sanctions and thereby enhance its status in the international society.

The sole difference of the outward deployment of post-truth politics from its successful practice domestically has to do with the fact that internationally the Putin regime does not enjoy the monopoly on mass media that it so swiftly introduced in Russia and must therefore operate in a pluralistic and competitive media environment. In this setting, publicising easily refutable lies, which is a common occurrence in the Russian media, is hardly a feasible strategy. For this reason, Russia opted for the purposeful contamination of the public sphere by a plurality of false and partly true facts or narratives, legitimised by the two conspiracist principles we encountered above: 'nothing is a coincidence' and 'nothing can be excluded'. The objectives of such operations may vary from undermining political figures allegedly hostile to Russia (Obama, Merkel, Macron), deflecting the blame for Russia's own actions onto others (the disinformation campaign after the downing of Malaysia Airlines Flight 17 and the Skripal poisoning), discrediting independent media or civil society organisations (BBC, White Helmets, Amnesty International), and so on. Without offering its own version of the truth, Russian interventions introduce into the public sphere so many competing 'truths' that the facts or narratives it deems disadvantageous to itself risk being drowned out or reduced to the status of mere opinions, neither more nor less true than the absurdities aired by Russian channels and pro-Russian 'useful idiots'. While domestically Russia exploits the advantages of controlled media to entirely exclude unwanted views and positions, internationally it undermines and discredits the liberal-democratic principles of free speech and media pluralism by re- or rather dis-ordering the public sphere according to the logic of equivalence that we described in Chapter 1. As expert evaluation is accorded the same epistemic status as the most toxic opinion, the public sphere no longer functions as the site of democratic debate but becomes a scrapheap of opinions expressed in the absence of any principle of adjudication between them.

By deploying this logic of equivalence worldwide, Putinism is simply doing internationally what has worked so well domestically. It would actually be surprising if Russia refrained from applying this strategy internationally: this would testify to a degree of autonomy of foreign policy from domestic politics that has hardly ever been observed in Russia or, for that matter, elsewhere. What is more troubling is that the successes in the use of this strategy internationally suggest that at least some Western societies appear to be particularly *receptive* to these disorientation and disinformation campaigns just as the Russian society was in the 1990s, which poses the question of the viability of their domestic democratic systems. In the early 1990s, the post-Soviet condition was interpreted along the lines of the Hegelian–Kojèvian end of history thesis (Kojève 1969), as the belated process of the emulation by postcommunist societies of the only legitimate model of sociopolitical development left worldwide (Fukuyama 1992; see also Prozorov 2009: ch. 1). From this perspective, however long, slow and tortuous the process of the Westernisation of Russia would be, its direction was indisputable.

Today, it is probably about time to admit that we must reverse the line of reasoning entirely. There is precious little evidence of any Westernisation of Russia, which has rather begun to resemble Central Asian or Middle Eastern autocracies (Bershidsky 2019). Instead, we may observe the contrary tendency of the Russification of the West, that is, the increasing prevalence in Western liberal democracies of processes, practices or styles that are familiar to us from the early postcommunist period, be it the degradation of the public sphere due to the spread of demagoguery and obscurantism, distrust in expertise and science, wide circulation of conspiracy theories, and so on. This does not mean, evidently, that the entire Western politics has been hijacked by Russian interventions, let alone the disappearance of the difference between Western liberal democracies and Russia's authoritarianism, but rather that these interventions could only succeed if they could rely on the pre-existing conditions favourable to this type of politics in the West itself.

Pomerantsev's chilling phrase 'We are all post-Soviet now' (Pomerantsev 2019a: n.p.) does not mean that we are all at the mercy of post-Soviet Russia, which might eventually lose the very struggle it has initiated, but that the post-Soviet condition unleashed the forces that easily spread in the political systems of the erstwhile antagonists of the Soviet Union. While the Russian intervention in the Brexit referendum or the US presidential election may have played a significant or even decisive role, it only became a worthwhile gamble for Russia because of the polarisation of the political space in the US and UK that had raised formerly marginal issues and forces to the forefront of the political agenda. The Soviet Union arguably refrained from intervening in Western elections not merely because it lacked the requisite expertise, but also because it had little to gain from a victory of a centre-right candidate or coalition over a centre-left opponent, or the other way round. Similarly, in the immediate aftermath of the Cold War the main contending forces in Western politics began to resemble each other more and more due to the ideological hegemony of neoliberalism, which made any intervention to help one defeat the other somewhat pointless. It was only after the rupture of this consensus after the 2008 economic crisis that the political space in Western democracies became increasingly polarised, marked by the decline of traditional centre-left and centre-right parties and the correlate rise of far left (Spain, Greece) and right (France, Italy, Austria) forces. Especially in the case of two-party systems and yes–no referenda, this polarisation was intensified even further, producing a binary choice between mainstream and extreme alternatives (Remain vs Leave, Clinton vs Trump). While Russia did not produce these binary constellations, it actively sought to amplify and weaponise them, intervening on the part of the extreme or anti-mainstream forces and deploying the variety of techniques that were so successful in the rise and consolidation of Putinism.

In this section we shall analyse the Russian perspective on this intervention, focusing on the writings of the already familiar Vladislav Surkov. After falling somewhat out of favour in 2011, Surkov was moved from overseeing Russian domestic politics to coordinating Russia's relations with the breakaway provinces of Ukraine and Georgia. In this new semi-international status, Surkov also moved on to address more global concerns in his writings, including the post-truth condition in the contemporary West.

In his 2017 article 'The Crisis of Hypocrisy' Surkov addressed the receptivity of the West to post-truth politics with the help of a somewhat unorthodox example – a song by the American heavy metal group Five Finger Death Punch, a band so critically reviled that few would admit to liking it even as a 'guilty pleasure'. Surkov discusses their song 'Wash it All Away' (see Five Finger Death Punch 2015) to illustrate the crisis of Western societies that was revealed in the 2016 election of Trump and the Brexit referendum.

According to Surkov, the current crisis of the West is nothing other than a revolt against hypocrisy. As such, hypocrisy lies at the foundation of all human coexistence, which presupposes some degree of self-limitation in the expression of one's opinions, preferences and interests and even the renunciation of some of them for the sake of peace and stability. The entire fabric of social life is constituted by reciprocal hypocrisy, whereby citizens agree to act 'as if' they believed in certain fundamental norms defining the social contract. Nonetheless, with the passage of time, the discrepancy between these norms and actual social practices becomes evident, which is when various social groups begin to revolt against the hypocritical character of these norms in the name of something new, presumably more real and authentic. The more complex the existing social order, the greater the demand for its simplification, as complexity begins to be viewed as merely sustaining the universal hypocrisy. Thus, the protagonist of the Five Finger Death Punch song has 'given up' on 'family', 'industry', 'media', 'democracy' and, ultimately, 'hypocrisy' and is now 'waiting for anyone to wash it all away' (Surkov 2017: n.p.).

Surkov expects this disposition to lead to the advent of a new 'tsar of the West', armed with 'artificial intelligence' and ready to dissolve the hypocritical structures and norms with a 'strong hand' (Surkov 2017: n.p.). In his reading, the contemporary predicament of the West is not that different from the disorientation that characterised the early postcommunist period in Russia, in which Surkov began his career, first as an advertising executive and then as a political mastermind. The opposition to the Soviet regime in the perestroika period also targeted the hypocritical character of the ideological edifice of the Soviet system that even the regime's authorities struggled to pretend to believe in. Conversely, the new cohort of postcommunist politicians from Boris Yeltsin to Vladimir Zhirinovsky and Alexander Lebed were, despite all their differences and for all their lack of finesse, lauded as those who 'tell it like it is'.

Yet, in the postcommunist context these new paragons of authenticity all turned out to be transitional figures, paving the way to Putin's regime that reconstructed the society on the basis of a new hypocrisy, this time of a statist and socially conservative kind. Thus, while Surkov certainly finds the juvenile protests against hypocrisy of the kind performed by Five Finger Death Punch exemplary, his approach excludes the possibility of a politics *without* hypocrisy, an authentic politics that would *not* rely on hypocrisy to constitute a new social reality. Thus, the new 'tsar of the West' would not be someone like Ivan Moody, the flamboyant yet plaintive singer of Five Finger Death Punch, but a strong-arm ruler to 'lead us out of all the chaos and all the lies'. The world-weary West, tired of its hypocritical 'political correctness', will eventually welcome its own version of Putinism.

In a 2019 article, 'Putin's Long State', Surkov reiterates and radicalises this provocative claim. While the bulk of the article offers familiar acclamations of Putin as the saviour of Russian statehood after the chaos and disorder of the 1990s, Surkov also notes that the West, which, convinced of the superiority of its liberal democracy, treated Russia with contempt in the 1990s, now begins to observe the Putinite model of the state with interest. Russia's 'information counter-attack' on the West only amplifies the West's own discontent with itself, the perception that all the slogans of liberalism and democracy were nothing but illusions, that power is actually exercised by the 'deep state', that sovereignty and national interests always trump globalisation and open borders, and so on. The Putinite model has great 'export potential', since it proclaims what the West itself had for a while secretly suspected but was too afraid to openly proclaim, aside from lowbrow metal bands, radio talk show hosts and reckless political entrepreneurs. 'De-globalisation, nationalism and re-sovereignisation', which Putin has forcefully affirmed at least since his 2007 Munich speech, are increasingly entering the mainstream of Western politics as well.

Nonetheless, just like in the article on hypocrisy, Surkov views the current phase of Western politics, often discussed in terms of populism, as a mere transitional stage that exacerbates the crisis of liberal democracy and must lead to its eventual demise:

[Distrust] and envy, used by democracy as priority sources of societal energy, necessarily lead to the absolutization of criticism and the increased level of anxiety. Haters, trolls and evil bots have formed the shrieking majority, having displaced from dominant position the formerly respectable middle class. No one believes in the good intentions of public politicians; they are envied and therefore viewed as vicious, deceitful or as outright scoundrels. There is a wide selection of scoundrels and confusing rules designed to lead the struggle between them to more or less of a tie. Thus emerges the virtuous system of checks and balances – a dynamic equilibrium of lowliness, the balance of greed, the harmony of trickery. If someone loses their head and behaves disharmoniously, the watchful deep state rushes to help and drags the renegade to the bottom with its invisible hand. (Surkov 2019: n.p.)

This description of the squalor of liberal democracy is familiar from both the Soviet propaganda tropes about the perpetually 'rotting capitalism' and the interwar diatribes against Anglo-American liberal democracy from European conservative-revolutionary commentators. While Russia is often viewed as supporting far-right populist forces in the West due to some convergence of values, Surkov's patronising description of the 'shrieking majority' rather suggests that these forces only serve as *accelerators* of the collapse of liberal democracy, which should make the Putinite model of the state more attractive to Western societies.

While the liberal-democratic model is utterly hypocritical, pretending to offer freedom of choice that has become meaningless, the Putinite model, in which any choice between alternatives is noticeably absent, is for Surkov at least distinguished by its greater honesty. There is no 'deep state' concealed by the rhetoric of human rights and civil liberties: state bureaucracy, including security police, is *all out there*, unconcealed and proud of its unconcealment. If there is anything 'deep' in this system, it is not the state but the *people*, withdrawn from the political scene and inaccessible to sociological surveys. It is this 'deep people' (ibid.) that forms the true basis of the Putinite state, since Putin's greatest feat was to begin to listen to and to understand this 'deep people' and build a new state in the way that would be adequate to this people's needs and wants.

In contrast to liberal-democratic systems, characterised by the interplay of complex and multilevel institutions, the Putinite state is sustained by the direct and informal communication between the leader and the people, exemplified by Putin's infamous annual multihour 'open line' call-in sessions, in which he listens to the complaints of 'ordinary people' and gives orders to resolve their problems. Surkov openly recognises that the political institutions borrowed from the West (parliament, parties, constitutional court, etc.) are in Russia [considered] as a matter of ritual, introduced so that we seem 'like every-one else' and the differences of our political culture do not appear so starkly to our neighbours, do not irritate and frighten them. They are like fancy clothing, worn when going out in public. The current model of the Russian state is built upon trust and rests on trust. This is its key difference from the Western model, which cultivates distrust and criti-cism. And that is the source of its strength. (Ibid.)

Surkov's text simultaneously dispels the hypocrisies of Western democracy and argues for the advantages of the hypocritical autoc-racy that he presents as an alternative. The foundation and sole legit-imation of this autocracy is the 'deep people', whose sheer 'depth' ensures its inaccessibility as a subject of politics and which only comes to presence as Putin's pleading interlocutor at carefully pre-arranged call-in sessions. With all other institutions reduced to ritu-als rendered void of all political meaning, Putin is the only subject in his own state, the only instance of reality that is neither mere façade, like the formal institutions, nor wholly withdrawn into the depths, like the people.

We have addressed the genealogy and the logic of the function-ing of this system in earlier works (Prozorov 2005, 2007, 2009, 2010), and its autocratic character has only become more visible since then. What we are interested in now is Surkov's rather more novel argument about the susceptibility of Western societies to the same model. While in a famous 2006 article Surkov advocated Putinite authoritarian 'sovereign democracy' (Surkov 2009) as an *alternative* to the liberal-democratic model that expresses Russia's civilisational difference *from* the West, in 2019 he offers much the same model as a possibly attractive model *for* the West itself to emulate. While Russia has been accused of interfering with Western elections, Surkov contends that what Russia has actually interfered with is the West's 'brain', and the latter 'does not know what to do with its own altered consciousness' (Surkov 2019: n.p.). What makes this interference possible is the epistemic and existential dis-orientation in Western societies, which has led them to question their own ideals, be they globalisation, open borders or responsibil-ity to protect. Yet, just as the uncertainty and contingency experi-enced in the Russia of the 1990s were a transient moment leading to the constitution of a new autocratic model, so the present Western revolt against hypocrisy that keeps waiting for someone to 'wash it all away' will only yield a Putin-like leader who will dismantle all

131

mediating institutions and communicate with the people directly as soon as they retreat into 'depth'.

On 29 August 2020 a demonstration of Covid dissidents took place in Berlin with over thirty thousand participants. Initially banned by the local government due to the concerns over the spread of the coronavirus, the event was nonetheless permitted by the local court. The protesters primarily came from extreme right, identitarian and even neo-Nazi movements and eventually sought to storm the steps of the Reichstag under Imperial black-white-and-red flags. The reporter at the event noted that 'the most beloved politician among the protesters was apparently Russia's President Vladimir Putin whose name was chanted repeatedly by hundreds of his fans' (Eckner 2020: n.p.). It is easy to note the incongruity in this position: while the protesters were presumably unhappy about the German corona-virus restrictions that they perceived as excessive, they chanted the name of the politician that spent the entire pandemic in isolation and implemented a far more draconian lockdown than Germany or, for that matter, most European countries. In the argumentative logic of discourse, the pro-Putin chants would therefore be easy to dismiss as uninformed, contradictory or simply stupid, yet in the expression-ist logic that defines post-truth the name 'Putin' no longer signifies any particular policy or standpoint, but only expresses the speak-er's resentment of the liberal-democratic system and the desire to destroy it. While the protesters justified their right to demonstrate with reference to the principles of liberal democracy, the content of their 'protest' was hostile to these very principles, further amplifying the incongruity of their position. Were such a demonstration to take place in Moscow, it would be violently suppressed by riot police and many of its participants sentenced to long prison terms. It is only liberal democracy that permits this self-styled 'deep people' to assert its existence on the surface on the political system, while a successful attack on it will inevitably lead to its retreat into the depths.

While he is often credited with inventing post-truth politics, Surkov approaches his invention functionally, not as a new condition that will succeed liberal democracy but as a *weapon* used to destroy it, which then can be abandoned in favour of a more avowedly autocratic model. Yet, even in this latter model we remain entirely beyond the dimension of truth. The rhetorically clumsy, if not out-right bizarre, idea of a 'deep people', foreclosed from all presentation aside from its periodic phoning in of its existence, demonstrates the utter indifference of this regime to any idea of truth, either as a foundation of its policies or as its legitimation. We may easily recognise the belonging of this idea to the conspiracist understanding of social reality that we have discussed above. In this understanding, the truth of a phenomenon is never on the surface but always hidden in the depths of the real, which enables the most outlandish interpretations to take hold, as long as they are backed by sufficient power and widely spread in the media. By the same token, the deep people is wholly withdrawn from presence in politics, hence it cannot ever be *re-presented* by the president, who instead brings the people to *presence* to begin with in the singular instances of communicating with it.

The people expresses its truth, bringing it out from the depths in which it dwells, only when it talks to the president in a call-in session – hence the truth is expressed in episodic and largely meaningless fragments, in which petty requests accompany rapturous acclamations. At other times, this truth can only be presented by the president himself, who alone 'hears and understands' the deep people, which repays him for this hearing and understanding with its trust. This is why Putin can be caught lying repeatedly, without its affecting his reputation domestically. His lies are held as true insofar as the people does not say otherwise, but since the people is 'deep' and presents itself only in carefully orchestrated circumstances, it can hardly present its objections to the way its truth is being told. The trust that Surkov places in the foundation of the Putin regime actually works in the inverse manner: rather than the people trusting the president, it is the president who trusts that the people will, in Pushkin's immortal line, remain 'silent'.

Surkov's argument may be rejected as tasteless hyperbole, yet it is highly significant for understanding the more global phenomenon of post-truth because of the explicitly anti-democratic approach of the author. Post-truth politics is sometimes defended against the overly snobbish and patronising tone of its critics as the expression of the authentic democratic intention against the depoliticised reign of experts and technocrats (see Kalpokas 2019: 115–116). Yet, Surkov's texts clearly demonstrate how the promotion of post-truth both within and outside Russia does not in any way contribute to greater democratisation, but serves to undermine democracy through excessive polarisation, cultivated distrust and existential disorientation, which pave the way for the lapse into autocracy that can no longer be criticised, since the enunciative modality from which this critique may be uttered has been discredited or devalued. Rather than give voice to the people, post-truth entails the retreat of the people into the depths, from which only an autocratic leader may occasionally bring it to presence.

Contemporary democratic theory has argued that rather than affirm the power of some substantial 'demos', liberal democracy dissolves every figure of the people into a plurality of voters that produce an utterly contingent electoral outcome (Lefort 1986, 1988; Nancy 2010; see also Prozorov 2019). In contrast to the totalitarian construction of the people in terms of racial or class identity that endows it with substantial being, liberal democracy posits the people as sheer appearance without any ground or foundation in being. The people only comes to appearance in elections and at this very moment becomes dissolved in a plurality of electoral preferences. It is against this idea of a merely apparent people that Surkov posits his notion of the 'deep' people, whose only difference from prior totalitarian constructions is that the people is endowed with an ontological status that is so 'deep' that it can no longer be defined in terms of class, race or any other determinate predicate. Against the constitutive superficiality of democracy, Surkov affirms the being of the people, which nonetheless retreats so far into the depths that it never comes to appearance, aside from occasionally phoning it in when conversing with the president. While democracy valorises the appearance of the people devoid of being, the Putinite state founds itself on the people whose being in the depths forecloses it from appearance.

Pussy Riot: How to speak in a non-equivalent manner

How could this slide towards authoritarianism in the post-truth era be resisted? What role could truth possibly play in this process if our being 'after' it is the very essence of the problem? What does truth even mean in the condition defined as post-truth? Our discussion of the rise of the post-truth disposition in Russian politics demonstrates that these questions are far from simple. While the deceitful claims of the Putin regime in a variety of spheres, from the revisionist history of World War II to the war crimes in Syria, have been debunked multiple times outside and within Russia, this debunking has not proven effective in undermining the regime that does not even pretend to tell the truth but operates in a manner indifferent to it, having dissolved it in a plurality of made-up conspiracies, false leads and sheer white noise intended less to indoctrinate than to disorient. While not reaching the same levels, the political strategies of the Trump presidency or the Orbán government in Hungary exhibit the same tendencies and remain largely immune to the efforts of fact-checking and debunking. The same goes for challenger parties not yet in power but increasing their support in Western societies despite the best efforts of mass media and civil society to challenge them on the terrain of truth.

From our perspective on post-truth as a regime of equivalence, this ineffectiveness is hardly surprising. After all, since post-truth does not introduce a new hegemonic ideology that would count as a 'new' truth but rather proceeds from the equivalence of all statements as mere opinions, it always already marks the space for the statements that oppose it, *but only as long as they are viewed as opinions in their own right*. In other words, any critique of false or deceitful statements by political actors is both rendered *legitimate*, by virtue of the principle of the freedom of self-expression, and rendered *ineffective*, by virtue of its reduction to the expression of yet another opinion that is neither better nor worse than the one it criticises. Moreover, insofar as the conspiracist disposition locates the truth of the statement beyond or beneath itself, it is also possible to attribute ulterior motives to any such critical opinion, framing it less as the contestation of what was said by others than as the expression of one's own self, one's standpoint or situation, with all the particular or even idiosyncratic interests and values that arise from it.

The same reduction is easily performed on the critique of post-truth claims from a meta-discourse position, which would interpret post-truth as the symptom or sign of something *beyond* itself, an ideological phenomenon whose understanding presupposes passing *beneath* the surface of its discursive claims towards the infra-structural level that determines them. It is easy to see that this ideology-critical exercise would actually add to the obfuscation already attained by the practitioners of post-truth by exposing their *hidden agenda*. The truth that this exercise would discover behind the claims of the practitioners of post-truth would only fortify the epistemological principle that sustains this disposition: truth is always elsewhere, beneath or beyond whatever is said. While their intentions may be diametrically opposed, the two genres share the desire to go beneath the surface, either to find an explanation or to obfuscate things even further, or, perhaps achieve the latter by doing the former (see Latour 2004: 228–30).

135

If neither *factual* nor *critical* modes of debunking appear to be effective, a different approach is called for, one that neither tirelessly debunks the claims everyone knows to be false nor explains the reigning falsities by relating them to a deeper truth but confronts the entire regime that enables the production of these claims. In the remainder of this chapter we shall analyse one example of a speech act that ventured and to a certain extent succeeded in rupturing the regime of equivalence in Putin's Russia, refusing to play along with the game of winks and smirks, where everything is said 'in quotation marks', 'as if not', undermining the statement in the very act of its enunciation.

On 21 February 2012 five young women belonging to the 'feminist-punk' group Pussy Riot entered the building of the Cathedral of Christ the Saviour in Moscow and proceeded to the soleas of the cathedral, where they ventured to perform a song entitled 'Mother of God, Drive Putin Away!' (Pussy Riot 2012). The entire performance lasted for 41 seconds, after which the band members were driven out of the building by the guards. The recording of this and a prior similar performance at a lesser-known Moscow church were then used in a music video that was posted on YouTube and various social networks, quickly gathering millions of views.

The song, which Pussy Riot labelled a 'punk prayer', features strident criticism of the complicity of the Russian Orthodox Church in the authoritarian regime in Russia ('the church's praise of rotten dictators'), focusing on the allegations of corruption in the Church establishment, the lavish lifestyles of Patriarch Kirill and other Church notables, as well as the reported links of the Church with the state security police in the Soviet and post-Soviet eras ('the head of KGB, their chief saint'). This criticism, expressed in the verses set to a punk rock song, is supplemented in the chorus with the injunction to Virgin Mary to 'become a feminist', 'join us in protest' and 'drive Putin away', set to the melody of a traditional Orthodox hymn.

On 26 February a criminal case was opened against the members of Pussy Riot, who were accused of 'hooliganism', a charge that in Russia carries a maximum sentence of seven years in prison. The hooliganism in question allegedly consisted in the purposeful offence of the religious sentiments of the employees and other attendees of the Cathedral of Christ the Saviour during the band's 41-second performance as well as millions of others who were presumably offended by watching the music video. On 4 March, the day of the Russian presidential elections, two of the band's members, Nadezhda Tolo-konnikova and Maria Alyokhina, were arrested, and the third one, Yekaterina Samutsevich, was detained on 15 March. All three were eventually charged with hooliganism and remained in prison custody until the trial that started on 30 July and ended on 17 August 2012 with the conviction of the three band members for hooliganism motivated by religious hatred and the sentencing of all three to two years in prison.

In the course of the trial, which was marked by extreme irregularities that led one of the defence lawyers to proclaim it 'worse than in Stalin's times' (see Elder 2012), the case of Pussy Riot received increased international attention. The Russian government was criticised for its handling of the case by numerous human rights activists and European politicians while the band received high-profile support from fellow musicians, from Madonna to Red Hot Chili Peppers. The case also became the object of intense political and sociocultural debates both inside and outside Russia, broaching such diverse questions as the continuing deterioration of the rule of law in Putin's Russia, the political role of the Orthodox Church, the balance between freedom of speech and respect for religious beliefs, the limits of artistic freedom and the excessively repressive justice system, the conditions of Russian prisons and the lifestyle of Patriarch Kirill, and so on.

And yet, the meaning of this event has remained elusive. Both the detractors of Pussy Riot and many of their supporters appear to share the interpretation of the band's 'punk prayer' as a parody, a prank, a blasphemous provocation targeting the Russian Orthodox Church and thus belonging to the long and distinguished tradition of the conflict between art and religion. This provocation may then be condemned as offensive to religious believers or defended as a constitutional right. Yet, the presentation of the case in terms of blasphemy and censorship, whereby what is at stake is the freedom of *all* speech (*isegoria*), arguably mutes the significance of the specific *kind* of speech act practised by Pussy Riot. Whom or what did Pussy Riot *really offend*? What is it about their punk prayer that simultaneously invited the full-blown assault of the entire repressive apparatus and attracted support from the most diverse of sources? To answer this question we shall venture an interpretation of this performance that systematically contrasts it with the logic of *blasphemy*, which we have already encountered in Chapter 2.

Throughout the trial, the prosecution forcefully advanced an interpretation of the Pussy Riot performance as a deliberate affront to the religious beliefs of Orthodox Christians, dismissing all references to the political content of the performance as irrelevant: 'The prosecutors do not believe the defendants' allegations that their actions in the church were not driven by hatred and enmity towards Orthodox believers, but were driven by political motives' (Nikiforov cited in Kostychenko 2012: n.p.). While the members of Pussy Riot and their lawyers insisted on the political significance of their performance, the prosecution sought to reduce it to a blasphemous act, a violation of Church ritual that was an offence to practising Orthodox Christians. In this attempt at depoliticisation, the prosecution went so far as to include in its case the references to the rules of liturgical rituals established in AD 363 by the Council of Laodicea (the prohibition for laypersons to sing in the ambon of the cathedral) and in AD 692 by the Quinisext Council (the prohibition of wearing 'comical' or 'satirical' clothing and performing 'pagan' practices in church). Disregarding the fact that the rules of neither Council are as yet incorporated into the Russian Criminal Code, the prosecution deemed them universally known and abided by in the country, which presumably makes their violation an instance of hooliganism.

Throughout the trial both the prosecution and the official media campaign against the band routinely compared their allegedly blasphemous performance to the anti-religious campaigns of the Bolsheviks in the 1920s and 1930s, the most extreme and infamous of which was the destruction of churches, including the original Cathedral of Christ the Saviour in 1931 (see Groys 2008: 101–22). Prosecutor Nikiforov explicitly referred to the band's actions in terms of 'abuse of God' (*bogohulstvo*), routinely comparing the band to the infamous Union of the Militant Godless, an anti-religious movement of the early-Soviet period (see Stites 1989: 101–22):

> With regard to the social danger of this crime, it is notable that also from the canonical standpoint of Islam such actions are unacceptable and call for public apology. Any temple carries holiness, a solemn atmosphere that those present in it must maintain. The bacchanalia of this sort throws a challenge to this. This testifies to the moral decline in the society. The keykeeper of the Cathedral has remarked on the similarity of the women's action to the Union of the Militant Godless in the 1920s, parodying processions and collective prayers that subsequently almost

led to the destruction of the Russian Orthodox Church. (Nikiforov cited in Kostychenko 2012: n.p.)

However understandable it might be as a rhetorical technique, the analogy drawn between Pussy Riot's prayer and Bolshevik anti-religious campaigns is entirely implausible. The iconoclastic drive of the art and politics of the 1920s sought to weaken the political and social influence of the Church through public education, propaganda and the counterforce of the new civil religion (Stites 1989: 109–14). In contrast, Pussy Riot's performance does nothing to undermine religion in general, or Orthodox Christianity in particular, but solely criticises its implication in contemporary this-worldly politics. There is certainly a difference between an anti-Putin prayer to Virgin Mary that calls on her to become a feminist and a poster of 'Virgin Mary with a bulging belly longing for a Soviet abortion' (ibid.: 107) or other favourite means of anti-religious propaganda in the early-Soviet period: the exhumation of entombed saints, the violent ridicule of such 'miracles' as 'weeping icons', the burning of the effigies of God, and parodies of Church liturgies set to indecent lyrics. While the parodies of the Union of the Militant Godless that set pornographic lyrics to liturgical music sought, successfully or otherwise, to make us laugh at what formerly filled us with awe, the prayer to Virgin Mary to drive Putin away clearly serves a rather different function that, moreover, would be seriously jeopardised by the ridicule of the addressee of the petition. Similarly, the lyrics describing the repressive and corrupt character of the Russian state and the complicity of the Church in this repression and corruption may hardly be termed comical or humorous, even in the more acerbic or satirical sense.

The same applies *a fortiori* to the final statements of the three Pussy Riot members during the trial, which are completely devoid of ridicule or spite but rather repeatedly refer to anger and pain that motivated their performance at the Cathedral of Christ the Saviour:

We are distressed that the great and luminous Christian philosophy is being used so shabbily. We are very angry that something beautiful is being spoiled. It still makes us angry and we find it very painful to watch. (Tolokonnikova 2012: n.p.)

Our motivation is more eloquently expressed in the words of the Gospel 'For everyone who asks receives, and he who seeks finds, and to him who knocks it will be opened.' I, and all of us, sincerely believe

139

that it will be opened for us. But, alas, so far the bars are closed on us. (Alyokhina 2012: n.p.)

It would therefore be entirely inappropriate to characterise the song and the statements of Pussy Riot as blasphemous. It is easy to see that their punk prayer does not fall under the conventional definition of blasphemy as 'pronouncing of injury or falsity on God' (Agamben 2009a: 41): there is no injury done to Virgin Mary in asking her to get rid of Putin or become a feminist. Yet, the performance of Pussy Riot is also clearly distinct from the wider, and more originary notion of blasphemy that we discussed in Chapter 2 with reference to Agamben's argument in *The Sacrament of Language* that approaches it as a deactivated or inoperative form of an oath: language spoken in vain. In the formal sense, the syntagm 'Mother of God, drive Putin away!' does not extract the divine name from semantic content, whereby it is uttered by itself and thus in vain, but, on the contrary, links it with a clearly defined object of petition. In the more substantive sense, the entire purpose of the performance is to *stop* the name of the Mother of God being uttered in vain in canonical prayers 'for rotten dictators' and the veneration of dubious relics ('the Virgin's belt') and to mobilise it in the struggle against the allegedly corrupt state and Church:

> [In] our performance we dared, without the Patriarch's blessing, to com-
> bine the visual images of Orthodox culture and protest culture, suggest-
> ing that Orthodox culture belongs not only to the Russian Orthodox
> Church, the Patriarch and Putin, that it might also take the side of civic
> rebellion and protest in Russia. (Samutsevich 2012: n.p.)

The charges of blasphemy and the offence of religious beliefs are entirely inappropriate, since the prayer in question is meant *seriously*, that is, Pussy Riot *really* want Virgin Mary to drive Putin away. It is precisely this seriousness that is properly offensive to the regime. While both political and clerical elites could probably live with parodic blasphemy of religious rituals, which would be a priori ineffective and 'in vain', what remains intolerable is the serious use of prayer. What the regime prosecutes is not an act of *styob*, travesty or ridicule, but the use of prayer as a *performative speech act*.

A prayer performs the *act* of praying, mobilising and transforming its discursive content into an actual petition. The speech act 'Mother of God, drive Putin away!' is thus a performative utterance that, unlike constative statement (e.g. 'Patriarch Kirill's watch costs USD30,000)', cannot be adjudicated as to its truth or falsity. Instead, it must be approached in terms of what Austin refers to as 'felicity' or 'infelicity', that is, success or failure in undertaking the action in question (Austin 1975: 14–45). This performative *efficacy* must in turn be distinguished from the *effects* of the action that are covered by the 'perlocutionary' dimension of the speech act, that is, whether a promise is kept, the threat succeeds in deterring, or whether the Mother of God does indeed drive Putin away (ibid.: 91). The illocutionary *force* of the action, which may be felicitous or not, does not pertain to its effects or consequences but solely to the undertaking of the action itself, which may either be completed successfully or end up void due to a number of possible 'infelicities'.

Austin's examples of performative utterances primarily refer to *conventional* acts, such as marriage, naming, opening a ceremony, and so on. The emphasis on conventionality also characterises his well-known threefold scheme for the felicity conditions of a speech act:

(A. 1) There must exist an accepted conventional procedure of uttering certain words in certain circumstances.
(A. 2) The persons uttering those words must be the accepted ones.
(B. 1) The procedure must be executed by all participants both correctly and
(B. 2) completely.
(C. 1) Where the procedure is designed for persons having certain thoughts or intentions, the persons in question must indeed have those thoughts.
(C. 2) Where a subsequent conduct is part of the procedure, the persons must conduct themselves accordingly. (Ibid.: 14–15)

The first two groups of conditions (A, B) are *external* to the speaker and refer to the *existence* of the conventional procedure of producing the act in question and its correct and complete *execution*. Even the internal or 'psychological' group of conditions (C) remains tied to this external procedure since it pertains to having thoughts or intentions *presupposed* by it or conducting oneself *in accordance* with its prescriptions. From this perspective, it is hardly surprising that any analysis of Pussy Riot's punk prayer as a performative act, an 'exercitive' or a 'behabitive' in Austin's tentative classification (see ibid.: 155–161), would proclaim this act to be 'infelicitous' in a number of ways.

141

It might be viewed as a *misfire* which both *misapplies* the procedure of prayer by introducing political content into it (A2) and *misexecutes* it with *flaws* pertaining to the band's inappropriate attire and manner of praying and *hitches* due to the band's being kicked out of the church after less than a minute (B1, B2). It is this aspect of misfire that the prosecution sought to prove with their references to the early medieval Church councils prescribing the proper procedure for prayer or other behaviour in the church. Alternatively, the performance may be viewed as an *abuse* of procedure due to the alleged *insincerity* of the performers, who, according to the prosecution, did not have the proper thoughts or intentions (C1) when praying to Virgin Mary but only sought to ridicule and humiliate other, genuine believers. Insofar as the felicity of a speech act depends on external conditions pertaining to the existence and correct execution of the conventional procedure, any act that is not in conformity with it remains void and is accessible only as an a priori ineffective parodic displacement (see ibid.: 16–18).

However, Austin's approach has been subjected to critical reinterpretations that emphasise the *contingency* of the conventional procedure. We need only recall Pierre Bourdieu's forceful restoration of the dimension of symbolic power as a condition of possibility of the external felicity conditions themselves (Bourdieu 1992: 73–4) or Jacques Derrida's demonstration of the impossibility of separating 'serious' from 'non-serious' or 'parasitic' invocations of performative formulae due to the general iterability of all linguistic marks (Derrida 1988: 15–18). The former reminds us that the force of performative formulae does not inhere in these formulae themselves but rather has the weight of the entire social order behind it, which delegates to some and not others the power of doing things with words. The latter demonstrates that this power must nonetheless presuppose, structurally and necessarily, the possibility of its own ruin in the proliferation of 'non-serious' (i.e. not properly socially authorised) use of performative formulae, whose condition of possibility is exactly the same as that of the most serious ones. If the procedure that authorises and contains the performative force of an utterance is itself a product of power and if there always remains a possibility of wresting this force away through iteration, then the conventional or ritualised form of the performative that Agamben (2005: 134) terms *performativum sacramenti* always coexists with *another* kind of performative, which is the 'other' of all convention or ritual and necessarily pre-exists it.

In his *Time that Remains* Agamben reconstructs this other kind of performative in a reading of the gospel (*euaggelion*) or the 'word of faith' in Pauline epistles: '[The] experience of the word of faith does not entail the experience of a denotative character of the word, its referring to things, but enacts its meaning through its utterance' (ibid.: 131). Yet, in contrast to the 'sacramental performative', which is both enabled by and itself reinforces the operation of the existing social order (*nomos*), the messianic 'word of faith' rather brings the *nomos* to fulfilment by deactivating it and rendering it inoperative.

Agamben terms this singular form of the performative *performativum fidei* and analyses it in the Foucauldian terms of 'veridiction' that we have addressed above in relation to the oath and its crisis. Thus, while Austin's definition of the performative insisted that it was necessarily *neither true nor false* but could only be felicitous or infelicitous, Agamben brings the question of truth back to the very foundation of the theory of performativity, reformulating the very distinction between constative and performative aspects of language in terms of truth. While constative statements are independent of the enunciating subject and their truth is evaluated by logical and objective criteria, in veridiction the subject constitutes itself through its truth-telling, 'linking itself performatively to the truth of its own affirmation' (Agamben 2009a: 57):

> [What] we today call a performative in a strict sense are the relics in language of this constitutive experience of speech – veridiction – that exhausts itself with its utterance, since the speaking subject neither pre-exists it nor subsequently linked to it but coincides integrally with the act of speech. When Paul, in Romans 10: 6–10 defines the word of faith (*to rema tes pistes*) not by means of the correspondence between word and reality but by means of the closeness of 'lips' and 'heart', it is the performative experience of veridiction that he has in mind. (Ibid.: 58)

By putting oneself at stake in one's own speech the speaker constitutes oneself as a subject, prior to any 'conventional procedure' that could regulate one's speech. Speaking in proximity of the lips and the heart is nothing other than swearing on the significance of one's words, speaking 'in all seriousness' and in this sense speaking truthfully. From this perspective, Austin's understanding of performatives as neither true nor false no longer holds true. It is perfectly possible to *truly* promise (just as it is possible to only pretend to promise, or to intend to break the promise at the very instant one makes it), *truly* demand, judge, and so on. The truth here pertains to the subject's *commitment* to its own discourse rather than to any conventional procedure, its identification as enunciating subject with the subject of the enunciated content.

It is only the sacramental performative that ventures to regulate this type of speech act by 'articulating it in precepts and semantic contents, [using it] as a means to ground contract and obligation' (ibid.: 134–5). Oaths and curses, religion and law venture to order and stabilise the experience of veridiction by imposing various versions of Austin's conventional procedure:

> The attempt to reconcile faith as the performative experience of a veridiction with belief in a series of dogmas of an assertive type is the task and at the same time the central contradiction of the Church, which obliges it, against the clear evangelical command, to technicalize oaths and curses in specific juridical institutions. (Ibid.: 66)

While it may serve to regulate the experience of veridiction, this technicalisation ultimately leads to the weakening of its performative efficacy: 'if the *performativum fidei* is completely covered by the *performativum sacramenti*, then the law itself stiffens and atrophies and relations between men lose all sense of grace and vitality' (Agamben 2005: 135). It is precisely this situation of atrophy that Maria Alyokhina, one of the convicted members of Pussy Riot, presented in her closing statement at the trial as the key motivation for the group's punk prayer: '[The] gospel is no longer understood as revelation, which it was initially, but as a kind of solid block which can be torn up into quotations and tucked anywhere, into any document, used for any purpose' (Alyokhina 2012: n.p.).

The accusation of blasphemy that was the central aspect of the prosecution's case must therefore be finally returned to sender, or, rather, to the protagonists of the punk prayer. Insofar as Pussy Riot target the atrophy of both state and Church, both law and religion, as a result of the separation of performative veridiction into a separate 'sacramental' sphere, it is ultimately *they* who accuse both the secular and clerical authorities of true blasphemy that takes the form of the combination of vain discourse and repressive regulation (see Žižek 2012).

And yet, Pussy Riot's performance is not exhausted by a *critique* of this reduction of the institution of the Church to sacramental conventions that deprive religion of its originary messianic vocation.

Precisely insofar as it takes the form of prayer and takes place at the site intended for prayer, it is an attempt to go beyond lamenting the demise of the 'word of faith' towards its actual *restitution*. Since the existing structures of secular and clerical authority have dispensed with veridiction in favour of the sacramental reproduction of the existing order, such a restitution can only take the form of a forceful act of veridiction, which would wrest away the illocutionary force of prayer from its atrophying confinement in the 'conventional procedure'. By neglecting or violating the conditions of the sacramental performative, the punk prayer is able to reach towards a more fundamental experience of the faithful performative, in which the subject puts itself at stake in affirming the truth of its enunciations. In this manner, veridiction 'open[s] up the space for gratuitousness and use as an expression of the subject's freedom' (Agamben 2005: 135). Such acts of veridiction offer perhaps the only meaningful experience of freedom in contemporary Russia, where the decline of freedom since the early 1990s has gone hand in hand with the negation of the existence of truth.

CHAPTER FOUR

The truth won't tell itself

Parrhesia: Disobedient discourse

In the preceding chapters we have addressed the internal logic of
the post-truth disposition, its philosophical interpretations and its
genealogical descent. We are now in a position to move from this
critical analysis towards a more affirmative task of outlining the
conditions for truth-telling in the age of post-truth. In the analysis
of Pussy Riot's punk prayer we have demonstrated how this act of
truth-telling is distinct from parody, blasphemy or ironic *styob*, but,
on the contrary, exemplifies a serious speech act in which the subject
puts itself at stake in their use of language. We have argued that this
act is characterised by a performative force that does not derive from
any 'sacramental' conventional procedure that would endow it with
efficacy but rather precedes and exceeds the institution of any such
procedure.

In this chapter we shall continue this line of argumentation in an
attempt to outline a more general theoretical model of truth-telling
adequate to the present post-truth era. We shall proceed by elucidating the effects of truth-telling in the context of affirmative biopolitics.
In Chapter 1 we have demonstrated how the post-truth constellation
poses a challenge to biopolitical governance without at the same time
contributing to a genuinely democratic politics. The generalisation
of the principle of *isegoria* in the regime of equivalence may undermine the truth claims involved in the rationalities of government but
not the exercise of power as such, which, as our discussion of postcommunist Russia in Chapter 3 has shown, may well unfold in an
autocratic and repressive manner in the absence of any truth claims.
We may now pose the question of whether *resistance* to post-truth
may also take a biopolitical form. By this we do not mean a merely

reactive reinforcement of the rationalities of biopolitical governance, whose facile injunctions to 'listen to the experts' got us into the post-truth predicament to begin with. On the contrary, what we are interested in is a modality of biopolitics that has been termed affirmative and associated not with the *objectification* of life in the apparatuses of government but rather with the *subjectivation* of living beings in resistance to and confrontation with these apparatuses.

While the discussions of affirmative biopolitics have largely focused on the work of Giorgio Agamben (2016) and Roberto Esposito (2008a), we suggest that a paradigm of a properly affirmative biopolitics may already be found in Foucault's late work on truth-telling in Antiquity, especially his final lecture course, *The Courage of Truth* (Foucault 2011). In this course, Foucault analysed the Cynic experience of truth-telling (*parrhesia*) as an irreducibly political experience, anticipating later theories of affirmative biopolitics by casting truth-telling as a practice of transformation of both one's life and one's world. By retracing Foucault's analysis of the Cynics, we shall also continue the line of inquiry begun in the analysis of the case of Pussy Riot, that is, the relation between truth and performativity, semantic truth content and pragmatic enunciative modality. We have already seen how the question of truth unexpectedly emerges in the act of speaking that was itself supposed to be beyond truth and falsity, its effectiveness guaranteed by a conventional procedure regulating its practice. While we are more accustomed to separating the semantic content of a speech act, which may be true or false, from the act itself, which cannot be adjudicated in these terms, it now appears that there is some truth involved in the very act of enunciation. The task of this chapter is to elucidate this aspect of truth-telling from the Cynics to the parrhesiasts of our times.

Foucault began his studies of veridiction in his 1980 course *On the Government of the Living* (Foucault 2014). Similarly to the lectures of the previous year, *The Birth of Biopolitics* (Foucault 2008), the course title is deceptive: just as there was nothing about the birth of biopolitics in the 1979 course, the 1980 lectures did not deal with the government of the living in any meaningful way, but from the outset adopted a new focus on what Foucault called 'alethurgy', the processes of the *manifestation of truth*. While both problematics clearly date back to the same source in *History of Sexuality I*, the difference between them is quite evident: the focus on the government of populations in European modernity is replaced by the concern with the individual subject governed through injunction to truth-telling in early Christianity. The shift appears even more definitive with the turn to Antiquity in the subsequent courses and volumes two and three of *History of Sexuality*. Even when the techniques of the self that Foucault analysed involved a variety of physical regimens (abstinence, diet, endurance), the recourse to these was guided by certain ethical ideals of the subject that gave one's life a positive form, to which one's 'natural' life was subjected in the name of the attainment of self-mastery or even renounced through purification and penance in the name of salvation (Foucault 1990b: 82–4; Foucault 2014: 114–41). While all Foucault's courses from 1980 to 1984 deal with forms of life in some sense, the first three courses clearly prioritise *forms* over *life*.

However, with the turn to the Cynics in the 1984 course *The Courage of Truth* things become more complicated for three reasons. Firstly, in these lectures the theme of life reappears with full force as the very *mode* of the manifestation of truth, which in turn is no longer contrasted with natural behaviours and desires but is expressed solely and immediately *through* them. Secondly, whereas *On the Government of the Living* concluded by demonstrating how the obligation to tell the truth in Christianity was inextricably tied to one's complete and permanent obedience to the other (Foucault 2014: 265–78, 307–8), Cynic *parrhesia* explicitly inverted this relationship: truth-telling is only possible as an act of *disobedience* in the face of all social norms and conventions. Finally, in contrast to prior forms of *parrhesia*, the veridiction of the Cynics was no longer a *condition* for practising politics or even an instrument for the attainment of political ends but rather became itself *immediately* political in effecting political transformation of the world through practising another life in accordance with truth (Foucault 2011: 217–19). In this manner, Foucault moved from the study of the governmental subjection of life to truth towards the analysis of the political subjectivation that overcomes this subjection by fully translating the truth into life itself.

Of course, Greek *parrhesia* was constitutively linked with life in all its forms, since it was distinguished from the statutory right of free speech (*isegoria*) precisely by the risk to the speaker's very existence that it involved (Foucault 2010: 157–9). Yet, with the Cynics, this necessary risk of veridiction is extended from words to the way of life itself:

[one] risks one's life, not just by telling the truth, and in order to tell it, but by the very way in which one lives. [. . .] One risks it by displaying it; and it is because one displays it that one risks it. One exposes one's life, not through one's discourses, but through one's life itself. (Foucault 2011: 234)

This formulation evidently resonates with the biopolitical problematic, albeit with an important twist: Cynic *parrhesia* no longer involves governmental power over the lives of its subjects but rather the power of one's *own* life that the subject mobilises and puts at stake in its truth-telling. Life is not merely the object but also the *subject* of biopower. Yet, what does it mean for life itself (in the unqualified and universal sense of *zoe*) to be the subject of power?

The name 'Cynic' is translated from Ancient Greek as 'dog-like'. While there are various explanations of this comparison, Foucault finds its basis in the bare life of the Cynics: Cynic *parrhesia* was wholly contained in 'the manifestation, in complete nakedness, of the truth of the world and of life' (ibid.: 183; see also ibid.: 242–4). While in Agamben's famous argument the Greeks constituted their positive form of bios by the *exclusion* of bare life, the Cynics made of this bare life itself the very *mode* of the manifestation of truth. Their destitute, brute and stripped mode of existence that was explicitly posited as 'animal' was intended not merely as an extreme form of self-assertion or self-fashioning but also as the manifestation, the bearing witness to the truth, whereby the body itself became 'the visible theatre of the truth' (ibid.: 179–80). It became such by redeploying in its very existence the familiar characteristics of truth in Ancient Greek philosophy. Foucault emphasises repeatedly that the Cynics did not introduce almost any innovation on the level of philosophical doctrine but rather borrowed the most conventional and widespread ideas, which they nonetheless subjected to a radical reinterpretation by relocating them to the level of life itself. In Foucault's reading, classical Greek philosophy defined truth in terms of four attributes: truth was *unconcealed, undistorted, straight* and *sovereign*. Rather than contest these attributes, the Cynics appropriated them as inherent in life itself, which evidently altered their conventional meanings.

Firstly, the Cynic's life 'is without modesty, shame, and human respect. It is a life which does in public, in front of everyone, what only dogs and animals dare to do, and which men usually hide' (ibid.: 243; see also ibid.: 252–5). This scandalous display of 'animal' behaviour that does not recognise social conventions and insists on the complete publicity of all its actions is perhaps the most famous aspect of Cynicism. Yet, this shameless or brazen life is only the literal and consistent application of the principle of unconcealment that defines the Platonic true *logos*. 'Applying the principle of non-concealment literally, Cynicism explodes the code of propriety with which this principle remained associated. As a result, the philosophical life appears as radically other than all other forms of life' (ibid.: 255). While the Platonic principle of unconcealment sought to secure the conventional and proper forms of life that had nothing to hide precisely because they were fully in accordance with the prevailing codes, the Cynics took this principle to the extreme, arguing that there could be nothing bad in whatever nature had endowed us with. For this reason, concealing any aspect of one's natural life, however 'dog-like' it might appear from the perspective of those codes, merely brings in untruth into one's life.

Second, the idea of true life as unalloyed or undistorted is converted by the Cynics into the principle of a life that is utterly indifferent to its own needs. The Platonic idea of a life purified from all disorder and discord, from all things material and physical, is 'revaluated' by the Cynics through the relocation of the ideal of purity towards the very domain of the physical and the bodily that it was supposed to be purified from. In this domain pure life is a life of poverty, stripped of everything superficial and inessential. For the Cynics poverty is an active principle going beyond mere indifference to wealth and contentment with one's own station. It is 'a real conduct of poverty' that is in principle unlimited, going further and further into dispossession in a quest for the absolutely indispensable (ibid.: 258).

Third, the Platonic principle of a straight life in accordance with the *logos* is converted into a life that accepts no law other than that of nature. Only what is natural is truly in accordance with the *logos*, hence all social conventions and codes must be abandoned, be they marriage, family or even the prohibition of incest. Nature or animality forms the new model that the human being must emulate to arrive at the true life. In Foucault's argument, animality becomes a

> material model in accordance with the idea that the human being must not have as a need what the animal can do without. [. . .] In order not to be inferior to the animal, one must be capable of taking on that animality as reduced but prescriptive form of life. Animality is not a given; it is

a duty. [. . .] Animality is an exercise. It is a task for oneself and at the
same time a scandal for others. (Ibid.: 265)

Similarly to poverty, animalisation is not a matter of a one-off act of
renouncing one's humanity but of the perpetual exercise that is to be
pursued in an aggressive or 'bestial' confrontation with the untrue
lives of others.

Finally, the Cynics simultaneously apply and reverse the Platonic
principle of the immutable and self-contained sovereignty of the true
life. The Cynic infamously proclaims himself the true 'king', precisely by virtue of his scandalous, dirty and beastly life. While in
Platonism and Stoicism the philosopher was often *compared to* a
king because he was capable of governing both his own soul and the
souls of others in accordance with the truth, the Cynic asserts that
he *is* the king, not metaphorically or ideally in a perfect world, but
in the here and now:

> Crowned sovereigns, visible sovereigns, as it were, are only the shadow
> of the true monarchy. The Cynic is the only true king. And at the same
> time, vis-à-vis kings of the world, crowned kings sitting on their thrones,
> he is the anti-king who shows how hollow, illusory, and precarious the
> monarchy of kings is. (Ibid.: 275)

And yet, rather than live a life of contentment and enjoyment, the
Cynic king submits his life to tireless tests in order to be able to take
care of others, lead them out of their untruth by his own manifestation of the true life. This care is undertaken in a characteristically
animalistic, violent manner, 'with a bark': 'the Cynic is of service in
a very different way than through leading an exemplary life or giving advice. He is useful because he battles, because he bites, because
he attacks' (ibid.: 279). For this reason the Cynic is compared to a
'guard dog', dedicated to service and saving others (ibid.: 243).

In all these four reversals the principle of animality remains crucial as a paradoxical *criterion* of truth. Foucault argues that ancient
thought generally approached animality as a 'point of repulsion' for
the constitution of the human being, an 'absolute point of differentia-
tion' that, in Agamben's later terminology, was 'inclusively excluded'
from the human as its negative foundation (Agamben 2004: 18–27).
A true life was then the life that successfully excluded, subjected or
dominated one's animal nature. In contrast, the Cynics transform
this negative foundation into a positive telos of human existence,

whereby animality is not a given to be mastered or conquered within oneself but a *model* to be attained in one's existence through courageous practices of truth-telling that break with established ways of living. And yet, there is nothing in this model that is not already *given* by nature, which therefore need not be subjected or dominated for this model to be implemented. On the contrary, the constitution of a true *bios* is conditioned by the prior grafting of its precepts onto *zoe* itself. Animality is not the other that must be subjected and mastered for a life of truth to be possible but rather the *manner* in which this life unfolds in the self. It is this use of animality that constitutes the true scandal of Cynicism: while there is nothing offensive in animal behaviour itself, which may, depending on the context, also be viewed as charming, innocent or stupid, the fact that the same old familiar truths that have hitherto prescribed a life of obedience could give rise to such a violent irruption is a genuine affront to the existing order.

Despite the fundamental identity between the ideational contents of the truths of the Cynics and their adversaries, the former's true life thus remains radically *other* than the life lived by the ostensible proponents of truth:

> [The] Cynic changes the value of this currency and reveals that the true life can only be an other life, in relation to the traditional life of men, including philosophers. [. . .] [It] is from the point of view of this other life that the usual life of ordinary people will be revealed as precisely other than the true. I live in an other way, and by the very otherness of my life, I show you that what you are looking for is somewhere other than where you are looking for it, that the path you are taking is other than the one you should be taking. (Foucault 2011: 314)

We may now understand the final words of Foucault's final lecture course: 'there is no establishment of the truth without an essential position of otherness; the truth is never the same; there can be truth only in the form of the other world and the other life' (ibid.: 340). However familiar it is in its nominal content, the truth is *made other* by its relocation from the domain of discourse towards the realm of life. In the very same movement life is also made *other* by the truth, attaining the status of a philosophical life without transcending or negating any of its natural dispositions. Finally, by disseminating the truth in its own transformed existence, this life can eventually change the world at large. While both Platonism and Christianity posited, in their own different ways, the existence of *the other world* beyond this one, the Cynics sought to attain another life right here in *this* world and thereby make it *otherwise* than it was. By virtue of their disobedience to all conventional moral codes, the Cynics made every act of veridictive subjectivation a part of the transformation of the wider world:

> Through this dissonant irruption of the 'true life' in the midst of the chorus of lies and pretences, of accepted injustice and concealed iniquities, the Cynic makes 'an other world' loom up on the horizon, the advent of which would presuppose the transformation of the present world. (Gros in Foucault 2011: 354)

While their orientation towards the transformation of the world renders Cynic *parrhesia* irreducibly political, their embodiment of the principles governing this transformation in life itself makes it unmistakably *bio*-political. Cynic *parrhesia* is biopolitical precisely and solely to the extent that it brings the power of one's life into play in one's affirmation of truth – it is an *exercise of biopower, whose object fully coincides with its subject.*

THE (BIO)POWER OF THE POWERLESS

It is hardly coincidental that Foucault develops his account of Cynic *parrhesia* at the time of his practical engagement with the struggles of the civil society in Poland. The resonance between Cynic *parrhesia* and the East European dissident practices of 'living within the truth' forms what Walter Benjamin termed a 'dialectical image', a constellation of past and present events, in which the past event acquires full intelligibility and thereby finds its fulfilment:

> The past can be seized only as an image which flashes up at the instant when it can be recognized and is never seen again. For every image of the past that is not recognized by the present as one of its own concerns threatens to disappear irretrievably. (Benjamin 1968: 255; see also Agamben 2005: 141–4)

For Benjamin past texts or practices are not immediately available for interpretation at any given moment, but acquire their full legibility or 'knowability' only in specific historical contexts that thereby themselves attain historical significance. While it is impossible to say whether it was the interest in the Cynics that led Foucault to actively support the Polish dissidents or it was this support that turned him to the study of Cynicism, the powerful resonance between discourses and practices that are two and a half millennia apart evidently endowed Foucault's final lectures with an ethico-political exigency that the immediately preceding courses arguably lacked.

Let us explore this exigency further by considering a key text of the East European dissident movement: 'The Power of the Powerless' (Havel 1985), written in 1978 by one of the leaders of Charter 77, Václav Havel, who would eventually serve as president of Czechoslovakia and the Czech Republic during 1989–2003. The essay takes up and elaborates the theme of living within the truth, first articulated in the context of dissident movements in the 1974 article by Alexander Solzhenitsyn entitled 'Live Not by Lies!' (Solzhenitsyn 2009). Havel begins with a famous example of a greengrocer who displays the official slogan 'Workers of the world, unite!' in his shop window, even though he certainly does not care much about the workers of the world and whether they choose to unite or not. He does so because he knows he is expected to do so and by doing so expects to be left in peace by the authorities, permitted to go about his daily business and enjoy whatever humble privileges his status confers:

> [Individuals] need not believe all these mystifications, but they must behave as though they did, or they must at least tolerate them in silence. For this reason, however, they must live within a lie. They need not accept the lie. It is enough for them to have accepted their life with it and in it. For by this very fact, individuals confirm the system, fulfil the system, make the system, are the system. (Havel 1985: 15)

To refuse to live a lie is then to suspend one's participation in this system. As Slavoj Žižek (2014: 141) has argued, Havel's concept of truth is not at all metaphysical, its entire content exhausted in one's *disengagement* from the reproduction of the official simulacrum. The proverbial greengrocer stops displaying the slogan, begins to distribute banned literature, speaks out at political meetings and joins the communities of others who refuse to live the lie. In this manner, the lie is revealed as a lie and truth is affirmed not as a hypothetical possibility of life in a brighter future but as a real form of life in the here and now. It is here that Havel takes an important step beyond the para-Soviet ethos of disengagement that we discussed in the previous chapter, which was content to recoil from the official lies into a variety of private practices without claiming for them the status of truth. While the late-Soviet subject was more likely to infer from the falsity of Soviet truths the inaccessibility of truth as such, thereby falling victim to the conspiracist discourses that claimed to access the inaccessible, Havel interprets these minor, unofficial, alternative or parallel forms of life as true in the sense of following the 'real aims' of life itself:

> [Between] the aims of the post-totalitarian system and the aims of life there is a yawning abyss: while life, in its essence, moves toward plurality, diversity, independent self-constitution and self-organization, in short, toward the fulfillment of its own freedom, the post-totalitarian system demands conformity, uniformity, and discipline. While life ever strives to create new and improbable structures, the post-totalitarian system contrives to force life into its most probable states. (Havel 1985: 15)

Living in truth must 'above all be an expression of life in the process of transforming itself', which calls for its withdrawal from the system, whose project of constructing a 'new life' ended up conflicting with the aims of life itself (ibid.: 30). These truths were not necessarily opposed to the official discourse of the system, which vainly presented itself as full of vitality and dynamism, fostering independence and innovation and otherwise concurring with the 'aims of life'. Just as the Cynics creatively reoriented the accepted truths of their time against the sterile and sedimented 'conventional procedures' regulating their enunciation, making them the source of a radically other life, Havel and other dissident authors sought to reclaim the possibility of a different life by recasting freedom, pluralism, diversity and other values as inherent in life itself.

What was important for both the Cynics and the dissidents was not *proving* the natural character of their truths, that is, their hypothetical origin in *zoe*, but rather *giving* the truths precisely this character, demonstrating their *viability* against the sterility of official simulacra, forming a *bios* of truth within the domain of *zoe*. This is why Havel repeatedly speaks of living within the truth as a 'natural', 'existential' and 'pre-political' mode of existence: 'For some time now, the problem has no longer resided in a political line or programme: it is a problem of life itself' (ibid.: 40). Yet, the true form of life is never simply given but must be *cultivated* through what

Havel calls the 'independent spiritual, social and political life of society', concretely manifested in the *parallel structures* in various social spheres: independent trade unions, theatres, universities, bookshops, rock clubs, and so on: 'What else are parallel structures than an area where a different life can be lived, a life that is in harmony with its own aims and which in turn structures itself in harmony with those aims?' (ibid.: 48).

Despite lacking any explicit oppositional orientation, these 'pre-political' practices, unfolding in the 'obscure arena of being itself', were perceived as extremely dangerous by Soviet and East European regimes (ibid.). Insofar as they expressed the desire for the truth in the very lives of their participants, things as innocuous as rock concerts, independent theatre performances, or public poetry readings could produce explosive political effects, undermining the carefully constructed simulacrum of the socialist form of life: 'Every free expression of life indirectly threatens the post-totalitarian system politically, including forms of expression to which, in other social systems, no one would attribute any potential political significance, not to mention explosive power' (ibid.: 23). Similarly to the Cynics, the transformation of the truth by its relocation to life produces both the reality of a different life and the possibility of a different world. It is easy to see that the dissident life within the truth manifests exactly the same features of truth as Cynicism did: it is *unconcealed* by virtue of refusing to live the lie, *unalloyed* by ceasing one's participation in the system, *straight* by virtue of being in accordance with the 'real aims of life' and, finally, *sovereign*, reclaiming its power from the system in ostensibly pre-political practices that nonetheless have potentially explosive political effects. The power of the powerless that Havel speaks of can only be *bio*-power, the power of and over one's life, which becomes the site of the confrontation between governmental rationalities and the subject's acts of veridiction.

Besides their 'critical' effect of demonstrating the failure of governmental biopower to fully translate its rationalities into life, which made the officially proclaimed 'new life' patently untrue, the practices of Charter 77 and other East European dissident movements also produced the 'affirmative' effect of demonstrating the capacity of the subjects of emergent civil societies to fashion their lives in truth at a distance from the regime. 'People have not only struggled for freedom, democracy and the exercise of basic rights

156

but they have done so by exercising rights, freedom and democracy' (Foucault 2000: 465). What was a perpetual illusion of governmental biopolitics, that is, the successful translation of the idea into life, became a reality in the veridictive practices of the dissidents, precisely because in the latter case biopolitics was no longer a matter of forcing the idea into life by overcoming resistance to it, which necessarily entails the resort of power to negativity that contradicts its very intention. Living within the truth exemplifies nothing less than a complete reversal of the biopolitical logic of real socialism, whereby the governmental forcing of truth into life gives way to the fashioning of a life of truth through active disobedience to governmental rationalities (see Prozorov 2016: 71–125).

From this perspective, 'living within the truth' is not merely *a* form of biopolitics among others but indeed its *paradigmatic* form, because it is able to avoid being contaminated with the negativity of sovereign power that forces its rationality within the life that resists it. In the parrhesiastic subject, be it the Cynic or the dissident, life and truth do not face each other as antagonists but rather become indistinct in their perpetual passage into one another. The parrhesiastic subject is therefore able to go one crucial step further than any governmentality that seeks to take hold of life and transform it in line with its own truths. It is not merely that resistance acquires a certain primacy in relation to power (Foucault 1990a: 95–6), but that the political subject acquires an autonomous *consistency* that goes beyond any notion of resistance. Strictly speaking, the parrhesiastic subject does not resist governmental biopower but demonstrates in its very practice of the true life how such power has always already *failed* to transform and govern its life, while the subject, by contrast, has *succeeded* in doing so by reclaiming its own biopower and applying it to itself. There is a fundamental asymmetry between biopolitical governmentality and the affirmative biopolitics of the parrhesiast, since even in the worst circumstances the latter is capable of that very productivity or creativity that the former tirelessly asserts but invariably lacks. 'Cynicism constantly reminds us that very little truth is indispensable for whoever wishes to live truly and that very little life is needed when one truly holds to the truth' (Foucault 2011: 190). Against the power that captures and governs life to adapt it to its rationalities it is always possible to live differently, even if from the perspective of these established forms this 'other life' appears shameful, violent or dirty.

157

TRUTH AS FORCE

We have seen how truth-telling was practised by the Cynics and East European dissidents against the hypocrisies and lies defining the regimes of their time, which, in very different ways, paid lip service to truth, while never practising what they preached. This dialectical image permits us to understand how truth-telling exemplifies an affirmative declension of biopolitics, empowering the subject to transform both their life and the world in which they dwell. Yet, there is also something about this image that risks becoming illegible in our present moment, namely the *prestige* accorded to truth in the societies in which the Cynics and the dissidents practised 'living in truth'. As we have argued in Chapter 1, it is precisely the lack or at least the weakening of this prestige that defines the post-truth condition. What is then the relevance of *parrhesia* in the post-truth era, in which truth is not merely not practised but also *not preached*? Can Foucault's account of *parrhesia*, which, as we have seen, remained highly relevant for the resistance to the socialist regimes of the twentieth century, also be adapted for the post-truth age?

As we have seen, in the Greece of the Cynics the philosophical truths of the time were not questioned as to their *existence* but rather upheld at a *distance* from the existence of those who affirmed them. It is this gulf between truth and life that the Cynics ventured to bridge in a singular way. The scandal of the Cynics consisted not in their 'animalistic' behaviours themselves, but in their insistence that this naked, poor and beastly life was much closer to the truth than the elevated discourses of the philosophers, who discussed truth in abstraction from life and on the basis of the mastery of their natural needs and desires. By the same token, Havel's 'living within the truth' acquired its affirmative force by wresting the truth, which the Soviet regimes identified with their own ideology to the extent that the official newspaper of the Soviet Communist Party was simply called 'Truth' (*Pravda*), away from these regimes and locating it in the myriad activities that were outside the regimes' control. While official ideology pretended to found its domination on the truth of Marxism-Leninism, dissident movements were able to show that the 'real aims of life' were better served by unofficial art, underground rock music, amateur poetry – almost anything *other* than the official ideology that had long since degenerated into lifeless dogmata.

In the age of post-truth, where truth loses its distinction and its privilege, this strategy is evidently disarmed. If truth does not exist, then nothing is attained by attempting to enact it in a purposefully confrontational manner, which would only strengthen the desire to dispense with it altogether. Similarly, since truth is not endowed with any privilege but rather ridiculed as naïve and old-fashioned, it makes little sense to protest this privilege and seek to bring truth down to the lowliest practices. Cynic provocations in today's permissive Western societies would cause little scandal and may be easily reappropriated by the existing order as a potentially lucrative subculture. Of course, not all societies are permissive and there are numerous sites in today's world where transgressions of the kind performed by Cynicism would retain their force and hence encounter significant sanctions. Yet, insofar as these sites are also increasingly permeated by the post-truth logic of equivalence, the strategy of Cynicism will find itself weakened there as well.

In the condition of post-truth, parrhesiastic affirmation must therefore take a rather different route, which targets not the *separation* of truth from life, which is not the problem that we are concerned with today, but the *denial* of truth as such, or rather the denial that truth is any different from an opinion and hence that it makes any difference. To recall the story of the emperor's new clothes, discussed in the previous chapter, the task of *parrhesia* is not to expose the hypocrisy and cowardice of those admiring the new clothes by bravely telling the truth about the emperor's nakedness, but to affirm that the latter statement is not just another opinion, entirely equivalent with those of the sycophants admiring the non-existent costume. In other words, the *parrhesia* of the post-truth age must force the *non-equivalence* of truths into the regime of equivalence and thereby render it inoperative. While the Cynics and the Soviet-era dissidents sought to bring the truth into their very lives, contemporary parrhesiasts must rather bring truth itself into existence in the regime constituted by its denial.

The post-truth regime of equivalence is based on the universalisation of the principle of *isegoria* and the exclusion of *parrhesia*. Anything can be said *as long as it means nothing*, makes no truth claims and has no significance. Every statement is acceptable as an opinion, whose meaning is beyond itself, in the properties of the speaking subject, who 'only says it' because of their religion, residence, citizenship, place of employment, financial interest, and so on. Any such opinion is admissible, as long as it also admits its diametrical opposite, which is substitutable for it. *Parrhesia* ruptures this regime of equivalence by insisting that *truth is not a matter of opinion*. In this manner, it introduces non-equivalence into the regime that only accepts *isegoria*, equal right to interchangeable opinions. To insist on the difference of truth from opinion is to refuse to accept the universal indistinction between the proverbial 'shades of grey' and reclaim the power to *distinguish* between democracy and authoritarianism, freedom and oppression, emancipation and conquest, truth-telling and vulgar trolling, and so on. This is why *parrhesia* continues to be a risky endeavour, just as it was in Ancient Greece, be it in the democratic assembly (Pericles), advising to the ruler (Plato) or confronting one's fellow citizens (Socrates, Diogenes). We observe this risk today not only in authoritarian regimes, where dissident discourse could result in death (Anna Politkovskaya, Boris Nemtsov), attempts at assassination (Alexei Navalny) or imprisonment (Pussy Riot, Yury Dmitriev), but even in liberal-democratic settings, where hate speech proliferates, particularly on social media, directed against figures engaged in truth-telling, from the Me Too campaigners to Greta Thunberg. The hateful response to truth-telling testifies to the continuing force of *parrhesia*, its potential to rupture the regime of equivalence.

Yet, how is this difference from opinion produced in the parrhesiastic discourse? How does one speak in a non-equivalent way? Let us recall the punk prayer of Pussy Riot. In asking Virgin Mary to drive Putin away, Pussy Riot were not speaking the truth in the sense of uttering a statement *corresponding* to reality: no such correspondence is even possible in imperative sentences such as a prayer. Nor were they merely expressing their *opinion* on the Orthodox Church, Putin or Virgin Mary. Nor was their act a matter of mere *parody* or ridicule of religious rituals. As we have seen, what drew attention to the Pussy Riot action was precisely that they appeared *serious* in the prayer to Virgin Mary to send Putin away. It is this seriousness that was particularly offensive to the regime that is used to laughing everything off as ultimately non-serious. By asserting their punk prayer as a serious speech act, Pussy Riot demonstrated the existence of something that cannot be filed away as a mere opinion, however oppositional or critical, and therefore remains in excess of the regime of equivalence. If there exist statements that are not equivalent to others, then the regime constituted by the assumption of the equivalence of all statements is revealed in its untruth. Since the insistence on the non-existence of truth was constitutive of this regime, then a statement that cannot be incorporated within it testifies to the presence of a truth value that exceeds it.

Yet, where is this truth value contained? Evidently, it is not in the locutionary *content* of the prayer, which contains nothing that could not be reduced to a particular preference and thus fitted into the regime of equivalence. Neither is it contained in the perlocutionary *effect* of the act, on which the jury is, as it were, still out. The truth value is contained neither in the words themselves nor in their hypothetical effects, but in the *force* with which they are uttered. What makes this prayer a felicitous speech act is the illocutionary force that renders its indifferent incorporation into the regime of equivalence impossible. It is received as *different* from the murmur of opinions, and this difference is *scandalous*. This scandal brings forth a response that goes beyond the mere recognition of yet another opinion: outrage, demand for retraction, ban, imprisonment, ridicule, harassment, denunciation, and so on. In short, to confront the regime of equivalence truth must serve as irritant, marking its non-equivalent status with its abrasive force:

> In *parrēsia* however, as if it were a veritable anti-irony, the person who tells the truth throws the truth in the face of his interlocutor, a truth which is so violent, so abrupt, and said in such a peremptory and definitive way that the person facing him can only fall silent, or choke with fury. (Foucault 2010: 54)

The requirement that the act of truth-telling must be scandalous, irritant or abrasive clearly renders truths context-dependent: there is no such thing as an objectively scandalous statement and many of the things viewed as scandalous in the time of the Cynics would only elicit yawns of boredom today. Similarly, an action like Pussy Riot's in a secular liberal democracy would barely be noticed by the authorities and would therefore struggle to maintain the interest of the audience. Not every act of profanity, ridicule or exposure amounts to truth-telling and many such acts are easily co-opted into the regime of equivalence as expressions of a particular *subculture* or a market niche: witness the incorporation of punk into mainstream pop or the sterility of allegedly transgressive practices in much of contemporary art. It is thus impossible to define from the outset the degree of abrasion or irritation that would suffice to rupture the regime of equivalence, hence every act of veridiction remains at the risk of being null and void, at best registered as an opinion.

Yet, what does this irritant force have to do with truth? We cannot grasp this force in terms of the familiar epistemological or logical theories that define truth in terms of correspondence, coherence or consensus. Abrasive or irritant statements might certainly sound incoherent and dissensual to an audience accustomed to euphonic sophistry, while statements in the form of injunctions, judgements, pleas or prayers cannot be investigated as to their correspondence to facts. It would be more helpful to compare this idea of truth with Badiou's (2005) understanding of truth as *fidelity* to the event, which we briefly addressed in Chapter 2. At first glance, the two notions could not be more different. It is difficult to see what acts of *parrhesia* are meant to be faithful *to*, other than themselves, and what event could have made them possible, other than their own eruption. And yet, precisely in this sense, acts of truth-telling correspond almost to the letter to Badiou's own formula of the event as a set comprised of the elements of the evental site and *itself* (see Badiou 2005: 201–10). By the same token, in addition to their semantic content acts of veridiction also enunciate their *own* nature as events of truth.

In his theory of performatives Austin provided a typology of speech acts based on their illocutionary force, distinguishing between verdictives, exercitives, commissives, expositives and behabitives (Austin 1975: 155–61). It is easy to see that the surplus force of truth can be produced in all five of these acts, though it is perhaps stronger in the first three: for example, *denouncing* a statement as untrue (verdictive), *demanding* that truth be told (exercitive), *promising* to speak the truth (commissive), *doubting* that a statement is true (expositive) and *apologising* for not speaking truly (behabitive). In all these cases we are dealing not merely with the locution of an utterance that may be true or false, but with the surplus exercise of illocutionary force that establishes the speaker's relation to the truth or untruth of the utterance: verdict, demand, promise, doubt or apology. While it cannot be assessed in terms of truth and falsity in the same way as the original utterance, this force nonetheless has an essential relationship with truth.

Let us recall the notion of 'emo-truth' discussed in Chapter 1. If the term is used to argue that emotive statements have taken the place of argumentative truth claims, then its use is somewhat problematic, since what distinguishes those emo-statements from arguments is presumably that they *cannot* be evaluated in terms of truth and falsity. Yet, it is also possible to use the term to refer to the emotive aspects of the illocutionary force that *accompanies* rather than replaces the semantic truth content of the statement, literally adding some 'emo' to the truth. In this sense, emo-truth would denote precisely the surplus force that *insists* on the truth of what it says in the very act of saying it. It thereby demonstrates the existence of that which the regime of equivalence has reduced to 'inexistence' (Badiou 2009a: 321–4). Truth-telling brings this 'inexistent' to speech, no longer as an opinion but as that which is non-equivalent to every opinion, that is, as truth. *What inexists as opinion has truth as its mode of being*, but only inasmuch as this truth is *forced* into discourse in a speech act that *both* says the truth *and* insists that what it says is the truth (see Badiou 2005: 400–6). Badiou uses the notion of forcing to describe the process of the transformation of the situation and its internal 'encyclopedia' of knowledge by, as it were, adding the indiscernible subset of truth to it and establishing its veracity within it (ibid.: 416–26). Similarly, in our approach forcing the truth transforms the regime that governs discourse by adding to it the kind of statement that was deemed to be inexistent in it and thereby making a difference in the order based on indifference.

This forcing is what separates *parrhesia* from *isegoria*, truth-telling from the free exercise of speech. It is important to reiterate that forcing pertains to the illocutionary force of the act (what one does *in* saying) and not its perlocutionary effect (what one achieves *by* saying it): the latter does not necessarily follow from the success of the former. This has important ethico-political consequences for grasping the significance of truth-telling, which is irreducible to the effects it might achieve. The scandal, irritation or disturbance brought about by truth-telling is in itself the desired effect, even as truth-telling might also have additional strategic goals: truth is, quite literally, *its own reward*.

Of course, one could not possibly tell the truth by illocutionary force alone: uttering conspiracy theories in a particularly irritating manner does not render them any more true, but only makes their falsehood even less bearable. Similarly, if the Cynics sought to embody not the familiar truths of their time but some novel, weird or deranged doctrine, their confrontational attitude would merely serve to amplify that doctrine's strangeness and move them even further to the margins of the society. Indeed, the locutionary content of the statement certainly matters in truth-telling, yet it does not in itself have performative efficacy and must therefore be complemented by the illocutionary force that alone may raise it to the level of truth. What is true is truth *insofar as it is told*. The truth won't tell itself, but depends on its being *told* for its *force*.

This understanding of truth-telling is neither circular nor tautological. The content of truth-telling *exceeds* the truth in question, yet this excess is hardly graspable in terms of semantic content, as if we were to add to the truth a certain surplus set of facts. To tell the truth one need not tell anything *other* than the truth, but must include the telling of the truth in the act of its enunciation. This inclusion clearly need not necessarily take the form of an auxiliary statement '. . . and that is the truth', but is rather attained through the illocutionary force of the enunciation, whereby one does not merely 'state' some recognisably true content, but *declares, insists, promises* or *protests* that one is telling the truth. It is in this dimension that the *parrhesia* proper to the post-truth era may unfold. The abrasiveness that defined the Cynic *parrhesia* thus remains timely for the age of post-truth, but its target shifts away from the hypocritical invocation of truth to the blanket denial of its existence. The parrhesiast of our times enacts, through its confrontational assertion of truth, the *difference* that truth makes in the regime that appears to make all claims indifferent.

Our emphasis on the 'telling' in truth-telling might appear to come at the expense of the specification of the notion of truth. What *is* this truth that must be told? If the argument of this book is at all correct, then this question is entirely beside the point. The regime of equivalence that characterises the post-truth condition does *not* discriminate between concepts of truth and epistemological theories but denigrates truth *as such*, the very *question* of truth irrespective of how it is conceptualised. As we have argued throughout the book, the post-truth condition is not defined by the debate on what truth *is* and the contestation or exclusion of some particular type of truth, but by indifference regarding its very existence. Consequently, our approach similarly brackets off the epistemological definition of truth in order to focus on the act whereby it is told. Once this perspective is adopted, it becomes easier to see that scientific truths asserted against climate change denialists and vaccination sceptics have a lot in common with the decidedly non-scientific truths affirmed by Pussy

Riot, if only because both are in need of being affirmed against the claims to the equivalence of all statements.

To summarise, in the act of truth-telling the *locutionary* content is represented by a statement claimed to be true by the speaker in accordance with some context-specific criterion (scientific method, internal coherence, non-contradiction, etc.). The perlocutionary effect aimed at by the act may consist in *gaining* the adherence of one's audience to this claim, the *restoration* of the consensus regarding the truth of this statement, the *weakening* of obscurantist discourse, and so on. Finally and most importantly for our purposes, the illocutionary force of this act consists in the *exception* this act takes to the regime of equivalence through purposefully confrontational, unconventional or unpredictable speech that renders the statement in question *non-equivalent* to any expression of opinion.

Distinguishing between these three aspects of any act of veridiction permits us to understand why acts of truth-telling so frequently combine the most neutral, well-known and often tedious facts on the level of semantic content with the most abrasive mode of enunciation: the latter is necessary precisely to endow with illocutionary force the truth content that is otherwise bound to be relegated to the status of an opinion equivalent to others. If truth must include its own telling in the act of its enunciation, its inclusion is no longer a neutral act but a rupture in the very regime that is constituted by its negation. Interestingly, this combination marks the inversion of the mode of discourse that arguably defines the post-truth disposition, that is, the combination of irritant content and a neutral, almost offensively appropriate form that we easily recognise from internet trolling, whose origins we addressed in the discussion of Lerner's *Topeca School* in Chapter 1. This phenomenon dates back to the early Holocaust revisionism, which ventured to present its denials of Nazi genocides as somehow validated by 'scientific methods' (see Lyotard 1988: 3–14). Racist discourses have similarly gained circulation by casting themselves as grounded in evolutionary biology, and the same strategy is widespread today in the pseudo-scientific discourses of climate change denialism, vaccination scepticism or Covid dissidence. Truth-telling and post-truth discourse thus seem to be diametrically opposed to each other: in the former neutral truth content is affirmed through abrasive speech, while in the latter utter falsehood is concealed by being presented as – what exactly? Not as truth, which would contradict the very logic of post-truth, but as

165

an *opinion* that is constructed through recognisable and respectable rules and therefore demands to be accepted.

Pseudo-scientific gibberish does not really hope to be accepted as a scientific truth, which would require its capacity to actually refute the existing truths. Instead, it is content with amplifying its circulation by being accepted as an *opinion*, which, because it is expressed in a neutral or pseudo-scientific form, has greater chance of acceptance than it would have had as an extremist rant. This discourse compensates for its untruth by its neutral or 'factual' presentation, while truth-telling compensates for its inexistence by its abrasive illocutionary force. *Parrhesia* enhances the force of truth, by forcefully insisting that it is speaking the truth, that what it says is not equivalent to a mere opinion. Truth denialism, in contrast, expands the circulation of falsehoods by suggesting that what it says is an opinion like any other and, in accordance with the logic of equivalence, has the same right of free circulation as other opinions.

This is why we insist that we can resist post-truth not simply by truth, but only by truth-*telling*, which adds to the sheer content of the truth the surplus force of its being said as such. To rupture the regime of equivalence, the act of veridiction must not merely speak the truth, which has already been negated in the regime of equivalence, but must, in this very act, *speak of its own speaking the truth*, affirm the truth that it says in the act of saying it.

GRETA THUNBERG: HOW TO FOLLOW THE SCIENCE

This approach has important implications in the contemporary context, where resistance to post-truth in the fields of climate change or vaccination scepticism often takes the admonishing form of telling us to 'listen to the scientists'. As we have argued throughout this book, it is hardly enough to appeal to the authority of truth, scientific or otherwise, in the condition defined by the weakening of this very authority. If the diagnoses of post-truth are at all correct, we are well past the point when appeals to science could work, and instead are in the situation where a *defence of science* is necessary, a defence that is not at all a scientific matter and cannot be undertaken solely with the tools of science or on the basis of the scientific method. In this defence, we cannot simply rely on scientific truths themselves, which have lost some of their performative efficacy that cannot be restored by repeating these truths in the same mode of enunciation.

166

It is particularly problematic to demand to 'listen to' or 'follow' the science in political debates. Science and politics belong to different genres of discourse (Lyotard 1988: 84, 135–7), and this difference is observable in the aspects of both content and form. In terms of content, statements belonging to the scientific discourse do not contain policy recommendations and are difficult to recast as such. There is no seamless transition from a *causal* argument of the kind 'if X, then Y' to a political *injunction* 'to avoid Y, we must refrain from X'. Science as such and even individual scientists may well be indifferent to the occurrence of Y and hence not eager to infer from the causal relationship between X and Y the need to refrain from X. Moreover, refraining from X may require a myriad of actions in a variety of fields not addressed by the science in question, which would make its practitioners incompetent in making strictly scientific statements about it. Statements made against X would therefore not count as scientific truths and would be reduced to mere opinions, equivalent to possible other opinions in defence of X.

This brings us to the aspect of form. A statement, formulated in accordance with the rules of scientific discourse (as impartial, supported by empirical evidence, reconstructible, etc.), does not make for a very useful instrument in political struggles even in the times more respectful of scientific truths. It is almost entirely useless in the polarised setting, in which one pole proudly constitutes itself as being tired of experts and the other pole is left with claiming expert discourse for itself, thereby depriving the latter of the universality it should possess and reducing it to the status of the particular opinion of the 'left', 'elites', 'cultural Marxists', and so on. Moreover, there are few instruments in the scientific discourse itself that would allow it to oppose and resist this reduction, which is only possible in a different type of discourse that does not merely tell the truth in its content but *includes* its own truth-telling in its very assertion.

This argument should be rigorously distinguished from the affirmation of the supremacy of politics over science, which devalues science and its truth claims in favour of political decisions that may break with these truths. While it is certainly possible in a democracy that a political decision would be made by legislative or executive authorities that is not in accordance with the scientific consensus (or the policy recommendations of scientists, which is a different type of discourse from science proper), this is by no means a necessarily laudable or desirable practice. Politics may trump science, but it does not need to, and there are good reasons to believe that it often should not. The gap between scientific statements and political decisions that we insist on is not intended to prevent any communication between science and politics (and make the latter autonomous from the former) but precisely the opposite, to make it possible to build *bridges* between them, which would hardly be possible if the two domains were indistinct or identical (see Lyotard 1988: 130–3).

To simply say 'follow the science' is therefore a poor political gesture (Bacevic 2020; Butler 2020). To resist post-truth through some form of dogmatic scientism is to misunderstand the political nature of the very problem of post-truth, which does not consist in the disputation of some truths in the name of some other, presumably untrue doctrine (religion, myth, ideology, etc.), but in the erasure of the very difference between truths and falsehoods by the reduction of all statements to opinions. It is impossible to reclaim the authority of science simply by claiming or suggesting to follow or listen to it: the problem is precisely that the performative efficacy of scientific truths is presently often too weak for this injunction to be followed. Moreover, in the context of democratic politics such a demand cannot but appear dangerously depoliticising if not outright authoritarian: while the content of scientific truths may be decided *within* the scientific discourse, the demand to follow or listen to science is not itself verifiable scientifically and is therefore to be resolved in another, political context, where other considerations (of justice, cost, responsibility, consent, enforcement) may be at stake, in addition to the truth or falsity of the science in question. This does not mean that scientific truths should have no effect on political decisions but only that this effect is always itself a matter of a political decision.

Even if it were possible to formulate a policy based strictly and solely on the existing scientific consensus (and there are many questions that could be raised with regard to this idea of scientific 'basis'), there would still be a need for the extra effort of translating this consensus into the victorious political project in a democratic setting. Science itself does not speak politically and its defence is not only a matter of and for scientists but of and for society as a whole. This is why the most effective defence of science today in the field of climate policy comes not from the climate scientists themselves but from Greta Thunberg, a Swedish teenager who claims no scientific expertise beyond that easily available to any interested observer. Thunberg does not speak *as* a scientist; she does not even try to speak *like* a scientist. Thunberg's discourse seeks neither the popularisation of climate science nor its translation into governmental policy. While the locutionary content of her discourse is often exhausted by the plea to 'go with the science', its illocutionary force consists in something else entirely – a deliberately irritant or abrasive act of the rejection of the current mainstream consensus, the condemnation of the betrayal of the future generations by political elites and the injunction to civil disobedience:

> You have stolen my dreams and my childhood with your empty words. And yet I'm one of the lucky ones. People are suffering. People are dying. Entire ecosystems are collapsing. We are in the beginning of a mass extinction, and all you can talk about is money and fairy tales of eternal economic growth. How dare you! For more than 30 years, the science has been crystal clear. How dare you continue to look away and come here saying that you're doing enough, when the politics and solutions needed are still nowhere in sight. (Thunberg 2019: n.p.)

Thunberg's speech acts mobilise the truth content of science on the locutionary level, yet seek to amplify its force by presenting it in a series of forceful judgements, demands and accusations, which are not reducible to any established political ideology that could be easily subsumed by the regime of equivalence. When politics proudly rids itself of experts and scientific discourse is unable to generate political projects, it takes a parrhesiast to demand that politics take its guidelines from what science has established as true. Thunberg's parrhesiastic speech derives its force of truth not from the repetition of the scientific consensus but from this demand to act on it politically. This is why if it so happened that the scientific claims about climate change that she relies on were to be revised considerably in a few years, Greta Thunberg would still have told the truth *today*. The truth-*telling* would hold true, even if the *truth content* would change.

Thunberg has arguably become so well-known because in her discourse the distinction, which is at the same time the articulation, between locutionary truth content and the illocutionary force of truth-telling is particularly striking. She expresses the truths belonging to the present scientific consensus with a pronounced anger that many consider disturbing (see Nicholson 2019). It is impossible to file it away as childish naïvety or idealism, since the content of her discourse is neither idealist nor naïve but rather in accordance with established knowledge. Yet, this content is delivered in such a forceful way that it cannot be dismissed as merely the repetition of what the scientists say. This is what makes Thunberg's discourse so irritating to climate change denialists, who can successfully deal with angry outbursts as well as reasoned scientific claims, but not with the combination thereof. This is why Donald Trump, the politician who has benefited most from mass expressions of anger, tries so desperately to pacify Thunberg, in his typically crass and bullying manner. 'She needs Anger Management', says the paragon of unmanaged anger, capitalising the nouns for no apparent reason (see Nicholson 2019).

Yet, Thunberg manages her anger quite well, famously appro-priating all the insults thrown at her in her Twitter bio: for exam-ple, 'A teenager working on her anger management problem . . .' (ibid.: n.p.) Her anger is thus not uncontrolled or unmanaged, yet it remains essential and could not be confused with a mildly ironic or sarcastic attitude, which would thoroughly undermine the illocu-tionary force of her discourse. This anger could not be replaced by ridiculing how stupid climate denialists are, by patronisingly trying to win them over by pretending to agree with them on something, by claiming neutral ground by 'merely' following the science, and so on. While all these responses may be acceptable in specific contexts, they would be unhelpful when dealing with the challenge of post-truth, since they are so easily accommodated by the regime of equivalence: opinion X denies climate change, opinion Y is unhappy with opin-ion X, considering its holders stupid, opinion Z tries to bring X and Y together to have an exchange of, what else, opinions, and so on. Yet, Thunberg is angry not with this or that opinion or its holders, but with the regime that remains indifferent to both the truth and its denial. She is not confronting anyone who happens to disagree with this opinion but the entire *order of discourse* that has made it an opinion to begin with. Her anger has, as it were, *nothing personal* about it.

This is why her speech is so abrasive: while the order of dis-course can easily accommodate the quaintest and most audacious opinions, it cannot include within itself the *negation* of its ordering principles. It must therefore reduce such statements to opinions – extreme, excessive and hyperbolic opinions, but opinions nonethe-less and therefore entirely harmless. This explains the proliferation of *ad hominem* attacks on Thunberg, which, in addition to testify-ing to the malice of the attackers in question, also demonstrate the desire to subsume the disruptive force of Thunberg's speech under her individuality and thereby reduce it to the expression of her idiosyncrasy – just as the conspiratorial mindset that we have addressed in relation to Russia insists that one only *says* something because of what one *is*. Yet, the attraction of Thunberg's discourse has nothing to do with her individuality – its locutionary content restates an all but universal scholarly consensus on climate change, while its illocutionary force consists in the angry disruption of the circulation of opinions that targets nothing but the regime of equivalence as such. Greta Thunberg says *nothing but the truth*, yet she also succeeds in bringing her own truth-telling to speech as such.

EQUALITY, EQUIVALENCE AND DEMOCRATIC LIFE

Our definition of the act of truth-telling in the post-truth context cannot but encounter an obvious objection. What about all the scandalous, irritating or abrasive statements made from the *other* side of the political spectrum: enthusiastic violations of 'political correctness', the gleeful trolling of establishment politicians or the mockery of 'mainstream media'? Aren't the parrhesiasts of our time rather the climate change deniers, vaccination sceptics, Russian Facebook trolls and, ultimately, the ceaselessly tweeting Donald Trump himself? What is it that separates the angry outbursts of Greta Thunberg from Trump's own belligerent rants? Isn't it all the same emo-truth, albeit deployed for different political ends? It is as if post-truth is itself becoming the new truth-telling.

This objection deserves to be considered in detail. Firstly, if *parrhesia* is approached as a practice of truth-telling and not in a more generic manner as 'straight talk' that 'says it all', it could not possibly be practised from the standpoint of truth-denialism, but must enunciate truth claims of its own. Merely abrasive or offensive speech, devoid of the *dictum* of truth affirmed in it, does not constitute *parrhesia* but only exemplifies the exercise of the free right to speech (*isegoria*), until it descends to the level of 'hate speech' that would be no longer protected by this right. Yet, the typical characteristic of post-truth discourses is precisely their indifference to the truth of their claims. It is not that their practitioners readily admit to the falsity of what they say, but that they dismiss the conventional protocols for the adjudication of the truth of their statements, be they peer review, expert evaluation, academic consensus, and so on, thereby obliterating the difference between truth and opinion, offering an opinion as if it were true or making a truth claim in the form of mere opinion, devoid of evidence or proof. Rather than speak truth to power at the risk of retribution, which was a central aspect of *parrhesia* in Foucault's reading, the discourse of truth denialism *seeks power* by expressing its opinion with no risk whatsoever, in the hope that it sticks, catches on, becomes shared, goes viral, and so on. This is *parrhesia* only in the most literal, etymological sense of the word: saying *everything*, not holding anything back – something captured better by the notion of *logorrhoea*.

Secondly, it is important to recall that just as the post-truth discourse pretends to have democratic credentials while in fact undermining democracy, it often simulates *parrhesia* by claiming to irritate the 'politically correct' consensus, 'telling it like it is' despite the wishes of vaguely defined 'elites' to conceal or remove the entire subject matter from the discussion. Yet, it would be a major distortion of the concept to view Trump, Steve Bannon, or even Surkov's favourite Five Finger Death Punch as modern-day parrhesiasts. *Parrhesia* has nothing to do with the expression of one's *particular* preferences or interests, be they deeply held or superficial. Even less does it consist in libellous and humiliating speech that seeks to *denigrate* the particular positions of one's opponents. To be worthy of the name, *parrhesia* must neither affirm nor challenge particular preferences but question the order of discourse *as such*, be it the gulf between philosophy and ordinary life in Ancient Greece in the case of the Cynics, the non-relation of official ideology to the 'real aims of life' in the case of Charter 77, or the equivalence of all statements in today's post-truth regime. The differentiating criterion between genuine and fake *parrhesia* is whether this 'frank' speech demands recognition as *a particular opinion* in the regime of equivalence or targets this *regime* itself, insisting on its non-equivalence. An opinion that is merely scandalous, extreme or marginal can still be incorporated into the regime of equivalence and thrive on its margins. In contrast, a truth claim does not belong to the margins. It is more extreme than any localisable extremity, by which we do not mean some unimaginable obscenity but rather an incongruity that affects the regime in its entirety and brings its operation to a standstill.

Thirdly, the rise of offensive or outright hateful speech in the post-truth era occurs for a different reason and has a different purpose than the abrasive discourse of truth-telling. This rise has been enabled by the pluralisation of sites of expression and disappearance of gatekeepers in mass media and the polarisation of political discourse in Western democracies, yet it would have made little sense outside of the shift from the logic of argumentation to the logic of expression, discussed in Chapter 1. Once it is no longer a matter of prevailing over one's opponent in a carefully regulated and mediated discursive setting but of expressing your identity or standpoint directly in a variety of formats to like-minded supporters, discourse tends to become increasingly more aggressive and obscene, without thereby becoming parrhesiastic in any way. 'Holding nothing back' does not here refer to frankness and sincerity that might sometimes cause offence but rather to the *weaponisation* of discourse, which must use all the rounds at its disposal, much like the technique of the spread in Lerner's *Topeca School*. Rehearsed vulgarity thereby takes the place of the abrasion that defines truth-telling.

This is why the true antonym of the parrhesiast is the *troll*, whose sole objective is to insult and hurt its target while always retaining its 'cool'. While Foucault's parrhesiast is beside itself with anger and indignation, which renders its discourse abrasive or tasteless to the refined audience accustomed to the arts of sophistry, the troll is offensively calm and even hyperbolically polite, which is precisely what is so irritating about them. The parrhesiast *suffers* the absence of truth, which leads it to an abrasive intervention intended to restore its status, while the troll wishes to render truth absent, which leads it to an at first glance similarly abrasive intervention, whose purpose is nonetheless diametrically opposed: to negate the existence of truth.

Thus, the 'authenticity' claimed and promoted by the champions of post-truth (Fieschi 2019: 35–9, 157–60) has nothing to do with the abrasive frankness of *parrhesia*. The authenticity that characterises today's self-styled populism arises from the *wilful transgression* of whatever is perceived as the politically correct norm regulating public discourse. Its shock value, arising from vulgarity, obscenity or hatefulness, serves to rupture the existing norms and hierarchies and to render equivalent what was not so. It takes the principle of *isegoria* to the extreme and only in this sense may be considered either democratic or populist. The 'authentic' here is simply the improper discourse that actively resists its own place in the discursive order and seeks to make itself equivalent to what is currently proper. It does not oppose the regime of equivalence but seeks to fortify it by making *itself* equivalent to the proper. Ultimately, we are dealing here with *disreputable* opinions that demand recognition as *reputable* opinions. This demand is not in itself illegitimate or unreasonable, but it has nothing to do with truth-telling.

In contrast, parrhesiastic truth-telling is not content with being recognised as having an equal right to speak, according to the principle of democratic *isegoria*. It would matter little to the parrhesiast to have its statements recognised as being 'as proper' as those of others. Greta Thunberg would not be satisfied in having her calls to action on climate change recognised as 'equal' to the opinions of climate change denialists. Similarly, Pussy Riot would probably not be content with having their punk prayer treated on par with the hypocritical prayers of the Orthodox officialdom. The parrhesiast is not content with being co-opted into the regime of equivalence but claims a hierarchy of their own, that is, between the truth that they utter and the numerous opinions to which they are indifferent, since they have no truth value and in this sense remain equivalent.

This brings us back to the question of the relation between truth and democracy that we raised early on in Chapter 1. Is the parrhesiast hostile to democracy? Is democracy rather not better served by the universalisation of freedom of speech that prevents any discourse from asserting their non-equivalence to others? The answer depends on whether democracy itself is defined in terms of equivalence or equality. The experience of today's post-truth politics demonstrates that it is possible, in principle, to live in the absence of truth, in a society where there are only particular opinions determined by partial interests. Yet, while all these opinions are equivalent, they remain unequal in their *power*. As we have seen, the affirmation of equivalence makes it difficult if not impossible to challenge this inequality of power: after all, why would we resist the hegemony of Putin, Erdoğan or Orbán, if all we can attain thereby is the hegemony of their opponents?

In contrast, the parrhesiast clearly refuses the idea of the equivalence of all statements, their truth claim only being meaningful as something *more* than an opinion. Yet, their discourse necessarily begins from the opposed position of saying something *less* than an opinion, because non-equivalent truth claims cannot be incorporated into the regime of equivalence and remain inexistent within it. In order to become something *more* than an opinion, it must compensate for this inexistence with surplus illocutionary force – hence its abrasive and irritant character. Does it then affirm inequality by ascending from being less to being more than opinion? Not exactly. Truth is not superior to this or that particular opinion: it is impossible to compare them since an opinion *cannot* be true or false by definition. What truth affirms is not inequality but *non-equivalence* between itself and the opinions that it is indifferent to. At most, it can be said that truth is superior to opinions *in general*, to *all* opinions, including mutually exclusive ones.

Yet, this affirmation of superiority is combined with the strongly egalitarian nature of truth itself. Precisely because truth is independent from one's identity or background, partial interests or particular predicates, it is *open to all* without any qualification. While opinions are particular by definition and hence attributable to specific identities, truth may traverse the most diverse identities without ever becoming reducible to them. While the particularistic regime of equivalence sustains inequality of power, truth-telling offers the possibility of *equality in truth*, which is conditioned only by one's subtraction from one's place in this regime that enables one to speak in the manner that does not merely express one's identity or standpoint. Badiou once presented as an alternative to the contemporary hegemony of democracy the idea of 'aristocracy for everyone' (Badiou 2011b): living in truth is superior to dwelling in particular opinions (hence the aristocratic aspect), but this superior way of being is not restricted to any particular group, attribute or predicate but is open to all without exception. Thus, while post-truth affirms the *equivalence of statements* sustained by the *inequality of power*, truth-telling affirms the *non-equivalence of statements* as a condition for *equality* offered by living in truth.

It is this emphasis on equality that connects our inquiry into post-truth with the argument we developed in *Democratic Biopolitics* (Prozorov 2019). In that book we defined democratic biopolitics as an ethos affirming the coexistence of forms of life under the conditions of *freedom, equality* and *community*, where no form of life may be posited as proper or necessary and hence no domination of some forms over others could be legitimate. We may now elaborate this idea in the post-truth context. While ostensibly pluralistic, the post-truth regime of equivalence in no way contributes to the improved equality of forms of life: the equivalence that it asserts exists only on the basis of the present inequalities of power and sustains these inequalities by dismantling the foundations for their contestation. Bracketing off and concealing these inequalities, the regime of equivalence offers those with political, economic and social capital the possibility to shift their aggression to the realm of language and practise it in the guise of pluralistic discourse, leaving those lacking such capital to express their aggression in a non-discursive fashion. By its very nature, the logic of equivalence removes all obstacles to the proliferation of this discursive aggression: hate speech and anti-hate speech regulations are rendered equivalent as opinions, hence none can dominate another, which in practice means that campaigns of trolling, blackmail or intimidation can go on without any meaningful sanction.

While this proliferation of toxic discourse may be formally in accordance with the principle of *isegoria* enshrined in democratic constitutions, it remains in contradiction with the more substantive understanding of democracy that, following John Dewey, we may call 'democratic life'. To recall, for Dewey democracy is 'more than a form of government; it is primarily a mode of associated living, of conjoint communicated experience' (Dewey 1985: 93). Rather than locate democracy in electoral procedures or institutional design, Dewey found it in the experience of coexistence of diverse identities and interests in the manner that seeks to reconcile individual and collective interests in a non-coercive, open-ended and experimental way.

In *Democratic Biopolitics* we have similarly approached democracy as an *ethos* in the original sense of a dwelling place, a space of coexistence of the most diverse forms of life in the absence of exclusion, hierarchy or domination. This coexistence is possible under two conditions. Firstly, it must be regulated by the principles of *freedom*, *equality* and *community* that guarantee, respectively, absence of domination, hierarchy and exclusion. Secondly, these principles must not remain mere transcendental prescriptions that have no bearing on concrete forms of life but must enter these forms of life themselves, enabling something like a democratic *manner* of living (Prozorov 2019: 133–40). We have argued that this democratic manner consists in the perpetual oscillation between one's *captivation* by a form of life and a distracted *withdrawal* from it so that one's dwelling in any form of life is always accompanied by the potentiality not to dwell in it, to abandon it for another, in a similarly non-definitive way. In this manner, the freedom to give one's life a certain form, the equality of these forms and their being in common are experienced, as it were, from *within* one's current form of life itself, making democracy an *experiment in living* and hence genuinely biopolitical in the affirmative sense.

How does truth-telling contribute to this ethos of democratic life? While the regime of equivalence entails the contamination of the democratic public sphere by toxic content, from fake news to hate speech, democratic biopolitics demands a certain *hygiene* of coexistence that limits the proliferation of this toxicity. To speak of hygiene in this context is of course to play on the traditional and literal understanding of biopolitics, which after all emerged by taking up such tasks as ensuring public hygiene in growing industrial cities and thereafter took on numerous additional objects and concerns (Foucault 2003: 239–63; 2015: 186–223).

Contrary to the approaches that view biopolitics in wholly negative terms and every attempt at hygiene as inherently repressive, we suggest that the present viral spread of post-truth, which contaminates public discourse and undermines civil society, calls for precisely a hygienic response, which ventures to protect the pluralism of forms of life, enabling their continuous (re)generation, free from subjection, domination or exclusion. The problem addressed by democratic biopolitics is how to let incommensurable forms be and keep open the space for new forms to arise and circulate. This evidently presupposes the possibility of intervention and regulation aimed at ensuring the equality of these incommensurable forms, which is entirely distinct from maintaining their equivalence under the condition of inequality. *Defending equality from a collapse into equivalence* – this is the ethos of democratic biopolitics.

While this hygienic intervention must evidently involve a plurality of legal and institutional mechanisms, it ultimately depends on social practices that sustain its ethos. As the experience of postcommunist Russia and other lapsed democracies of the post-truth age demonstrates, all legal procedures can be swiftly rendered void of meaning by authoritarian governments and all institutional designs can be twisted to serve the ends opposed to those they were designed for. It is here that truth-telling, of the kind practised in various contexts by Pussy Riot and Greta Thunberg, like Socrates, Diogenes or Jesus before them, becomes so important. To press the metaphor of hygiene further, their irritant and abrasive discourse functions in the mode of disinfectant, which might certainly sting, but thereby protects against the further contamination of the public sphere.

Evidently, this does not mean that democratic life is only possible if we all try to be as irritating to each other as possible. The abrasive discourse of truth-telling may well retreat to the margins in a vibrant public sphere in which forms of life circulate as free, equal and in common. Yet, this discourse returns to the foreground when this circulation is suspended either due to the emergence of *hegemonic* forms of life that elevate themselves over others or as a result of the weakening of the regulative principles of freedom, equality and community, whereby *plural* forms of life withdraw into themselves and strive to protect their particularity against contamination by the other. These hegemonic and pluralistic forms of *identitarianism*, which we observe respectively in Putin's Russia and today's Western democracies, easily feed into and turn into one another. A regime exercising hegemony or oppression domestically may well present itself as a victim internationally – witness the Putin regime's endless lamentations about 'NATO expansion' that it claims to be threatened by. Conversely, a minoritarian form of life in a pluralistic society may well be extremely repressive or exclusionary within its own domain, negating on the inside the principles that enable its existence on the outside.

The relative weight of an identity or form of life matters little. What is important are the effects of its retreat into itself, which Agamben aptly termed the 'deficit of existence' (Agamben 1993: 43), and withdrawal from the democratic space of freedom, equality and community. Once these principles cease to regulate the coexistence of particular forms of life, this coexistence can either be eliminated entirely through authoritarian domination or governed according to the logic of equivalence. Again, the two are not mutually exclusive: as we have seen, the increasingly authoritarian regime in Russia has not abandoned its earlier truth denialism for some form of official ideology, but only began to rely on this denialism more extensively, even deploying it as a tool of foreign policy. Once the regime of equivalence sets in, it becomes increasingly difficult to affirm democratic principles against the slide into authoritarianism, since these principles are immediately converted into opinions expressing one's particular identity rather than serving as the enabling conditions for the coexistence of these identities. It is here that truth-telling emerges as the indispensable (though of course not invincible) instrument of the reassertion of democratic principles and thus the reinvigoration of democratic life.

Truth-telling need not be reduced to any of its particular forms, be it that of the Cynics, Socrates, Greta Thunberg or Pussy Riot. Nor must its addressee necessarily be an authoritarian ruler or a flamboyant demagogue. Parrhesiastic practices may also target more impersonal governmental rationalities that venture to found themselves on the 'best available science' through a selective adoption of some elements of the prevailing scientific consensus. These attempts at foundation are doubly depoliticising, insofar as they seek both to efface the dissenting voices within the scientific discourse in question and erase their own status as political decisions by claiming to be merely 'following the science'. As a result of this depoliticisation, the conditions of democratic life are undermined, as equality gives way to the privilege of what is (at best) a temporary consensus, freedom is weakened by the injunction to abide by this consensus, and community is ruptured by the exclusion of what- or whoever does not seem to be abiding by it. At first glance, this hegemony based on scientific truth seems to be furthest away from the regime of equivalence that truth-telling targets and rather resembles the (good?) old days of 'pre-post-truth' politics. Nonetheless, we should bear in mind Carl Schmitt's famous dictum: 'depoliticization is a political act in a particularly intense way' (Schmitt 1998: 227). By selecting particular elements from the existing scientific consensus and deciding to use them as a foundation for a specific policy, which no science could authorise in and by itself, governmental agencies exercise the same 'freedom of choice' that defines the pluralistic regime of equivalence, in which truth claims are available as commodities on the market that one selects and adopts: this is our truth, where is yours?

In this setting, truth-telling practices have an important role to play in insisting on the political nature of these depoliticising decisions, reminding us of the contestation and controversies around and within the 'best available science', as well as of the impossibility of a direct translation of this science into policy. In this manner, truth-telling practices continue to highlight the non-equivalence of truth, its irreducibility to an object of consumer choice. By insisting, in the force of their own discourse, that there is *more* to truth than freely chosen or consensually upheld statements, these practices both question governmental practices as to their truth and, even more importantly, subject them to a persistent test in terms of the conditions of democratic life. Does the putative foundation of governmental practices on truth sustain and enhance the coexistence of forms of life under the conditions of freedom and equality or does it rather violate these conditions, imposing a hegemonic or a pluralistic form of identitarianism?

Truth-telling practices are performative speech acts that effectively serve as the bulwark against the universal spread of the regime of equivalence and the resultant nihilism of social life. However minor and marginal they might appear, they insist that this equivalence is *not all there is*, which means that the regime of equivalence can never be as general or universal as it pretends to be. Taking a stand against universal equivalence is sufficient proof that this equivalence is in fact not universal but remains *limited*.

This is why truth-telling itself is characterised by a *singular universality*. This is not the vapid universality of the lowest common denominator, but, on the contrary, an extremely *partial* universality that presents itself as a scandalous exception to the logic of general equivalence. At first glance, this scandalous stance is yet another standpoint of the kind valorised by standpoint epistemologies, whose ambivalent relation to post-truth we have addressed in Chapter 1. Yet, in contrast to the identitarian standpoints that follow the expressionist logic, nothing in particular is expressed in the parrhesiastic standpoint other than one's taking a *stand* against the regime of equivalence. This stand is entirely indifferent to identitarian predicates and the knowledge arising from one's situation. Neither these predicates nor this knowledge offers the parrhesiast any grounding, authority or privilege. What sustains the discourse of truth-telling is rather its *subtraction* from all particular predicates and all situated knowledge, which could all be reduced to particular opinions in the regime of equivalence (see Prozorov 2013b: 13–18).

The discourse of truth-telling does not seek to *express* anything of its situation or standpoint, nor does it seek to *oppress*, *suppress* or *repress* any such expression. Even less is it trying to *impress* the audience in the manner of the sophist or *depress* it in the manner of the social critic. Instead, it simply *presses* on with its point. This is what makes it universally accessible: while we all have our particular situations and standpoints and sometimes struggle to understand the situations and standpoints that are unfamiliar to us, we can very easily understand what it means to *bracket off* this situation, to speak without support from a standpoint, not on one's home turf and out of one's depth. Only because the experience of such subtraction is understandable from within any situation, forceful enunciations from this subtractive locus may succeed in bursting the bubble of universal equivalence with the singular universality of concrete truths.

CODA

On error

What comes after truth? It can only be error. Truth liberates the possibility of error, which is entirely foreclosed from the regime of opinions. 'There can be no wrong opinion' – what a stifling and even
suffocating statement this is! What could be more oppressive than
this impossibility of ever being wrong? How can anything significant
exist in the absence of the possibility of error? It is precisely because
no possibility of error is accepted that opinions are so uninteresting
and their exchange is nothing more than idle talk, whose contents
are forgotten as soon as they are enunciated.

*

Truth has been long thought of as something already attained, as a
set of laws or facts that can be learned or that one can be tested on.
It has thus become something tedious and oppressive, so that eventually many have become enamoured of swindlers and thugs who
proclaimed its non-existence. When truth is something already given
or already known, it is easier to dispense with, especially if a life
without it is not something yet experienced and hence quite irresist-
ible as a mirage.

*

Yet, truth may also be thought of as a process, a search, a quest that
has no guarantee of success in the form of laws to be set in stone,
but which guarantees the possibility of error, not in the sense of the
already given false facts or erroneous laws, but the very process of
errancy, of wandering and alteration, of self and other, of self *as*
other. In this sense, truth is not given and is defined precisely by

181

this *non-givenness*, a *not-yet*, which opens a possibility that might eventually amount to nothing much, but might also initiate a most profound transformation.

*

This is why we should not oppose truth to error, as if we knew all the truths there were and all the errors that might be, but rather must view the established facts of truth and falsity as effects of errancy, which is also always an errancy *in* truth, that is, an errancy that pre-supposes truth as one of its destinations and which would have no reason to go on, were it firmly established that truth did not exist. Indeed, if this non-existence were to be firmly established, what would it be established *as*? As a truth, perhaps?

*

Perhaps, this is all truth is – the *reason to go on*, not the reason why something is what it is, not even the reason why there is something rather than nothing, but the reason why something can be *otherwise*, why it can alter itself, not in accordance with any law but as a mat-ter of errancy, by sheer virtue of going on, persisting in existence and hence necessarily exiting itself rather than merely insisting on staying the same. Truth is always *after itself*, pursuing its own latest altera-tion. To be after truth is to pursue it in its own pursuit of itself, to err on the side of non-equivalence.

Bibliography

Agamben, G. (1991), *Language and Death: The Place of Negativity*, Minneapolis: University of Minnesota Press.

Agamben, G. (1993), *The Coming Community*, Minneapolis: University of Minnesota Press.

Agamben, G. (1998), *Homo Sacer: Sovereign Power and Bare Life*, Stanford: Stanford University Press.

Agamben, G. (1999a), *End of the Poem: Studies in Poetics*, Stanford: Stanford University Press.

Agamben, G. (1999b), *Potentialities: Selected Essays in Philosophy*, Stanford: Stanford University Press.

Agamben, G. (2000), *Means without End: Notes on Politics*, Minneapolis: University of Minnesota Press.

Agamben, G. (2004), *The Open: Man and Animal*, Stanford: Stanford University Press.

Agamben, G. (2005), *The Time that Remains: A Commentary on the Letter to the Romans*, Stanford: Stanford University Press.

Agamben, G. (2007a), *Infancy and History: On the Destruction of Experience*, London: Verso.

Agamben, G. (2007b), *Profanations*, New York: Zone Books.

Agamben, G. (2009a), *The Sacrament of Language: An Archaeology of the Oath*, Stanford: Stanford University Press.

Agamben, G. (2009b), *The Signature of All Things: On Method*, New York: Zone Books.

Agamben, G. (2016), *The Use of Bodies*, Stanford: Stanford University Press.

Allison, R. (2008), 'Russia Resurgent? Moscow's Campaign to "Coerce Georgia to Peace"', *International Affairs*, 84(6): 1145–71.

Alterman, E. (2004), When Presidents Lie: A History of Official Deception and *its* Consequences, New York: Viking.

Alyokhina, M. (2012), 'Closing Statement', <http://freepussyriot.org/content/masha-alyokhinas-closing-statement> (accessed 30 August 2020).

Andersen, K. (2017), 'How America Lost its Mind', *The Atlantic*, September, <http://www.theatlantic.com/magazine/archive/2017/09/how-america-lost-its-mind/534231/> (last accessed 23 February 2021).

Anderson, P. (2007), 'Russia's Managed Democracy', *London Review of Books*, 29(2), <https://www.lrb.co.uk/the-paper/v29/n02/perry-anderson/russia-s-managed-democracy> (last accessed 23 February 2021).

Arendt, H. (1973), *The Origins of Totalitarianism*, New York: Harcourt.

Arendt, H. (1992), *Lectures on Kant's Political Philosophy*, Chicago: University of Chicago Press.

Arendt, H. (1998), *The Human Condition*, Chicago: University of Chicago Press.

Arendt, H. (2006), *Between Past and Future*, New York: Penguin Classics.

Asmus, R. (2010), *The Little War that Shook the World: Georgia, Russia and the Future of the West*, Basingstoke: Palgrave.

Austin, J. L. (1975), *How to Do Things with Words*, Cambridge, MA: Harvard University Press; Oxford: Oxford University Press.

Bacevic, J. (2020), 'There's No Such Thing as Just "Following the Science" – Coronavirus Advice is Political', *The Guardian*, 28 April, <https://www.theguardian.com/commentisfree/2020/apr/28/theres-no-such-thing-just-following-the-science-coronavirus-advice-political> (last accessed 23 February 2021).

Badiou, A. (1999), *Manifesto for Philosophy*, New York: SUNY Press.

Badiou, A. (2001a), *Ethics: An Essay on the Understanding of Evil*, London: Verso.

Badiou, A. (2001b), *Saint Paul: The Foundation of Universalism*, Stanford: Stanford University Press.

Badiou, A. (2005), *Being and Event*, London: Continuum.

Badiou, A. (2009a), *Logics of Worlds*, London: Continuum.

Badiou, A. (2009b), *Pocket Pantheon*, London: Verso.

Badiou, A. (2011a), *Second Manifesto for Philosophy*, London: Polity.

Badiou, A. (2011b), 'The Democratic Emblem', in G. Agamben, A. Badiou, D. Bensaïd, W. Brown, J.-L. Nancy, J. Rancière, K. Ross and S. Žižek, *Democracy in What State?*, New York: Columbia University Press.

Baker, P. and S. Glasser (2005), *Kremlin Rising: Vladimir Putin's Russia and the End of Revolution*, New York: Simon & Schuster.

Belton, C. (2020), *Putin's People: How the KGB Took Back Russia and Then Took on the West*, New York: Farrar, Straus and Giroux.

Benjamin, W. (1968), *Illuminations*, New York: Harcourt.

Bershidsky, L. (2019), 'Putin's Russia is a Middle-Eastern Country', *Moscow Times*, 8 October, <https://www.themoscowtimes.com/2019/10/08/putins-russia-is-a-middle-eastern-country-a67624> (last accessed 23 February 2021).

Bertelsen, O. (2017), *Revolution and War in Contemporary Ukraine: The Challenge of Change*, New York: Columbia University Press.

Bourdieu, P. (1992), *Language and Symbolic Power*, London: Polity.

Brown, W. (2015), *Undoing the Demos: Neoliberalism's Stealth Revolution*, New York: Zone Books.

Bunin, I. (2001), 'Karnavala Ne Budet: Politicheskie Budni Bolshoi Reformy', *NG-Stsenarii*, 6(62).

Butler, J. (2015), *Notes Towards a Performative Theory of Assembly*, Cambridge, MA: Harvard University Press.

Butler, J. (2020), 'Follow the Science', *London Review of Books*, 42(8), <https://www.lrb.co.uk/the-paper/v42/n08/james-butler/follow-the-science> (last accessed 23 February 2021).

Cassiday, J. and E. Johnson (2013), 'A Personality Cult for the Postmodern Age: Reading Vladimir Putin's Public Persona', in H. Goscilo (ed.), *Putin as Celebrity and Cultural Icon*, London: Routledge.

D'Ancona, M. (2017), *Post-Truth: The New War on Truth and How to Fight Back*, New York: Random House.

Dawisha, K. (2015), *Putin's Kleptocracy: Who Owns Russia*, Simon & Schuster.

Dean, M. and K. Villadsen (2016), *State Phobia and Civil Society: The Political Legacy of Michel Foucault*, Stanford: Stanford University Press.

Derrida, J. (1985), *Margins of Philosophy*, Chicago: University of Chicago Press.

Derrida, J. (1988), *Limited, Inc.*, Chicago: Northwestern University Press.

Derrida, J. (1998), *Of Grammatology*, Baltimore: Johns Hopkins University Press.

Dewey, J. (1985), *The Middle Works 1889–1924, Vol. 9: Democracy and Education*, Edwardsville: Southern Illinois University Press.

Eckner, C. (2020), 'Germany's Far-Right and the Rise of the Anti-Corona Protests', *Spectator*, 31 August, <https://www.spectator.co.uk/article/germany-s-far-right-and-the-rise-of-the-anti-corona-protests?fbclid=IwAR26whemHKqz11uAQ6L82lDoncldCTzGnQk-Zer18vE_N3O3017FZuntgpE> (last accessed 23 February 2021).

Elder, M. (2012), 'Pussy Riot Trial Worse than Soviet Era', *The Guardian*, 3 August, <http://www.guardian.co.uk/world/2012/aug/03/pussy-riot-trial-russia> (last accessed 23 February 2021).

Esposito, R. (2008a), *Bios: Biopolitics and Philosophy*, Minneapolis: University of Minnesota Press.

Esposito, R. (2008b), 'Totalitarianism or Biopolitics? Concerning the Philosophical Interpretation of the 20th Century', *Critical Inquiry*, 39, 633–45.

EUvsDisinfo (2020), 'Who Benefits from "Cui Bono"?', *EUvsDisinfo*, <https://euvsdisinfo.eu/who-benefits-from-cui-bono/> (last accessed 23 February 2021).

Fedorov, A. (2001), 'Vladimir Putin: Vypolnimo li Zadumannoye?', *Nezavisimaya Gazeta*, 73(2383).

Feyerabend, P. (2010), *Against Method: Outline of an Anarchistic Theory of Knowledge*, London: Verso.

Fieschi, C. (2019), *Populocracy: The Tyranny of Authenticity and the Rise of Populism*, Newcastle: Agenda.

Five Finger Death Punch (2015), 'Wash it All Away', <https://genius.com/Five-finger-death-punch-wash-it-all-away-lyrics> (last accessed 23 February 2021).

Forti, S. (2015), *New Demons: Rethinking Power and Evil Today*, Stanford: Stanford University Press.

Foucault, M. (1977), *Discipline and Punish: The Birth of the Prison*, New York: Knopf.

Foucault, M. (1981), 'The Order of Discourse', in R. Young (ed.), *The Post-Structuralist Reader*, London: Routledge.

Foucault, M. (1989), *The Archaeology of Knowledge*. London: Routledge.

Foucault, M. (1990a), *History of Sexuality. Volume One: An Introduction*, Harmondsworth: Penguin.

Foucault, M. (1990b), *History of Sexuality. Volume Two: The Use of Pleasure*, New York: Random House.

Foucault, M. (2000), 'The Moral and Social Experience of the Poles', in M. Foucault, *Power: Essential Works of Foucault 1954–1984*, vol. 3, ed. J. D. Fabion, New York: New Press.

Foucault, M. (2003), *'Society Must be Defended': Lectures at the Collège de France 1975–1976*, London: Picador.

Foucault, M. (2006), *Psychiatric Power: Lectures at the Collège de France 1973–1974*, Basingstoke: Palgrave.

Foucault, M. (2008), *The Birth of Biopolitics: Lectures at the Collège de France 1978–1979*, Basingstoke: Palgrave.

Foucault, M. (2010), *The Government of Self and Others: Lectures at the Collège de France 1982–1983*, Basingstoke: Palgrave.

Foucault, M. (2011), *The Courage of Truth: Lectures at the Collège de France 1983–1984*, Basingstoke: Palgrave.

Foucault, M. (2014), *On the Government of the Living: Lectures at the Collège de France 1979–1980*, Basingstoke: Palgrave.

Foucault, M. (2015), *The Punitive Society: Lectures at the Collège de France 1972–1973*, Basingstoke: Palgrave.

Foucault, M. (2017), *Subjectivity and Truth: Lectures at the Collège de France 1980–1981*, Basingstoke: Palgrave.

Fraser, N. (1995), 'Foucault on Modern Power: Empirical Insights and Normative Confusions', in B. Smart (ed.), *Michel Foucault: Critical Assessments*, vol. 5, London: Routledge.

Fukuyama, F. (1992), *The End of History and the Last Man*, New York: Free Press.

Galeotti, M. (2014), 'The "Gerasimov Doctrine" and Russian Non-Linear War', *In Moscow's Shadows* (blog), 6 July, <https://inmoscowsshadows.wordpress.com/2014/07/06/the-gerasimov-doctrine-and-russian-non-linear-war/> (last accessed 23 February 2021).

Gaman-Golutvina, O. (2000), 'Byrokratia ili Oligarkhia: Politicheskiy Protsess Priblizilsya k Tochke Bifurkatsii', *NG-Stsenarii*, 3(48).

Gaman-Golutvina, O. (2001), 'Ot Koronatsii k Inauguratsii ili ot Inauguratsii k Koronatsii: Istoki i Sovremennye Osobennosti Rossiyskoi Tendentsii Kontsentratsii Vlasti', *Nezavisimaya Gazeta*, 80(2390).

Gemes K. (1992), 'Nietzsche's Critique of Truth', *Philosophy and Phenomenological Research*, 52(1): 47–65.

Gerasimov, V. (2013), 'Tsennost' Nauki v Predvidenii', *Voyenno-Promyshlennyy Kurier*, 26 February, <http://vpk-news.ru/articles/14632> (last accessed 23 February 2021).

Gillespie, S. (2008), *The Mathematics of Novelty: Badiou's Minimalist Metaphysics*, Melbourne: re.press.

Grant, T. (2015), *Aggression against Ukraine: Territory, Responsibility and International Law*, Basingstoke: Palgrave.

Grebowicz, M. (2007), 'Standpoint Theory and the Possibility of Justice: A Lyotardian Critique of the Democratization of Knowledge', *Hypatia*, 22(4): 16–29.

Groys, B. (2003), *Iskusstvo Utopii*, Moscow: Khudozhestvenny Zhurnal.

Groys, B. (2008), *Art Power*, Cambridge, MA: MIT Press.

Gudkov, L. (2001), 'Russia: A Society in Transition?', *Telos*, 120: 9–30.

Hale, H. E. (2014), 'Russian Nationalism and the Logic of the Kremlin's Actions on Ukraine', *The Guardian*, 29 August, <http://www.theguardian.com/world/2014/aug/29/russian-nationalism-kremlin-actions-ukraine> (last accessed 23 February 2021).

Harding, S. (1991), *Whose Science/Whose Knowledge?*, Milton Keynes: Open University Press.

Harsin, J. (2015), 'Regimes of Post-Truth, Postpolitics and Attention Economies', *Communication, Culture and Critique*, 8(2): 327–33.

Harsin, J. (2017), 'Trump l'Œil: Is Trump's Post-Truth Communication Translatable?', *Contemporary French and Francophone Studies*, 21(5): 512–22.

Hartsock, N. (2004), 'The Feminist Standpoint: Developing the Ground for a Specifically Feminist Historical Materialism', in S. Harding and M. Hintikka (eds), *The Feminist Standpoint Theory Reader: Intellectual and Political Controversies*, New York: Routledge.

Havel, V. (1985), 'The Power of the Powerless', in J. Keane (ed.), *The Power of the Powerless: Citizens and the State in Central-Eastern Europe*, London: M.E. Sharpe.

Heit, H. (2018), 'There Are No Facts . . .: Nietzsche as Predecessor of Post-Truth', *Studia Philosophica Estonica*, 11(1): 44–63.

Hekman, S. (1997), 'Truth and Method: Feminist Standpoint Theory Revisited', *Signs: Journal of Women in Culture and Society*, 22(2): 341–65.

Holmes, S. (1997), 'What Russia Teaches Us Now: How Weak States Threaten Freedom', *The American Prospect*, 33: 30–9.

Illarionov, A. (2007), 'Silovaya Model' Gosudarstva', *Kommersant*, 53: 4.

Interfax Editorial (2012), '*Pussy Riot* Is Guilty of Hooliganism – Prosecutors (*updated*)', 7 August, <http://www.interfax-religion.com/?act=news&div=9660> (last accessed 23 February 2021).

Judis, J. (2016), *The Populist Explosion: How the Great Recession Transformed American and European Politics*, New York: Columbia Global Reports.

Kakutani, M. (2018), *The Death of Truth: Notes on Falsehood in the Age of Trump*, New York: Tim Duggan Books.

Kalb, M. (2015), *Imperial Gamble: Putin, Ukraine and the New Cold War*, Brookings Institution Press.

Kalpokas, I. (2018), 'On Guilt and Post-Truth Escapism: Developing a Theory', *Philosophy and Social Criticism*, 44(10): 1127–47.

Kalpokas, I. (2019), *A Political Theory of Post-Truth*, Basingstoke: Palgrave.

Kellner, D. (2016), *American Nightmare: Donald Trump, Media Spectacle and Authoritarian Populism*, Rotterdam: Sense.

Keyes, R. (2004), *The Post-Truth Era: Dishonesty and Deception in Contemporary Life*, New York: St. Martin's Press.

Kharkhordin, O. (1997), 'Reveal and Dissimulate: A Genealogy of Private Life in Soviet Russia', in J. Weintraub and K. Kumar (eds), *Public and Private in Thought and Practice: Perspectives on a Grand Dichotomy*, Chicago: University of Chicago Press.

King, C. (2008), 'The Five Day War: Managing Moscow after the Georgia Crisis', *Foreign Affairs*, 87(6): 2–11.

Kojève, A. (1969), *Introduction to the Reading of Hegel: Lectures on the Phenomenology of Spirit*, Ithaca: Cornell University Press.

Kostychenko, E. (2012), 'Sedmoi Den' Slushaniy po Delu Pussy Riot', *Novaya Gazeta*, 7 August, <http://www.novayagazeta.ru/news/58806.html> (last accessed 10 August 2020).

Kotkin, S. (2017), *Stalin, Vol. II: Waiting for Hitler, 1929–1941*, New York: Penguin.

Kryshtanovskaya, O. (2005), *Anatomia Rossiyskoi Elity*, Moscow: Zakharov.

Laclau, E. (2005), *On Populist Reason*, London: Verso.

Laclau, E. and C. Mouffe (1985), *Hegemony and Socialist Strategy*, London: Verso.

Latour, B. (1993), *We Have Never Been Modern*, Cambridge, MA: Harvard University Press.

Latour, B. (2004), 'Why Has Critique Run Out of Steam? From Matters of Fact to Matters of Concern', *Critical Inquiry*, 30: 225–48.

Lefort, C. (1986), *The Political Forms of Modern Society: Bureaucracy, Democracy, Totalitarianism*, Boston: MIT Press.

Lefort, C. (1988), *Democracy and Political Theory*, London: Polity.

Lemm, V. (2014), 'The Embodiment of Truth and the Politics of Community: Foucault and the Cynics', in V. Lemm and M. Vatter (eds), *The Government of Life: Foucault, Biopolitics and Neoliberalism*, New York: Fordham University Press.

Lerner, B. (2019), *The Topeca School*, New York: FSG Originals.

Levitsky, S. and D. Ziblatt (2018), *How Democracies Die*, New York: Penguin.

Lucas, E. (2008), *The New Cold War: How the Kremlin Menaces both Russia and the West*, London: Bloomsbury.

Lyotard, J.-F. (1988), *The Differend: Phrases in Dispute*, Minneapolis: University of Minnesota Press.

Lyotard, J.-F. (2009), *Enthusiasm*, Stanford: Stanford University Press.

Mance, H. (2016), 'Britain Has Had Enough of Experts, Says Gove', *Financial Times*, 3 June, <https://www.ft.com/content/3be49734-29cb-11e6-83e4-abc22d5d108c> (last accessed 23 February 2021).

Meillassoux, Q. (2014), 'Decision and Undecidability of the Event in *Being and Event I and II*', *Parrhesia*, 19: 22–35.

Mikhailova, T. (2013), 'Putin as the Father of the Nation: His Family and other Animals', in H. Goscilo (ed.), *Putin as Celebrity and Cultural Icon*, London: Routledge.

Mishra, P. (2017), *The Age of Anger*, New York: Farrar, Straus and Giroux.

Mouffe, C. (2013), *Agonistics*, London: Verso.

Mounk, Y. (2018), *The People vs Democracy: Why Our Freedom is in Danger and How to Save it*, Cambridge, MA: Harvard University Press.

Mueller, J.-W. (2016), *What is Populism?*, Pittsburgh: University of Pennsylvania Press.

Nancy, J.-L. (2010), *The Truth of Democracy*, New York: Fordham University Press.

Nancy, J.-L. (2015), *After Fukushima: The Equivalence of Catastrophes*, New York: Fordham University Press.

Nemtsov, B. (2000), 'Budushee Rossii: Oligarkhia ili Demokratia', *Nezavisimaya Gazeta*, 237(2299).

Nicholson, R. (2019), 'Emotional Incontinents Like Trump Can't Cope with Her Controlled Anger', *The Guardian*, <http://www.theguardian.com/commentisfree/2019/dec/14/emotional-incontinents-like-trump-cannot-cope-with-greta-thunberg-controlled-anger> (last accessed 23 February 2021).

Nietzsche, F. (1977), *The Portable Nietzsche*, New York: Viking.

Ostrovsky, A. (2017), *The Invention of Russia: The Rise of Putin and the Age of Fake News*, New York: Penguin.

Parmar, I. (2012), 'US Presidential Election 2012: Post-Truth Politics', *Political Insight*, 3(2): 4–7.

Pavlovsky, G. (2000), 'Proshai Belovezhje!', *Nezavisimaya Gazeta*, 235(2297).

Pavlovsky, G. (2014), *Sistema RF v Voine 2014: De Principatu Debili*, Moscow: Evropa.

Pavlovsky, G. (2019), *Ironicheskaya Imperiya: Risk, Shans I Dogmy Sistemy RF*, Moscow: Evropa.

Pelevin, V. (1992), *Omon Ra*, Moscow: Vagrius.

Pelevin, V. (1999), *Generation P*, Moscow: Vagrius.

Pomerantsev, P. (2015), *Nothing is True and Everything is Possible: The Surreal Heart of the New Russia*, London: Faber and Faber.

Pomerantsev, P. (2019a), 'Rudy Giuliani Welcomes You to Eastern Europe', *The New York Times*, 5 October, <https://www.nytimes.com/2019/10/05/opinion/sunday/putin-trump-ukraine.html> (last accessed 23 February 2021).

Pomerantsev, P. (2019b), *This is Not Propaganda: Adventures in the War against Reality*, London: Faber and Faber.

Prozorov, S. (2005), 'Russian Conservatism in the Putin Presidency: The Dispersion of the Hegemonic Discourse', *Journal of Political Ideologies*, 10(2): 141–3.

Prozorov, S. (2007), 'The Paradox of Infra-Liberalism: Towards a Genealogy of "Managed Democracy" in Putin's Russia', in H. Wydra and A. Woell (eds), *Democracy and Myth in Russia and Eastern Europe*, London: Routledge.

Prozorov, S. (2009), *The Ethics of Postcommunism: History and Social Praxis in Russia*, Basingstoke: Palgrave.

Prozorov, S. (2010), 'Ethos without Nomos: The Russian–Georgian War and the Post-Soviet State of Exception', *Ethics and Global Politics*, 3(4): 255–75.

Prozorov, S. (2013a), *Ontology and World Politics: Void Universalism I*, London: Routledge.

Prozorov, S. (2013b), *Theory of the Political Subject: Void Universalism II*, London: Routledge.

Prozorov, S. (2016), *The Biopolitics of Stalinism: Ideology and Life in Soviet Socialism*, Edinburgh: Edinburgh University Press.

Prozorov, S. (2019), *Democratic Biopolitics: Popular Sovereignty and the Power of Life*, Edinburgh: Edinburgh University Press.

Prozorov, S. (2020), 'Foucault and the Birth of Psychopolitics: Towards a Genealogy of Crisis Governance', *Security Dialogue*, online first, <https://doi.org/10.1177/0967010620968345> (last accessed 23 February 2021).

Pussy Riot (2012), 'Mother of God, Drive Putin Away!', <http://freepussyriot. org/content/lyrics-songs-pussy-riot> (accessed 2 August 2020).

Pynnöniemi, K. and A. Racz (2016), *Fog of Falsehood: Russian Strategy of Deception and the Conflict in Ukraine*, Helsinki: Finnish Institute of International Affairs.

Reddaway, P. and D. Glinski (2001), *Tragedy of Russia's Reforms: Market Bolshevism against Democracy*, New York: United States Institute of Peace.

Samutsevich, E. (2012), 'Closing Statement', <http://freepussyriot.org/ content/katja-samutsevich-closing-statement-criminal-case-against-feminist-punk-group-pussy-riot> (accessed 17 August 2020).

Schmitt, C. (1998), 'Strong State and Sound Economy: Address to Business Leaders', in R. Cristi, *Carl Schmitt and Authoritarian Liberalism*, Cardiff: University of Wales Press.

Schwartzbaum, A. (2018), 'Art of the Headline: Kommersant's Wordplay Masters', *BMB Russia*, 27 February, <https://bearmarketbrief.word-press.com/2018/02/27/art-of-the-headline-kommersants-wordplay-masters/> (last accessed 23 February 2021).

Shevtsova, L. (2001), 'Vybornoe Samoderzhavie pri Putine: Perspektivy i Problemy Evolutsii Politicheskogo Rezhima', *Moscow Carnegie Centre Briefings*, 3(1).

Shevtsova, L. (2002), 'Mezhdu Stabilizatsiei i Proryvom: Promezhutochnye Itogi Pravleniya Vladimira Putina', *Moscow Carnegie Centre Briefings*, 4(1).

Solzhenitsyn, A. (2009), 'Live Not by Lies!', in E. Erickson Jr and D. Maloney (eds), *The Solzhenitsyn Reader*, Wilmington: Intercollegiate Studies Institute.

Stites, R. (1989), *Revolutionary Dreams: Utopian Vision and Experimental Life in the Russian Revolution*, Oxford: Oxford University Press.

Surkov, V. (2009), 'Nationalization of the Future: Paragraphs *pro* Sovereign Democracy', *Russian Studies in Philosophy*, 47(4): 8–21.

Surkov, V. (2017), 'Krizis Litsemeria', *Russia Today*, <https://russian. rt.com/world/article/446944-surkov-krizis-licemeriya> (last accessed 23 February 2021).

Surkov, V. (2019), 'Dolgoe Gosudarstvo Putina', *Nezavisimaya Gazeta*, 11 February, <http://www.ng.ru/ideas/2019-02-11/5_7503_surkov.html> (last accessed 23 February 2021).

Tallis, B. (2016), 'Living in Post-Truth', *New Perspectives. Interdisciplinary Journal of Central & East European Politics and International Relations*, 24(1): 7–18.

Tesich, S. (1992), 'A Government of Lies', *The Nation*, January, 6–13.

Thunberg, G. (2019), 'Transcript: Greta Thunberg's Speech at the U.N. Climate Action Summit', *NPR*, 23 September, <https://www.npr.org/2019/ 09/23/763452863/> (last accessed 23 February 2021).

Timofeevsky, A. (1991), 'Puzyri Zemli', *Stolitsa*, 46–7, <https://openuni.io/course/1/lesson/5/material/107> (last accessed 23 February 2021).

Tolokonnikova, N. (2012), 'Closing Statement', <http://freepussyriot.org/content/nadia-tolokonnikovas-closing-statement> (last accessed 17 August 2020).

Vatter, M. and V. Lemm (eds) (2014), *The Government of Life: Foucault, Biopolitics and Neoliberalism*, New York: Fordham University Press.

Volkov, V. (2002), *Violent Entrepreneurs: The Use of Force in the Making of Russian Capitalism*, Ithaca: Cornell University Press.

Walzer, M. (1986), 'The Politics of Michel Foucault', in D. C. Hoy (ed.), *Foucault: A Critical Reader*, Oxford: Basil Blackwell.

Weinberg, J. (2019), 'Brazilian Government to Defund Philosophy in Public Universities', *Daily Nous*, 26 April, <http://dailynous.com/2019/04/26/brazilian-government-defund-philosophy-public-universities/> (last accessed 23 February 2021).

Williams, C. (2017), 'Has Trump Stolen Philosophy's Critical Tools?', *The New York Times*, 14 April, <https://www.nytimes.com/2017/04/17/opinion/has-trump-stolen-philosophys-critical-tools.html> (last accessed 23 February 2021).

Wolin, R. (1994), 'Foucault's Aesthetic Decisionism', in B. Smart (ed.), *Michel Foucault: Critical Assessments*, vol. 3, London: Routledge.

Yablokov, I. (2018), *Fortress Russia: Conspiracy Theories in Post-Soviet Russia*, London: Polity.

Yurchak, A. (2006), *Everything Was Forever until it Was No More: The Last Soviet Generation*, Berkeley: Berkeley University Press.

Žižek, S. (1989), *The Sublime Object of Ideology*, London: Verso.

Žižek, S. (2012), 'The True Blasphemy: Slavoj Žižek on Pussy Riot', *Dangerous Minds*, 10 August, <https://dangerousminds.net/comments/the_true_blasphemy_slavoj_zhizhek_on_pussy_riot> (last accessed 23 February 2021).

Žižek, S. (2014), *The Universal Exception*, London: Bloomsbury.

Index

193

EU representative:
Easy Access System Europe
Mustamäe tee 50, 10621 Tallinn, Estonia
Gpsr.requests@easproject.com

www.ingramcontent.com/pod-product-compliance
Lightning Source LLC
Chambersburg PA
CBHW071534300326
41935CB00049B/1466